Counterrevolution

Counterrevolution

The Role of the Spaniards in the Independence of Mexico, 1804-38

BY

ROMEO FLORES CABALLERO

Translated by

JAIME E. RODRÍGUEZ O.

UNIVERSITY OF NEBRASKA PRESS · LINCOLN

Publishers on the Plains

UNP

Copyright © 1969 by El Colegio de México
Translation © 1974 by the University of Nebraska Press
International Standard Book Number 0-8032-0805-7
Library of Congress Catalog Card Number 75-172037
Manufactured in the United States of America

To María Elena, Milena, and Aldo

Contents

vii

Abbreviations

AGN	Archivo General de la Nación, Mexico City
BN	Ramo de Bienes Nacionales, AGN
C	Ramo de Consolidación, AGN
H	Ramo de Historia, AGN
JE	Ramo de Justicia Eclesiástica, AGN
RC	Ramo de Reales Cédulas, AGN
BAGN	*Boletín del Archivo General de la Nación*
HAHR	*Hispanic American Historical Review*

Preface

The role of the Spaniards as prime movers of the colonial economy and the events that led to their replacement by the creoles are the major themes discussed in this work. It also discusses the validity of the widely accepted thesis that the expulsion of the Spaniards soon after Independence bankrupted Mexico and allowed foreigners to obtain control of the new nation's economy. It is, however, my contention that the economic contraction that so severely afflicted Mexico in the 1820s would have occurred whether or not the Spaniards had been ousted. The men from Spain did indeed enjoy a prominent economic position in New Spain during most of the colonial epoch, but by the beginning of the nineteenth century their fortunes had declined. A rising, ambitious creole class had begun to direct the region's economic affairs and to profit from them.

Although events are placed in historical perspective, the emphasis is on economic and political matters. What is offered in this book is a new interpretation of a vital and much-discussed theme—an interpretation intended to provoke further discussion and research on the topic. Rich opportunities for continuing research in this general realm remain open to scholars. We know, for instance, very little about the sources of financial support received by the Mexican insurgents, or of the political alignments among the creole oligarchy during the rebellion. The political implications of these questions are clear, but equally as important, the answers will tell us much about the economic situation in Mexico at that time. We also lack a meaningful understanding of the impact of the Royal Law of Consolidation which occurred just prior to the outbreak of the revolt, yet we know that it was a fundamental cause of the discontent that propelled Mexico toward Independence.

Despite these and many more unanswered questions, we are beginning to gain new and important insights into the entire Independence period of Mexican history. My general conclusions concerning the expulsion of the Spaniards have not greatly changed since 1969, when the book was first published by El Colegio de México. However, I have not hesitated to incorporate in this volume many of the suggestions for improvement made to me by readers of my earlier endeavor. In this regard, I am especially indebted to my friend and colleague Professor Jaime E. Rodríguez O., who not only has produced an excellent translation, but who also helped me to reorganize and clarify several sections of the book so that they would be more comprehensible to readers of English. Professor Rodríguez himself has researched certain aspects of the same period of Mexican history, and his general knowledge of the events that occurred undoubtedly helped to improve my presentation.

Romeo Flores Caballero

El Colegio de México
Mexico, D.F.

Translator's Note

Whenever possible, I have attempted to retain the author's style, but in all cases, clarity has been my principal objective. This book was originally written for a Mexican public which could be expected to know its national history. As a result, references were made to people and events without explanation. For the translation, I have provided clarification as needed, and as the great differences in the logic of Spanish and English necessitated a certain reorganization of parts of the book, the enumeration of footnotes is not the same in the English edition as in the Spanish version.

I am grateful to two friends and former colleagues, both of California State University, Long Beach: William F. Sater, who read the entire translation in its earlier versions and offered incisive criticism, and Keith I. Polakoff, who read most of the translation, also offering valuable criticism. Finally, I thank my wife, Linda Alexander Rodríguez, for important criticism and much needed encouragement.

Jaime E. Rodríguez O.

University of California
Irvine, California

Counterrevolution

ONE

The Spanish Population of Mexico, 1790-1821

Spaniards living in Mexico occupied a prominent place in the so-cial, economic, and political life of the country during the first three decades of the nineteenth century.[1] In order to evaluate their in-fluence on events in that critical period, it is necessary to examine both the size of the group and its role in Mexican society. The num-ber of Spaniards is difficult to determine with any certainty, how-ever, despite the existence of published studies on the subject.

The census of 1793, initiated by Viceroy Juan Vicente Güemes de Pacheco, the second count Revillagigedo, estimated that the total population of the Viceroyalty of New Spain numbered 4,483,680 in-habitants.[2] Ten years later Alexander von Humboldt estimated the populace at 5,764,731,[3] and by 1808 he considered it "very probable" that the population exceeded 6,500,000.[4] In 1810, when the War of Independence began, Fernando Navarro y Noriega calculated, in his *Memoria sobre población,* that there were 6,122,915 persons in Mexi-co.[5] The following year Juan López Cancelada, while admitting that no one really knew the size of the population, stated in his *Ruina de la Nueva España* that some census reports placed it at 5,900,000 and that "the general opinion, and probably the most accurate one," estimated it at an average of 6 million.[6]

Humboldt divided the population according to origin—Europeans, creoles, Indians, and castes (those of mixed blood)—calculating 75,000 Spaniards; 1 million creoles; 2.3 million Indians; and approxi-mately the same number of castes.[7] According to his estimates, the capital of the kingdom housed slightly more than 106,000 residents, including 2,118 Spanish men and 217 Spanish women, 21,338 creole men and 29,033 creole women, 11,232 Indian men and 14,371 Indian women, and 2,598 mulatto men and 4,136 mulatto women. The remaining 7,832 men and 11,525 women were not classified.[8] Navarro y Noriega divided the 1810 population of 6,122,915 as follows: 1,097,928 Spaniards and creoles, 3,676,281 Indians, and 1,348,706 castes.[9] Thus there were 18 whites, including both creoles and Spaniards, 60 Indians, and 22 castes per 100 persons. At the beginning of the independence government, Tadeo Ortiz de Ayala calculated that the population of Mexico had reached 9,940,000, including the inhabitants of Guatemala, which he estimated at 1½ million.[10]

The figures in the previous paragraphs, in spite of their indisputable importance, must be accepted with some reservation. The authors based their calculations on the Revillagigedo census, and, although it was one of the best taken in that era, it suffered from a number of deficiencies. Father José de Alzate, an eminent scholar of viceregal Mexico, was the first critic. He classified it as one of the "most unfounded productions which has ever come off the press," that it included "various items totally contrary to reality," and that in a word it was "a census of babbling and confusion rather than of population."[11]

Humboldt was aware of the problems with the Revillagigedo census, and it is possible that he had taken Alzate's observations into account. But Humboldt's calculations also were marred by a tendency to overgeneralize.[12] The estimate of the European population clearly reflects this error. According to Navarro y Noriega, the Revillagigedo census listed 7,904 Europeans.[13] Humboldt, on the other hand, estimated that 75,000 Spaniards lived in New Spain.[14] Navarro y Noriega, who doubted the German scholar's figures, reexamined Revillagigedo's census critically, and later, after considering several reports omitted from the general census, such as the one on immigration, he asserted that "no more than 15,000 Europeans could be counted" in 1810.[15] Humboldt had erred in assuming that the ratio of Spaniards to creoles in Mexico City was valid for the entire viceroyalty. That ratio was not general, since the majority of Spaniards tended to concentrate in the capital, as Humboldt himself observed.[16]

The Royal Tribunal of the Mining Guild also disagreed with Humboldt's estimate. In a report to the king explaining the inability of the residents of New Spain to name representatives to the Cortes (the Spanish parliament), it declared that "European Spaniards had raised their number without reason" to 75,000.[17] Lucas Alamán also considered Humboldt's figure to be extremely exaggerated.[18] Finally, Bishop Manuel Abad y Queipo raised the figure to 200,000

Europeans,[19] while Ortiz de Ayala estimated 100,000.[20]

This author reexamined the population statistics for the cities of Guanajuato, Oaxaca, Orizaba, and Jalapa contained in the Revillagigedo census. The census differentiated what it classed as Spanish families from Indians and castes. Further, it divided the Europeans into "pure" and "mixed" families, "pure" referring to those in which both husband and wife were European, and "mixed" to families in which either the husband or the wife was a creole and the other Spanish. This division made it possible to isolate the data relating to the European population and to discover the name, age, place of origin, marital status, and occupation of the principal members of each family. From the place of origin we can see the difference between those classified as Spanish and as European. The first were born in the colony and the second in Spain or other European countries.

It is easy to understand why most of the census's critics showed greater concern for the elite Spanish and creole families than for the bulk of the population. Aside from their prestige and power, they were the best-educated people; therefore their segment of the census was less likely to include the types of errors first discovered by Alzate and later corroborated by Ortiz de Ayala. Alzate noted that many individuals and families hid from the census takers. Some concealed themselves, "fearful and in panic" lest their children be taken away to populate the coasts of northern California; others feared that their fathers, husbands, or sons would be forced to join the army. Alzate asserted that "the name census alone . . . fills them with such horror that married women call themselves widows; mothers hide their young children; sisters hide their brothers; and some families even move from house to house, always fleeing from the census takers."[21]

The results of the author's study of the population statistics of the four previously mentioned cities are contained in Tables 1-4.

The results obtained from an analysis of these tables as well as the observations made about the 1793 census indicate that Navarro y Noriega's estimates are more correct than those of Humboldt. The estimates of the age of the Spanish population made in Table 2, the fact that Spanish immigration was small or nearly nonexistent because of the Napoleonic Wars, Spain's prohibition of "voluntary expatriation" of her subjects from New Spain to the peninsula,[22] and the large number of Europeans killed during the first years of the War of Independence suggest that the number of Spaniards calculated by Navarro y Noriega must have been less than 15,000.

TABLE 1

General Summary of Pure and Mixed Spanish Families,
Number of Europeans, and Total Population

Cities [a]	Families	Population	Europeans
Guanajuato	8,128	28,963	254
Oaxaca	2,957	10,504	212
Orizaba	1,896	8,360	120
Jalapa	2,369	8,768	97
Totals	15,350	56,595	683

Source: Archivo General de la Nación, Ramo de Padrones. Orizaba, vol. 19; Guanajuato, vols. 30, 31, 32, 33; Oaxaca, vol. 13; Jalapa, vol. 20.

[a] Including haciendas and nearby ranches. In the case of Oaxaca, it includes the village of Antequera.

TABLE 2

Ages of the European Residents

Ages	Guanajuato	Oaxaca	Orizaba	Jalapa	Total
13-20	25	20	5	4	54
21-30	58	37	20	11	126
31-40	52	53	30	20	155
41-50	41	48	36	31	156
51 & older	30	44	30	28	132
Totals	206	202	121	94	623

Source: Archivo General de la Nación, Ramo de Padrones. Orizaba, vol. 19; Guanajuato, vols. 30, 31, 32, 33; Oaxaca, vol. 13, Jalapa, vol. 20.

TABLE 3

Marital Status of the European Population

Civil Status	Guanajuato	Oaxaca	Orizaba	Jalapa	Total
Married	48[a]	72[b]	60[c]	47[d]	227
Widowed	9	19	5	5	38
Bachelors	134	101	55	45	335
Totals	191	192	120	97	600

Source: Archivo General de la Nación, Ramo de Padrones. Orizaba, vol. 19; Guanajuato, vols. 30, 31, 32, 33; Oaxaca, vol. 13; Jalapa, vol. 20.

[a] All married to creole women.
[b] Four marriages between Europeans.
[c] Two European women married to creoles and two marriages between Europeans.
[d] Two Europeans married to mestizo women and two Europeans married to European women.

This would be true even if one takes into account the fact that the Spaniards had a longer life expectancy than the rest of the population. In 1793, Humboldt estimated that for every 100 inhabitants of Mexico City, 18 Spaniards, 8 creoles, 7 mulattos, 6 Indians, and 6 castes lived to the age of 50 or longer.[23] Miguel María de Azcárate observed that of the 2,338 Spaniards who then lived in Mexico City, 90 percent were 17 or older, 415 were between 25 and 40, 645 were between 40 and 50, and 642 were older than 50 years of age.[24] The importance of these calculations lies in the fact that the majority would have died by the time independence was achieved.

After 1810 any significant population movement was directly related to the War of Independence. The Spanish emigrated from the areas of combat and, in general, from New Spain. Ortiz de Ayala pointed out that the only emigration from Mexico was Spanish and that "an average of 800 to 1,000 left every year."[25] By the same token, immigration to New Spain was also dominated by Spaniards, especially military men. According to Lucas Alamán, by the end of the colonial period Spain had sent 8,500 expeditionary soldiers to Mexico.[26] If one accepts Navarro y Noriega's estimate of 15,000 Spaniards in Mexico in 1793, subtracts those who died and those who emigrated, and adds the expeditionaries as well as the few others who arrived after 1810, then one may conclude that there were probably about 15,000 Spaniards in Mexico at Independence. Of these, about half were military men, approximately 1,500 clergy, and the remainder bureaucrats, merchants, and a few landowners.

A brief analysis of social conditions in New Spain reveals that this small group of Spaniards occupied the upper strata of society along with the wealthy creoles. The Europeans dominated commerce and the bureaucracy, which they used to further their interests and those of their monarch. The creoles, given the hereditary nature of their property, were primarily involved in mining and agriculture. These two groups were the guiding forces behind the economy, politics, and society.

TABLE 4

Occupations of the Europeans

Occupation	Guanajuato	Oaxaca	Orizaba	Jalapa	Total
Merchants	78	83	34	43	238
Cashiers	67	41	8	10	126
Royal Officials	18	28	21	10	77
Land Owners	1[a]	4	6[b]	3[a]	14
Military	5	9	4	5	23
Clergy	2	1	16	1	20
Miners	51	3	—	—	54
Others	14[c]	6[d]	16[e]	12[f]	48
Totals	236	175	105	84	600

Source: Archivo General de la Nación, Ramo de Padrones. Orizaba, vol. 19; Guanajuato, vols. 30, 31, 32, 33; Oaxaca, vol. 13; Jalapa, vol. 20.

[a] Farmer.
[b] Four tobacco growers and two farmers.
[c] Seven vintners, two servants, one barber, one tailor, one butcher, one licensed surgeon, one confectioner.
[d] One architect, one broker, one carpenter, one student, one engraver, one ranch manager.
[e] Five factory workers, two operators, four sugar mill employees, one schoolteacher, one servant, one dyer, and two unemployed invalids.
[f] Three vintners, two tailors, one barber, one schoolteacher, one surgeon, one broker, and two with "various jobs."

The Spaniards controlled the principal posts in public administration, the Church, the judiciary, and the army. Father Servando Teresa de Mier noted that the following public officials were Spanish: the viceroy and all his dependents (except his secretary, who was creole); the president of the merchant's guild and the consuls; the assessor general of the viceroyalty; the superintendent of the mint; the treasurer general, as well as the administrator, of the *alcabala* (sales taxes); the chief clerk of customs; the director, the treasurer, and the chief clerk of the General Administration of Tobacco; the officials of the General Treasury; the treasurer and the accountant general of the lottery; all the intendants; the director of mining; the *alcaldes ordinarios*; the *corregidor*; the superintendent of the city; the director of the General Administration of the Mails; the smelter general of gold and silver; the secretary of the university, who held "a lifetime post with many perquisites"; the stewards of the Royal Hospital and San Andrés Hospital, "who have large incomes"; and the director of the Anatomical Amphitheater. In the Church the following were peninsulares: the archbishop; all the bishops but one; the chaplains; the stewards of the richest nunneries and their familiars, secretaries, prosecretaries, and clerks; the inquisitors and their secretaries; the treasurer, the nuncio, the keeper, the dean, the archdean, the cantor, the treasurer, and various canons and prebends of the capital. Europeans in the judiciary included: the regent and most of the judges of the Audiencia, the magistrates of the courts, the three state attorneys, the vicar general, the provisor, the judge for testaments and pious works, and the special judge of the Acordada. Although there were some creoles in the army, the following were Spaniards: the colonels of Guanajuato, Valladolid, Texas, Oaxaca, and Puebla; the colonel of the Tlaxcala battalion; the colonel of the battalion of the merchants of Mexico; the commander of the baker's squadron; the captain general; the lieutenant general; all the commanders of the ten brigades of the kingdom; all the colonels and sergeants major of all the regular as well as provincial regiments; the major of the fortress of San Juan de Ulúa, and the commander of the shipyards.[27]

While a substantial number of other foreigners participated, the peninsulares dominated commerce. The Spanish merchants retained their privileged position because of the monopoly they enjoyed with those merchants in the mother country who traded with New Spain, even though, as José María Quirós stated, trade with Spain was not as large as commonly believed and did not have much influence over

the "internal flow of currency in the kingdom."[28] Furthermore,
though other foreigners had 20 million pesos invested at rates of 15 to
20 percent in Mexico's trade,[29] Spaniards remained dominant. Those
peninsulares who did not arrive as employees or relatives of
merchants in the peninsula came to New Spain while very young to
begin their careers with the help of their compatriots in the colonial
retail business. While many remained single, some married creoles because of the almost total absence of Spanish women.[30] In time, these
men lost their ties with Spain. The few who contracted marriage with
rich creole women became powerful members of the colonial
oligarchy by managing their wives' fortunes.[31]

Textile manufacturing and winegrowing, among the most important industries at the beginning of the nineteenth century, were
controlled by Spaniards. In some instances, especially in the case of
textiles, the industry was completely dependent upon Spanish capital.
Some capitalists, like the merchants of Puebla, also owned cotton
lands which enabled them to control their tenants' production as well
as that of other cotton planters.[32] Since the industry could not com-
pete in the world market, it was oriented toward domestic
consumption.

Despite the advantages which Spanish merchants enjoyed, however, the creoles generally possessed greater wealth. They owned the
mines, then considered the colony's most important enterprise.[33]
Mexicans also dominated agriculture and livestock raising, which
might be considered the true mainstays of the economy, since they
employed the majority of the population.[34] López Cancelada, though
he exaggerated, calculated the number of creoles engaged in agriculture at 350,000 "rich farm owners."[35] Félix María Calleja, moreover,
denied that the Europeans controlled the colony's riches,
characterizing such assertions as "infamous lies, falsehoods, slander,
and errors." He further alleged that there were thousands of wealthy
Mexicans among the nobles, the merchants, and the great landowners who had both the ability and the character necessary to make
their own fortunes or to preserve what they had inherited.[36]

While it was generally believed that mining was Mexico's greatest
source of wealth, many observers have argued the contrary. Ortiz de
Ayala maintained that the mining industry really did not affect the.
"true prosperity of the nation"; rather, he believed that agriculture
was "the basis of a truly reliable opulence." Humboldt agreed with
Ortiz de Ayala that "the true prosperity" of Mexico did not depend

upon the vicissitudes of a foreign trade subject to the vagaries of European politics, but upon agriculture, which he described as "the fundamental source of the nation's life."[37] José María Quirós, secretary of the *consulado* (merchants' guild) of Veracruz, observed that agricultural production was valued at 227,500,000 pesos, while estimating mineral output to be worth only 27,000,000 pesos. Thus, it was agriculture, rather than commerce or mining, which generated the wealth of New Spain.[38] Since the creoles controlled both agriculture and mining, the truly great fortunes were theirs.

Thus, though Europeans controlled the bureaucracy, commerce, and some industry, they were neither the wealthiest nor the best-educated segment of society. The Spaniards' education, according to José María Luis Mora, was "very scanty."[39] Alamán did not consider them enlightened as a class.[40] Humboldt also thought them "without education and without intellectual development."[41] And Lorenzo de Zavala maintained that the core of their knowledge could be epitomized in the maxim "Be silent and respectful toward the king and the Inquisition."[42]

Although it was the creoles and not the Spaniards who constituted the best-educated part of the colony, their careers were limited because the only professions available to them were law and the clergy. Those who had not inherited fortunes, or who failed to become wealthy through their own efforts, occupied only mediocre positions in the civil and military bureaucracy or the less important curacies in the Church.

The creoles and the Spanish colonial oligarchy, although often in agreement on economic issues, were divided socially and politically. The creoles, the largest colonial landowners, had the closest ties with the people and controlled the city councils. Thus their strength and support came from the colony itself. By the very nature of their activities, the Spaniards derived their power from the mother country. So although they were not popular, they controlled the most powerful colonial institutions, such as the *consulados*. Under these circumstances it is not strange that the Spaniards, rather than the creoles, responded more rapidly to the frequent requests for aid from Spain. Initially their large contributions were voluntary. Later, especially when the Crown—ignorant of the true state of New Spain's economy—imposed the Law of Consolidation of 1804, they reacted differently. The oligarchies coexisted as long as the mother country could dominate the colony. This uneasy truce ended at the beginning of the nineteenth century when the colony saw Spain so weakened that she had to solicit funds from Mexico in order to meet her European commitments and maintain her imperial power and prestige.

More affluent, better educated than the rest of the population, yet conscious of being second-class citizens in their own country, the creoles awaited an opportune moment to rebel against Spanish administration. With those successful mestizos who comprised the small middle class, they capitalized on ancient but hitherto dormant grievances against Spain, and began to strive for a separate national identity. The creoles, who had no direct ties with Spain, began calling themselves Americans. According to Humboldt, after 1780, they could be heard to say with pride: "I am not a Spaniard, I am an American," words which, as that scholar noted, "were symptoms of the revival of ancient grievances."[43]

The majority of the prerevolutionary society consisted of mestizos, Indians, and castes. The latter two groups, who provided the labor necessary for the oligarchy to maintain its control and enjoy its privileges, lived in abject poverty. Without hope, living in absolute misery and ignorance, they were ready to follow their creole leaders in search of redemption and political emancipation.

The general population's only direct contact with the political system was through the king's bureaucrats, as they administered justice. Most creoles and mestizos saw the pomp and prestige of the monarchy only through the celebrations conducted by the viceroy and his officials. These fleeting contacts with Spanish administration had at one time been sufficient to satisfy them. But at the turn of the century they became disgruntled as they aspired for autonomy.[44] This sense of alienation, in conjunction with various economic abuses, provided a receptive audience for liberal principles among the colonials, especially among the dissatisfied creoles. Moreover, as a result of the independence of the United States and the French Revolution, liberal ideas spread more easily and widely than ever. Spain had not prevented her people from participating in the Enlightenment; neither could she prevent her colonies from imitating the example of the republicans to the north. These events coincided with the collapse of the Spanish empire, once the most powerful in the world.

In 1808, fearing that Viceroy Iturrigaray would take the lead in separating Mexico from the mother country because of the French invasion of Spain, the Europeans arbitrarily jailed him. To the tiny minority of peninsulares it was necessary to act in order to preserve their social, economic, and political interests. With this in mind, they embarked upon a program which, according to Justo Sierra, could be described as "New Spain for the Spaniards." This totally conflicted with the insurgents' desire of a "New Spain for the Mexicans."[45]

NOTES

1. The terms *European, peninsular,* and *Spaniard* are used interchangeably in this work to refer to persons residing in Mexico who were born in Spain. Similarly, *Spain, peninsula,* and *metropolis* refer to Spain. At no time will the term *Spaniards* refer to Spaniards living and acting in Spain, still less to creoles or the rest of the population of Mexico.

2. Alexander von Humboldt, *Tablas geográfico-políticas del reino de la Nueva España que manifestan su superficie, población, agricultura, fábricas, comercio, minas, rentas y fuerza militar. Por el Barón de Humboldt, presentada al excmo. señor virrey don José de Iturrigaray* (Mexico, 1822), p. 5; hereafter cited as Humboldt, *Tablas*.

3. Ibid., p. 6.

4. Alexander von Humboldt, *Ensayo político sobre el reino de la Nueva España*, 5 vols. (Mexico, 1941), 2:25; hereafter cited as Humboldt, *Ensayo político*.

5. Fernando Navarro y Noriega, *Catálogo de los curatos y misiones de la Nueva España, seguido de la Memoria sobre la población del reino de la Nueva España (primer tercio del siglo XIX)* (Mexico, 1943), pp. 68-69; hereafter cited as Navarro y Noriega, *Catálogo*.

6. Juan López Cancelada, *Ruina de la Nueva España si se declara el comercio libre con los estranjeros. Exprésanse los motivos. Quaderno segundo y primero en la materia por D. Juan López Cancelada* (Cadiz, 1811), p. 9; hereafter cited as López Cancelada, *Ruina*.

7. Humboldt, *Tablas*, p. 12.

8. Humboldt, *Ensayo político*, 2:118.

9. Navarro y Noriega, *Catálogo*, p. 65. Critics of the first edition of this work indicated that the figures used in the text were wrong. When Navarro y Noriega's figures were checked, the error was discovered. Therefore, correct totals are used in this English edition.

10. Tadeo Ortiz de Ayala, *Resumen de la estadísca del Imperio Mexicano* (Mexico, 1822), p. 19; hereafter cited as Ortiz de Ayala, *Resumen de la estadísca*.

11. Correspondence between Father José Antonio Alzate and Viceroy Revillagigedo concerning population and consumer goods of Mexico City may be found in the Archivo General de la Nación (hereafter cited as AGN), Ramo de Historia (hereafter cited as H) vol. 74, exp. 1, fol. 72.

12. See, among others, the criticisms of Navarro y Noriega, *Catálogo*, pp. 14-15; Ortiz de Ayala, *Resumen de la estadística*, p. 24; more recently, Hugh Hamill, *The Hidalgo Revolt: Prelude to Mexican Independence* (Gainesville, Fla., 1966), p. 19; Victoria Lerner, "La población de la Nueva España," *Historia Mexicana* 17 (January-March, 1968): 327-46.

13. Navarro y Noriega, *Catálogo*, p. 13.

14. Humboldt, *Ensayo político*, 2:26.

15. Navarro y Noriega, *Catálogo*, p. 14.

16. Humboldt, *Ensayo político*, 2:121.

17. Juan E. Hernández y Dávalos, *Colección de documentos para la historia de la guerra de independencia de México de 1808 a 1821*, 6 vols. (Mexico, 1879-1882), vol. 2, doc. 224, 450. Hereafter cited as Hernández y Dávalos, *Colección*.

18. Lucas Alamán, *Historia de Méjico desde los primeros movimientos que prepararon su independencia el año de 1808 hasta la época presente*, 5 vols. (Mexico, 1849-1852), 5:811. Hereafter cited as Alamán, *Historia*. However, he also considered that there were 70,000 Spaniards. See ibid., 1:30.

19. Manuel Abad y Queipo, "Informe dirigido a Fernando VII," in Alamán, *Historia*, 5:691.

20. Ortiz de Ayala, *Resumen de la estadística*, p. 25.

21. "Contestaciones . . . ," AGN, RH, vol. 74, exp. 1, fols. 27-28.

22. Decree of January 20, 1806, AGN, Ramo de Reales Cédulas (hereafter cited as RC), vol. 197, leg. 4, fol. 1; also, *Gazeta de México* 14, no. 38, p. 307.

23. Alexander von Humboldt, *Tablas políticas del reino de Nueva España que manifiestan la superficie, población, agricultura, comercio, minas, rentas y fuerza militar, primer bosquejo*, AGN, H, vol. 72, fol. 28.

24. Miguel María de Azcárate, *Noticias estadísticas que sobre los efectos de consumo introducidos en esta capital en el quinquenio de 1834 a 1838, presenta el comandante de rentas unidas de México, coronel retirado del ejército M.M.A.* (Mexico, 1839). These estimates are for 1790.

25. Ortiz de Ayala, *Resumen de la estadística*, p. 20.

26. Alamán, *Historia*, 5:18-19. Elsewhere he calculated that of the 40,000 soldiers of New Spain, 12,000 "were from regiments that came from Spain" (Ibid., 4:436).

27. Servando Teresa de Mier, *Historia de la revolución de la Nueva España, antiguamente Anáhuac, ó verdadero origen y causas de ella, con la relación de sus progresos hasta el presente año de 1813* (London, 1813), p. xv.

28. José María Quirós, *Memoria de estatuto. Idea de la riqueza que deban a la masa circulante de Nueva España sus naturales producciones en los años de tranquilidad y su abatimiento en las presentes conmociones . . . leída en la primera junta de gobierno celebrada en 24 de enero de 1817* (Veracruz, 1817), p. 18; hereafter cited as Quirós, *Memoria de estatuto*.

29. Manuel Abad y Queipo, "Representación a nombre de los labradores y comerciantes de Valladolid de Michoacán, en donde se demuestra con claridad los inconvenientes de que se ejecute en las Américas la real cédula de 26 de diciembre de 1804, sobre enagenación de bienes raíces y cobro de capitales de capellanías y obras pías, para la consolidación de vales," in Hernández y Dávalos, *Colección*, vol. 2, docs. 262, 862. Fifteen or twenty million pesos was approximately half the amount of money circulated in the commerce of New Spain. This figure does not take into consideration the contraband trade by foreigners. See also Miguel Lerdo de Tejada, *Comercio esterior de México desde la conquista hasta hoy* (Mexico, 1853), doc. no. 14; Robert S. Smith, "Shipping in the Port of Veracruz, 1790-1821," *HAHR* 23 (February 1943): 13-15; John H. Hann, "The Role of Mexican Deputies in the Proposal and Enactment of Measures of Economic Reform Applicable to Mexico," in Nettie Lee Benson, ed., *Mexico and the Spanish Cortes, 1810-1822* (Austin, 1966), pp. 153-84.

30. See Tables 3 and 4.

31. José María Luis Mora, *Obras sueltas,* 2d ed. (Mexico, 1963), p. 76; Alamán, *Historia,* 1:22. Among the most notorious were Gabriel de Yermo, Juan López Cancelada, Félix María Calleja, and Lucas Alamán's father.

32. "Apuntes estadísticos de la intendencia de Veracruz, relaciones," cited in Robert Potash, *El Banco de Avío de México: El fomento de la industria, 1821-1846* (Mexico, 1959), pp. 20-23.

33. Alamán, *Historia,* 1: 68-69. This does not mean that the Spaniards were excluded from mining and agriculture. Yermo and Calleja, who were great landowners, achieved that position because of their wives' inheritances.

34. Alamán, *Historia,* 1: 227-28.

35. López Cancelada, *Ruina,* p. 10.

36. Humboldt, *Ensayo político,* 3: 12-175.

37. Ortiz de Ayala, *Resumen de la estadística,* 64.

38. Quirós, *Memoria de estatuto,* p. 28.

39. Mora, *Obras sueltas,* p. 77.

40. Alamán, *Historia,* 1: 25.

41. Humboldt, *Ensayo político,* 2: 117.

42. Lorenzo de Zavala, *Umbral de la independencia.* (Mexico, 1949), 86.

43. Humboldt, *Ensayo político,* 1: 80.

44. Miguel Ramos Arizpe, *Memoria, que el Doctor D. Miguel Ramos de Arizpe, cura de Borbón, y Diputado en las presentes Cortes Generales y Extraordinarias de España por la provincia de Coahuila, una de las cuatro Internas del Oriente en el Reyno de México, presenta a el augusto Congreso, sobre el estado natural, político y civil de su dicha provincia, y las del Nuevo Reyno de León, Nuevo Santander y los de Texas, con exposición de los defectos del sistema general, y en particular de sus gobiernos, y de las reformas, y nuevos establecimientos que necesitan para su prosperidad* (Cádiz, 1812), p. 30.

45. Justo Sierra, *Evolución política del pueblo mexicano* (Mexico, 1950), pp. 107-8.

TWO

The Royal Law of Consolidation

Relations between Spain and New Spain underwent fundamental changes in the period between the viceregency of the second count Revillagigedo and the beginning of independence in 1810. During this time the mother country found it increasingly difficult to raise the revenues necessary to maintain its position as a world power, while the colony was enjoying unprecedented prosperity. Spain had experimented with various methods of alleviating its financial difficulties,[1] but none of them had proved wholly successful. In times of crisis, Spain had frequently appealed to its subjects in Mexico, who had provided assistance. As long as the requests were for voluntary aid, the oligarchy of New Spain supported the mother country. But when Spain's urgent needs outstripped the willing cooperation of its subjects, the Crown resorted to forced loans and other measures.

Of all its American possessions, Mexico yielded the greatest dividends to Spain. The northern colony not only accounted for two-thirds of its imperial revenue, but also supported Spanish colonies in the Caribbean, Louisiana, and Florida. This does not include the occasional contributions which Mexico granted more freely in times of prosperity.[2] However, as the colony's prosperity increased, so also did the creoles' misgivings toward Spaniards and the government. According to Mora, "the desire for independence went hand in hand" with material progress.[3]

Spain's declaration of war on England on December 12, 1804, substantially aggravated the peninsula's already weak financial condition. It was necessary to raise funds to finance the war as well as to service Spain's foreign debt. Since the home government's resources were rapidly being exhausted, it was imperative that the colonies, especially New Spain, assist the mother country.[4] However, the colony's response was inadequate; many people were tired of sending their wealth to support Spain's interminable European conflicts. The creoles, especially the educated, ceased to identify Spain's interests with their own and began to question the authority of the Spanish monarchy.[5]

Faced with a critical need for money, the Crown took desperate measures. On December 26, 1804—only fourteen days after declaring war—Spain decreed the Royal Law of Consolidation, an act which provoked grave economic, social, and political consequences in her American possessions. Significantly, this first attack against the wealth of the Mexican Church took place half a century before the reform laws of Benito Juárez's government.

On the eve of independence, the Church was the richest and most powerful institution in Mexico. Its wealth was primarily associated with the possession of land. Nevertheless, the private capital that the church administered exceeded the real estate in value, and therefore played a more important part in its power and influence.[6] Bishop Abad y Queipo, for example, contended that, excluding the lands of some regular orders, the Church derived its income from investments and loans to merchants, farmers, and miners.[7] Humboldt, supporting Abad y Queipo, wrote that the landed wealth of the Mexican Church did not exceed 2½ million to 3 million pesos, but its investments amounted to more than 44 million pesos.[8] Ortiz de Ayala substantially agreed with these figures, estimating that the Church's land was worth about 5 million pesos, while, as of 1804, the Church held 45 million pesos in mortgages on private properties. The interest from these loans paid for pious works, chaplaincies, legacies, and gifts to convents.[9] Mora disagreed with Humboldt, who did not have information on all the bishoprics, and argued that it was necessary to "more than double" Humboldt's calculations since the Church's total wealth was not less than 75 or 80 million *duros*. However, this figure is somewhat exaggerated because it includes income from legacies of various regular orders.[10]

The Royal Law of Consolidation had first been promulgated in Spain in 1798. When pressing financial need forced the government to implement it again in 1804, it was extended to the empire. "Peace has been maintained by the force of Millions—which are diminishing as debts are paid," stated the introduction of the decree. "Many more are necessary to cover those that remain and to meet the innumerable obligations of the Crown and of the defense of the kingdom." The

king, "having ascertained in Spain the utility and advantageous effects" of the law, therefore resolved that the government seize and
auction the real estate belonging to the pious works regardless of "its
nature or condition." The proceeds from its sale together with other
wealth that might belong to pious works were to be deposited in the
Royal Amortization Fund at a "just and equitable interest."[11]

Although the disentailment and sale of its real estate would not
have substantially affected the Church's wealth, by including its liquid
capital the law posed "grave economic consequences." The Church
was the financial nerve center of New Spain. Its capital came from
diverse sources, the most important being the investments of the Tribunal of Chaplaincies, Testaments, and Pious Works.[12] The wealthy
commonly endowed the tribunal with a bequest of between two and
six thousand pesos to establish a chaplaincy or some philanthropy
called a pious work. The tribunal then invested the sum, usually at 5
percent, providing an income for the pious work or for the chaplain,
who was obliged in turn to celebrate a certain number of masses
annually for the well-being of the benefactor's soul.[13] There were
thousands of such chaplaincies and pious works in New Spain, and as
a consequence the tribunal had amassed enormous capital. Since
these endowments were in cash, the tribunal controlled large sums of
liquid capital, which it invested in order to obtain income, and thus it
had become one of the principal sources of investment capital in the
colony. Farmers, merchants, and miners frequently borrowed from it.
The Tribunal of Chaplaincies did not have legal title to the bequests,
but held them in trust, merely administering the funds, making loans,
and collecting and disbursing income to the beneficiaries.[14] In addition to the Tribunal of Chaplaincies, convents, monasteries, religious
orders, brotherhoods, and colleges also received gifts of land or large
sums of money which were invested in a similar fashion.

As a general rule, these institutions lent their money to all sectors of the population, including individuals as well as public institutions. As Michael Costeloe indicates, there was some reluctance to
lend to the government because it was a poor credit risk, often failing
to repay its debts.[15] Most ecclesiastical institutions required land as
collateral, but on a few occasions they accepted the guarantees of
prominent borrowers.[16] The loans were generally made for periods of
five to nine years, at a rate of interest which varied between 5 and 6
percent. When debtors were delinquent in their payments, the Church
usually did not foreclose, but either extended the payment period or

renegotiated the contract.[17] Under this happy arrangement the beneficiaries received a regular income from the endowment, the Church
did not require large staffs to manage the funds, and the debtors
never repaid the principal, instead passing the debts on to their
children. Thus the Church became an investment bank and the
motivating force in New Spain's economy.

Foreign events shattered this routine economic activity and the
traditional practice of allowing the renewal of contracts. The Royal
Law of Consolidation threatened to ruin New Spain because it
demanded that the Church put not only its lands but also its capital
at the disposal of the Crown. The government, trying to minimize the
effects of such a forced loan, offered to return the capital eventually
and to pay 3 percent annual interest. As collateral it offered to mortgage its income from the tobacco monopoly, the *alcabala* tax, and
other revenues.

The Crown disguised the true reason for promulgating the Law of
Consolidation when it stated that it needed "considerable and
immediate aid to alleviate the misfortunes of hunger, pestilence, and
other calamities which Divine Providence has inflicted in these last
years." But regardless of its motive, the Spanish government needed
the funds and provided incentives for their collection. It established
subordinate committees of consolidation composed of viceroys, presi-
dents of Audiencias, archbishops and bishops, regents of Audiencias,
a deputy, and a secretary, who would also act at times as accountant.
The decisions of the committees were to be implemented immediately.
If appeals were made, they were to be forwarded directly to the
monarch through the Council of Castile, although such appeals were
not to delay or suspend the confiscations. In no case could the subordinate committees exempt any property from confiscation without
consulting and receiving approval from the sovereign. The committees were obliged to investigate "promptly and meticulously" all
pious works and chaplaincies in their districts, even if they were
"collective or familial," listing their landed property, capital, and
bonds. Moreover, in order that the information be complete, all
scribes, administrators, majordomos, renters, priests, parishioners,
regular prelates, and all those who might provide pertinent information were required to cooperate with the committee. All must provide
their information within one month "without the slightest opposition
or reluctance and with the accuracy consistent with honor and good
conscience."[18]

The properties of churches and religious communities were excluded from the confiscation, but possessions in their trust, the revenues from which paid for pious obligations, suffrage, worship, or other works of charity, were not exempted. This was true even if such possessions were commingled with their legal properties, or if they were assigned to them by virtue of patronage, administration, or any other reason. Trust properties, including those which might have been acquired by later donations or purchased with trust income, could be confiscated. In this group were properties of the Third Order of St. Francis, brotherhoods, hermitages, sanctuaries, hospitals and houses of mercy, and similar institutions.

The law provided that rural and urban properties under mortgage to chaplaincies or pious works and whose payments were delinquent would be accepted for "adjustment," provided some cash payment was made and the rest paid according to terms agreed upon by the Subordinate Committee of Consolidation. If these obligations were not met, the committee could sell the properties at auction. The law further specified that a buyer who could pay two-thirds of the value of a confiscated property in cash need not wait for an auction but might buy it from the committee. Those properties, sold at auction and valued at between ten and twenty thousand pesos, were to be paid for half in cash and the remainder within one year; those valued at between twenty and fifty thousand pesos, one-fourth in cash and the remainder in five years; and those worth between fifty and one hundred thousand, one-fifth in cash and the remainder in six or seven years. The judges might decide what amount should be paid in cash for any property valued at more than one hundred thousand pesos, but the remainder had to be paid within ten years. In order to encourage buyers, all such transactions were exempted from taxation.

The law prohibited judges, appraisers, representatives of pious works, deputies, and those who participated in the auctions from buying properties; but since the Crown realized that the effectiveness of the law depended upon the willingness of the bureaucrats to carry out their obligations in the face of strong pressures which powerful interests might bring to bear upon them, the king provided a series of incentives. Members of the superior committee in Spain would receive one-half of 1 percent of the amount collected. Members of subordinate committees, the viceroy, governors, and bishops would receive the same amount, in addition to their salaries as committee members. The state attorney of the subordinate Audiencias would receive three hundred pesos, those of the capital, five hundred. The accounting secretary would also receive one-half of 1 percent; the royal officials and the principal deputy would receive one-fourth of 1 percent of the amount collected in the provinces.[19] The Crown hoped these incentives would keep officials from attempting to obstruct the execution of the law.

The Spanish government thus required the Church and the colony to sacrifice themselves to the higher interests of the Crown. The Law of Consolidation would have totally disrupted Mexico's economy in good times, but its effects threatened to be even more devastating because New Spain was suffering from a severe and protracted agricultural crisis.[20] Merchants, land owners, miners, small farmers, retail store owners, and the countless *menu peuple* who were delinquent in their payments sought to circumvent the law or to have it annulled. The colony's most influential groups and institutions led the protest against its implementation, beseeching the Crown in petitions known as representations to reconsider. The language of these representations, while respectful, was charged with a sense of desperation. Indeed, the word *ruin* appears in every petition submitted to the monarch.

The colonists tried to have the law rescinded on the ground that the wealth of the Mexican Church, unlike that of the Church in Spain, was invested productively in the nation's economy. Bishop Abad y Queipo argued that while taking the lands and capital from the Spanish Church might have helped the mother country by allowing it to utilize such wealth more effectively, the same would not be true in Mexico, where the Church was contributing to the well-being of New Spain's economy. He also maintained that in Spain the Tribunal of Chaplaincies had little wealth, but in Mexico it was the chief source of investment capital. The Bishop further observed that nearly all of the two hundred thousand persons engaged in agriculture, mining, and commerce operated with funds borrowed from the Church, moreover, very few of those who owned property controlled more than a third of the capital they utilized in their activities. Thus, although confiscating the capital of pious works had little effect in Spain, in Mexico it would cause economic disaster. The bishop insisted that the Law of Consolidation therefore be suspended.[21]

The mining tribunal supported Abad y Queipo's arguments, adding that the Tribunal of Chaplaincies and Pious Funds did not have title to funds, but merely held them in trust, acting as administrator for the beneficiaries. It concluded with the statement that in New Spain the capital of the pious funds should be considered "the moving force behind agriculture, mining, commerce, and industry."[22] The City Council of Mexico also joined in making strong protests against the law, concluding for the same reasons given in the other representations that the Crown's experience in Spain was not applicable to Mexico.[23]

While most of the representations agreed that Church wealth was not based on land, they could not agree on the value of clerical investments. The ecclesiastical cabildo of Valladolid believed the funds of the pious works amounted to approximately 27 million pesos, held in the following manner:

	Millions
Archbishopric of Mexico	9.0
Bishopric of Puebla	6.0
Bishopric of Michoacán	4.7
Bishopric of Guadalajara	3.0
Bishopric of Sonora, Durango, and Monterrey	1.0
Bishopric of Oaxaca and Campeche	1.0
Real estate	2.0
Total	26.7[24]

The mining tribunal, on the other hand, estimated the Church's capital at 40 million pesos,[25] and Abad y Queipo calculated that the capital of the pious funds totaled 44½ million pesos, distributed as follows:

Diocese	*Millions*
Mexico	9.0
Puebla	6.5
Michoacán	4.5
Guadalajara	3.0
Durango, Monterrey, and Sonora	1.0
Oaxaca and Yucatán	2.0
Pious works in the churches of regular orders of both sexes	2.5
Total invested capital of churches and religious communities of both sexes, which must be turned over by decree of the Committee of Consolidation in Mexico	16.0
Total	44.5[26]

The City Council of Mexico calculated the funds of the pious works at 50 million pesos, of which 25 million were concentrated in the diocese of Mexico; there were between 18 and 19 million pesos "in cash dispersed" elsewhere.[27] The representation of Tehuacán placed the real value of the pious funds much higher, at about 70 million pesos.[28] But as the Pátzcuaro city council indicated, the wealth of the pious funds was not in cash but in investments and therefore took on "the abstract and hypothetical value of the [mortgaged] real estate."[29]

Although the Royal Law of Consolidation affected all sectors of the economy, farmers were the hardest hit. Their business was subject to vicissitudes of weather and other factors beyond their control which often drove them into debt. The *hacendados* of Mexico City, among the most powerful in the colony,[30] assured the Crown that they were the ones who needed Church funds most, and as a group, they were the ones most heavily in debt.[31] They argued that although commerce might not need money from the pious funds, miners and farmers needed it desperately.[32] The Puebla city council agreed with the Mexico City landowners, emphasizing the farmers' dependence on the pious funds with the observation that those funds were the only source of aid in times of crisis, since there were no pawn shops or individual lenders to whom the farmers could turn.[33] The representation of Mexico City[34] reinforced these arguments and suggested that nine-tenths of the farmers and ranchers, as opposed to possibly two-thirds of the merchants and miners, would suffer from the application of the Law.[35]

The number of property owners threatened with confiscation was considerable. Some maintained that 90 percent of all real estate, especially rural properties, was mortgaged to the pious works.[36] Those not so encumbered were rare, since most had been mortgaged for several generations. Some properties had been pledged for as long as 250 years.[37] Perhaps as many as ten to thirty thousand families would suffer.[38] The greatest harm would fall on those with limited resources; although wealthy families would be affected, they had the means to tide them over the crisis. And as the mining tribunal explained, they were not the ones most active in the economy. It was the countless small farmers, merchants, and miners who really sustained Mexico's economy; they were the ones who would be ruined by the law. Indeed, the mining tribunal argued that the rich generally represented "an obstacle . . . to enterprise."[39]

Thus it seemed that if the royal law were implemented, very few people could meet its conditions.[40] Under such circumstances, it was likely that most mortgaged property would be confiscated and sold at public auction. But who could guarantee that an auction would attract any buyers since, according to the Valladolid city council, no one had any money with which to purchase the confiscated real estate?[41] Farmers and businessmen in Mexico City believed that since so many properties would be confiscated there would be a glut on the market. They added that only 6 percent of Mexico City's real estate was classified as rural and the remaining urban land would be "difficult to sell."[42] The mining tribunal noted that the value of mortgaged properties in New Spain was about 50 to 60 million pesos, while there were only between 14 and 16 million pesos in circulation.[43] The Puebla city council noted that "there were so many attractive haciendas [being auctioned] that the market was saturated."[44] As a result, the few wealthy men able to buy confiscated property could actually set their own prices by not purchasing until values declined drastically.[45]

It was estimated that Spain would raise about seven hundred thousand pesos annually from the execution of the Law of Consolidation. This was not a large sum—Spain normally derived 8 to 10 million pesos in taxes from Mexico—but the war with England had disrupted trade, diminishing the Crown's revenues along with the merchants' profits. Mexico had generally experienced an adverse balance of payments with Spain, resulting in the constant flight of specie, and because of the currency shortage, New Spain's authorities were forced to increase the production of the mint. The measure was useless, however, since silver generally left the colony faster than it could be mined and coined. The Law of Consolidation threatened to add an even greater burden by further reducing Mexico's already scarce specie. The ecclesiastical cabildo of Valladolid warned that because of the multiplier effect, the colony's financial market would suffer a tenfold contraction if the law were implemented and the royal treasury would lose 3 million pesos a year in taxes.[46] The City Council of Mexico argued that under such circumstances smuggling would increase, depriving the mother country of an estimated 10 million pesos.[47] Thus, although Mexico would be forced to exert a maximum effort in order to survive and to meet its commitments to Spain, there was no guarantee that the sacrifice would be productive. If the Law of Consolidation were carried out, Mexico's economy might be destroyed; yet the results could well be less income for the Crown than normal taxes were already providing.[48]

The threat of the Law of Consolidation had grave political consequences. Spain's subjects in Mexico had always before come to the assistance of the mother country in periods of crisis, at times using some funds from the pious works.[49] However, the potentially crippling effects of the law shook their faith in the ideal of a "just monarch directing his people toward prosperity and happiness." They warned him that they, his subjects, would suffer the most if the law were implemented.[50] It was not that they were reluctant to assist the Crown in a time of need: they offered to provide the king large gifts. They simply did not want to be ruined in the process. Later, when they saw that their protests were having little effect, they yielded, but with great resentment.[51] The representatives of the province of Tepeaca informed His Majesty that they could not possibly pay their debts "in one, or ten, or fifty years." Bitterly they put their properties at the king's disposal "to sell them, burn them, or do what he wanted with them."[52] Others, seeing that nothing could be done to save their estates, abandoned all hope and suspended their activities to await the inevitable.[53] However, most of those affected by the law reacted strongly, refusing to give up their efforts to prevent its implementation. Since nothing could be done for the moment, they caustically thanked His Majesty for his "tender mercy." They had lost faith in the Crown and awaited an uncertain future. Between 1800 and 1810 Mexico experienced what Richard Herr has called "the real revolution of the late eighteenth century," the "destruction of the state of mind necessary for the continuation of the old order—which occurred in France before 1789 . . . [and] in Spain between 1792 and 1801."[54]

As the king's representative in Mexico, Viceroy José de Iturrigaray answered the protests against the Law of Consolidation. In reply to the representations of the Royal Mining Tribunal and the City Council of Mexico, he declared that the Crown's decisions regarding the nationalization of property belonging to the Tribunal of Chaplaincies and Pious Funds was final. The law was based on a factual analysis of the country's economy, he explained, and was designed to promote "general well-being." He added that he was displeased by the "radical" assertions that the Law of Consolidation was impractical and that its effects would be disastrous. He warned the petitioners that they were guilty of giving unsolicited counsel and advised them to refrain from "acting as the spokesmen of the entire kingdom," because they were not authorized to do so.[55] Upon receiving the viceroy's letter, the City Council of Mexico replied that they could not understand how such a demonstration of their "love and loyalty towards the sovereign could excite anger in Your Excellency." Arguing forcefully that their opinion also was based on "a factual analysis" and that it was their duty to make it known since no law was unchangeable, they reminded the viceroy that their representations had been addressed to the Supreme Committee of Consolidation and strongly requested that the petitions be forwarded to Spain for consideration.[56]

In the midst of this acrimonious debate, Iturrigaray received a letter from the bishop of Durango not only supporting the viceroy's stand but also offering, "if it is necessary, all my services and means so that the king's intentions will not be frustrated."[57] The powerful Consulado of Mexico also offered its cooperation, stating that instead of creating difficulties, as had other organizations, it would seek to implement the law.[58] That, however, was not a simple matter.

When the Viceroy learned that a petition was being circulated in Mexico City in support of the "Representation of the Landowners and Farmers of Mexico," he ordered the judge commissioner of the Royal Acordada Tribunal to apprehend the person soliciting the signatures in order to interrogate him.[59] The culprit turned out to be Camilo de Mesa, a merchant from Cuernavaca, who confessed that he was collecting the signatures on behalf of the marquis of San Miguel de Aguayo, the marquis of La Colina, the marshal Castilla, Juan Cervantes Padilla, and Pedro González Noriega. Fifty-four powerful landowners had signed the petition, among them: Gabriel de Yermo, Diego Rull, Ignacio Obregón, Manuel Rincón Gallardo, the marquis of Santa Cruz de Iguanzo, and the wealthy Fagoagas, José Mariano, and José María. In attempting to exonerate himself, Camilo de Mesa revealed that he was soliciting the signatures at the request of Lic. Luis Gonzaga Ibarrola, "secretary of the king and of the Royal Tribunal of the Consulado, who had persuaded him to do it because of their friendship."[60] Because such powerful persons were involved, Iturrigaray requested advice from his civil and fiscal state attorneys. In "a very secret letter," he explained that the incident was nothing less than a "premeditated attempt to suspend, divert, or frustrate the king's law."[61]

The state attorneys realized that the matter was serious, not only because of the Crown's need, but also because of the "lively and very strongly worded representations of respectable Europeans" and Mexicans, who, seeing their interests threatened, had banded together in order to be heard.[62] The counselors agreed that grave social and economic consequences might result from the implementation of the Royal Law of Consolidation and recommended that it be applied "with the greatest latitude possible." If the matter were not handled "gently and with all the care which justice and the commonweal require," they were sure that "innumerable ills would be perpetrated."[63] The attorneys felt that the protests had been made in good faith and that Iturrigaray had no reason to believe that the petitioners showed a lack of respect.[64] However, the lawyers were not lenient with Bishop Abad y Queipo, whose representation included a plan to ameliorate taxation in the kingdom. Because it was critical of Spanish government, they felt it to be "extremely disrespectful and insolent." The state attorneys concluded by recommending an investigation to determine the number of farmers indebted to the pious funds, a measure they considered an indispensable preliminary to any decision.[66]

The Church was the chief victim of the law, but it was as divided as the rest of society. While a few dignitaries were willing to assist the viceroy in carrying out the law, others were hostile. The ecclesiastical cabildo of Valladolid and the diocese of Puebla led the opposition.[67] After repeating the litany of ills Mexico would suffer if the Law of Consolidation were implemented, they wondered about the future security of their wealth. "Can we flatter ourselves," they asked, "with the certainty that new demands will not be thought up in the future and that hereafter we will be able to enjoy quietly and peacefully the possession of the remainder of our goods?"[68] This was a question which no one could answer.

Despite the warnings and protests, the Royal Law of Consolidation was first applied on September 6, 1805. The Subordinate Committee of Consolidation, the body charged with the application of the law, was composed of the following Spaniards: Diego Madolell, who had been named in Spain as secretary and accountant; Viceroy José de Iturrigaray; Archbishop Francisco Javier Lizana; Regent Pedro Catani; Intendant Francisco Manuel de Arce; the state attorney of the royal treasury, Javier de Borbón; and the principal deputy, Antonio José Arrangoiz. They assembled weekly to decide which cases would be appealed.[69]

The execution of the Law of Consolidation affected all sectors of

the population and not just Spaniards, as one distinguished historian implies;[70] it is true, however, that those Spaniards hurt by the law, including some powerful members of the oligarchy, were the most vociferous in their complaints.[71] The majority of those injured by the law were creoles, and the most vulnerable were not the wealthy and powerful, but the numerous owners of medium-sized and small holdings who were unable to raise the money needed to liquidate their debts. Notices of foreclosures and auctions of cattle ranches, haciendas, and all types of enterprises filled the pages of the *Gazeta de México* and the *Diario de México* during 1807 and 1808.[72] The sections of Bienes Nacionales and Consolidación of the Archivo General de la Nación are filled with the appeals of those who sought to save their property.[73] Perhaps the most interesting is the litigation carried on by members of the oligarchy, some of whom had actively participated in the protests against implementation of the law and a few of whom were suspected of personal antagonism toward the viceroy. The protests came from prominent families and persons such as the Fagoaga, Yermo, Iguanzo, Castilla, Heras y Soto, Arze, Rivascacho, the Marqués del Valle, Rull, Barquena, the count of Regla, Valenciana, and Domínguez. All of them either owed money to the pious funds or had offered their names and property as security for someone else. Besides these families, the law also threatened institutions such as the Consulado of Mexico.

The final decision on such cases was reserved for a special committee presided over by the viceroy. When the debts were acknowledged, the debtors, following the provisions of the law, made a large initial cash payment and paid the rest within a term of nine to sixteen years. The Fagoaga family, including Juan Bautista, José Juan, and José Mariano, were compelled to pay 60,000 pesos.[74] Antonio González Alonso, heir to the marquis of Santa Cruz de Iguanzo, agreed to remit 30,000 pesos, although he asked for a reduction in the amount due.[75] The marquis of San Miguel de Aguayo agreed to an "adjustment" of more than 450,000 pesos.[76] Diego Rull agreed to pay 50,000 pesos.[77] The marshal Castilla, one of the most influential Spaniards, was forced to pay 116,000 pesos on terms.[78] Juan Vicente Arze, who had been the director of the lottery, was assessed for 20,000 pesos, which could not be collected because he was then on duty as intendant general of the army in Venezuela.[79] The heirs of the marquis of Rivascacho divided among themselves debts of 82,446 pesos.[80] The owners of the Marquisate del Valle had to provide 30,000 pesos which they owed to pious works.[81] The count of Valenciana was forced to pay almost 60,000 pesos.[82] The Consulado of Mexico acknowledged a debt of 250,000 pesos which it had inherited from the will of Captain Francisco Zúñiga and which had been provided for the support of an orphanage. However, in this case the committee decided to file away the folder without collecting the debt "so that the good effects [of the orphanage] would continue to operate in the future."[83] Unlike the others, Sebastián Heras Soto bought a hacienda, one mortgaged for 28,000 pesos.[84] However, he was one of the very few buyers; most people were too deeply in debt to be able to purchase the property being auctioned.

The most famous case concerned Gabriel de Yermo, whose vast riches were derived from his creole wife's inheritance, which he had maintained and increased.[85] Along with the family properties, Yermo inherited the family debts—in some cases the capital and property were mortgaged. In addition, Yermo had allocated funds to chaplaincies on his own and had cosigned for various friends who wanted to borrow from the funds of the pious works. Father Mier estimated that Yermo owed the treasury between 60,000 and 80,000 pesos in liquor taxes besides the 400,000 pesos which he had to turn over to the government under the Law of Consolidation.[86] I have found documents which bring Yermo's debt to more than 200,000 pesos. Yermo defended himself in all the judgments against him. In the cases in which he was only the guarantor, he pressured the debtors to pay the debt.[87] He recognized his debts to chaplaincies and paid them.[88] In other cases his excuse was legitimate and as a result he was absolved.[89]

There were, however, instances when the rigor with which the Law of Consolidation was applied went beyond the limits of the probity and justice which the state attorneys had recommended to the viceroy. A case began on January 13, 1806, in which Yermo was required to pay 131,200 pesos he owed to the College of Saint Ignatius Loyola. The subordinate committee presided over by Iturrigaray recommended to the royal commissioner that he collect the debt from Yermo only after seeking legal counsel and "with due consideration for the logic of common law and judicial opinion." The royal commissioner, however, failed to give Yermo the committee's decision in person, and on February 15 the committee ruled that if the debt were not paid, the authorities should seize the valuable Temisco hacienda without "permitting the slightest recourse, even for an instant, which might obstruct compliance with the inviolate decision . . . [of the committee]." On March 1, Yermo, seeing himself seriously threatened, agreed to pay the debt. Yet the committee considered his request untimely and decided to name a receiver to administer the hacienda of Temisco. When Yermo protested the manner in which the produce and profits of the hacienda were handled, the committee named a majordomo to supervise the property.[90] On March 24 it accepted Yermo's proposal to pay 15,000 pesos in cash and the rest within nine years, but the transaction was never carried out.

In yet another petition on the same subject, Yermo argued that the Law of Consolidation did not apply because his late uncle and father-in-law had been involved only as guarantors and the amount given had not been for pious works but to feed the religious members of the college and to defray the expenses of the infirmary. The matter was turned over to the *corregidor* of Querétaro on April 29, 1807, and the case concluded on October 1, 1808, only fifteen days after Yermo led the rebellion which overthrew Viceroy Iturrigaray.[91] Eventually Yermo recovered his hacienda without paying the debt.

The Royal Law of Consolidation was officially in effect from September 6, 1805, until January 4, 1809. Lucas Alamán estimated that it brought 10,656,000 pesos into the treasury, not including other income belonging to the consolidation, such as annuities, *nuevo noveno,* and tithes.[92] The author of "Noticias de la Nueva España en 1805" calculated that from 1805 to 1808 the Royal Consolidation Fund received 10,507,957 pesos in revenues from the confiscation and sale of pious works. If the revenues from *noveno,* annuities, and tithes are included, this figure reaches 11,118,813.90 pesos.[93] Original documents in the section of Consolidación of the Archivo General de la Nación demonstrate that the royal treasury of New Spain received 12,080,291.70 pesos from the archbishopric of Mexico and all the dioceses of New Spain. That amount is approximately one-fourth of the wealth attributed to the Church. The funds originated from the following sources:

Archbishopric of Mexico
General Fund (September 6, 1805, to December, 1806) 2,749,585.90
General Fund (1807)   1,525,028.44
General Fund (1808)   1,525,028.44
Ecclesiastical Annuities   102,131.25
Nuevo Noveno (1808)   82,514.55

Enterado (1809)		89,310.34
Annuities		11,061.18
Nuevo Noveno		117,670.09
	Total	6,202,330.16

Bishopric of Puebla

General Fund (up to 1808)		2,218,044.97
Annuities		46,044.11
Nuevo Noveno		57,340.30
	Total	2,322,110.38

Bishopric of Valladolid

General Fund (up to 1808)		1,068,804.27
Annuities (1808)		23,000.00
General Fund (1809)		34,875.31
Annuities (1809)		17,316.44
Nuevo Noveno		55,483.54
	Total	1,199,479.56

Bishopric of Guadalajara

General Fund (1808)		954,841.06
Annuities		12,863.25
Nuevo Noveno (1808)		23,069.66
General Fund (1809)		1,450.00
Annuities		14,967.37
Nuevo Noveno (1809)		99,808.05
	Total	1,106,999.39

Bishopric of Durango

General Fund (up to 1808)		145,479.96
Ecclesiastical Annuities		1,865.50
Nuevo Noveno (1808)		16,446.66
Nuevo Noveno (1809)		17,098.98
	Total	180,891.10

Bishopric of Monterrey

General Fund (up to 1808)		61,445.00
Nuevo Noveno (1808)		11,064.06
General Fund (1809)		62,379.28
Nuevo Noveno (1809)		27,581.19
	Total	162,469.53

Bishopric of Oaxaca

General Fund (up to 1808)		566,103.78
Annuities (1808)		2,596.09
Nuevo Noveno (1808)		12,546.70
General Fund (1809)		25,340.88
Nuevo Noveno (1809)		2,068.92
	Total	608,656.37

Bishopric of Yucatán

General Fund (up to 1808)		163,025.00
Annuities (1808)		7,565.14
Nuevo Noveno (1808)		5,962.09
General Fund (1809)		95,059.95
Annuities (1809)		5,161.43
Nuevo Noveno (1809)		6,156.62
	Total	282,930.23
	Total Amount	12,080,291.70

These are the most complete statistics available and may be considered fairly accurate, although the reliability of some of the figures, such as those recorded for the archbishopric of Mexico for the years 1807 and 1808, may be questioned.[94]

The Royal Law of Consolidation faced many administrative difficulties; for example, there were complaints that administrators had not remitted all the revenues to the treasury.[95] Within the limitations arising from internal and external circumstances, however, it can be said that the law was discharged efficiently. This may be attributed to the incentives the Crown provided, which have been estimated to have cost 500,000 pesos,[96] or about 5 percent of the total. Besides that amount, which did not enter the consolidation fund, approximately 300,00 pesos were deducted to pay the interest on the funds of pious works—for which the Crown was now responsible.[97]

The money collected was not forwarded to Spain immediately, despite the urgency with which the law had been decreed and the Crown's imperative need for funds. No remittances were sent in 1805 because Spain was at war with England, and the sea lanes were in enemy hands; the same difficulty was encountered later during the war with France. It was not until after Iturrigaray's fall that the funds raised by the Law of Consolidation arrived in the peninsula. The first remittance, of 9 million pesos, was approved by Viceroy Pedro Garibay on October 28, 1808.[98] The second, 2 million pesos, was approved on January 26, 1809.[99] Both remittances were made with the cooperation of the navy of England, then an ally.[100] They were sent in violation of Article 45 of the law, which specified that neither the viceroy, the supreme committee, nor any other judge or tribunal could dispose of the funds, regardless of the "major need and urgency [which might exist], even if they were to be returned rapidly, unless ordered to do so by the king."[101] By that time, however, the king of Spain was a prisoner in France.

The implementation of the Law of Consolidation produced serious consequences, economic, social, and political. Many of the fears expressed in the representations were borne out; the economy suffered seriously because many debtors abandoned their farms and the value of real estate declined by half.[102] Furthermore, foreign trade was blocked by the wars, first against England and later against France. Spain appeared unable to resolve her European problems and the colony resented more than ever the constant outflow of her products. The Spanish government, which until then had been considered a unifying force, became a divisive factor whose political and economic failures provoked schisms among her subjects in New Spain. The Royal Law of Consolidation was the last straw. It caused serious friction between the Spanish government and the oligarchy.

The viceroy was blamed for the results of the law as well as for other long-standing problems. Most Spaniards who had resided in the colony longer than Iturrigaray grew distrustful of him. They believed him partial to the creoles and therefore a threat to the dependent relationship with the mother country and to their stability within the colony. As a result, judges and bishops, supported by the peninsular oligarchy, men who would never attack the king, decided to remove the threat to themselves by overthrowing Iturrigaray.

The viceroy was but one of many obligated to apply the law. Indeed, the Subordinate Committee of Consolidation was the body truly responsible for its implementation. Notwithstanding the benefits which accrued to the viceroy as well as other members of the committee, the monarchy frequently pressured and urged the viceroy to obtain money for the funds of consolidation. The Supreme Governing Commission of the Crown asked that Iturrigaray be indefatigable in enforcing the law. Mier, Alamán, and Mora all agree that when imprisoned, the viceroy had various letters from Spanish ministers demanding the execution of the law and the prompt remittance of 9 million pesos.[104]

Iturrigaray was neither the best nor the worst viceroy to govern New Spain. His misfortune was having been appointed to the post during one of the most critical moments in the history of Spain and Mexico. The innumerable accusations that he was opportunistic, venal, and egotistical could well have been applied to most of the previous viceroys. His predecessor, the marquis of Branciforte, was "venal and cynical," yet he has not been discredited like Iturrigaray, even though the scandalous abuses he perpetrated have been widely recognized.[105] Humboldt said that any unscrupulous executive who came to America had every opportunity to enrich himself, because he could dispense patronage, control the distribution of mercury used in silver mining, and grant special privileges to trade with neutral powers in time of war.[106] Contrary to general belief, there is no evidence that Iturrigaray was any more corrupt than his predecessors. In fact, he seems to have been a reasonably good administrator, as may be seen in the press. The *Gazeta de México,* the *Jornal de Comercio,* and the *Diario de México* supported him; the second paper, which belonged to Veracruz merchants, praised him for his dedication to efficient government.[107] In 1806, the *Diario de México* found proof of "his goodness, his tenderness, and his mercy" when Iturrigaray dedicated a hospital built by contributions he obtained from both the Spanish and creole oligarchy.[108] By 1808, however, these feelings had changed completely.

Spain's political and economic crisis had a profound effect upon peninsulares in Mexico. A few eventually concluded that, given the mother country's economic weakness, defeat in the European conflict was inevitable.[109] Others, however, reacted violently against Francophile Spaniards and had them incarcerated for ideological reasons, even though the latter might have resided in New Spain for twenty or thirty years.[110] Most Spaniards in Mexico were already divided over peninsular politics between those who favored Godoy and those supporting Ferdinand; the Law of Consolidation exacerbated these dichotomies. Even the clergy was divided. The bishop of Puebla and the cabildo of the vacant see of Valladolid bitterly opposed the law, while the archbishop of Mexico and the bishop of Durango supported the viceroy in his implementation of it.

Other economic measures besides the Law of Consolidation caused friction among the Spaniards. Needing money to sustain his administration, Iturrigaray decided to increase the taxes of the meat suppliers of Mexico City. The largest suppliers, Yermo and the marquis of Aguayo, protested through the civil state attorney, Ambrosio Sagarzurieta. The attorney requested that the viceroy grant him a public audience, a petition which Iturrigaray refused on the ground that, as the marquis of Aguayo's son-in-law, Sagarzurieta could not be impartial. From then on the offended state attorney "bore a grudge" against the viceroy.[111]

The viceroy was also at odds with the powerful *consulados,* which were composed of the richest Spanish merchants. Because of the wealth and power they derived through their monopoly of trade and their close and direct relations with Spain, the *consulados* sought to control Mexico by influencing appointments to the bureaucracy, including such high officials as the viceroy. As a result they generally lacked respect for all local authority.[112] Traditionally, there was a bitter rivalry between the Consulado of Veracruz and the Consulado of Mexico, but they put their differences aside when the Law of Consolidation threatened their mercantile interests or when the bureaucracy did not respond to their wishes.[113] This occurred during Iturrigaray's administration because the viceroy was a partisan of Godoy, while the merchants and their supporters in Spain belonged to the rival pro-Ferdinand faction.[114] The merchants' hostility toward him did not disturb Iturrigaray. He feared no one because he was strongly supported in court and believed he was in a position to do as he wanted.[115]

The equilibrium existing between the merchants and the viceroy ended in May, 1808, when Napoleon's invasion of Spain tipped the balance in favor of the merchants. Along with the judges, who were considered the leaders of the Spanish party, they awaited an opportune moment to overthrow the viceroy and choose a candidate more amenable to their interests. News of Godoy's downfall and the accession of Ferdinand VII reached Mexico in June. Knowing that his power had depended upon Godoy's support, Iturrigaray decided to play his trump card: he suspended the Law of Consolidation.[116] By this action he hoped to win the support and loyalty of the inhabitants of New Spain. Within weeks, news arrived that the Spanish monarchs were imprisoned in France and the Spanish people were fighting a war of national liberation against French imperialism. The viceroy called for unity, exhorting the people of New Spain to aid the mother country. Then he began to prepare the colonial army in case the

French should attempt to conquer the kingdom.

The viceroy's moves did not mollify his enemies, who regarded his activities with misgivings and questioned his loyalty to the Crown. Most of all, the Spaniards believed that their interests would be threatened so long as Iturrigaray remained in power. Since the peninsular oligarchy rejected the viceroy, the wealthy creoles took every opportunity to win his favor. They purchased high military commissions and important civil posts in order to gain access to Iturrigaray's inner circle. Although the creole oligarchy already controlled the City Council of Mexico, they wanted to undermine the Spaniards' influence with the viceroy, thus gaining more power for themselves. The Spanish judges and merchants hoped to prepare the way for Iturrigaray's ouster by discrediting him in public. They criticized him for incompetence and circulated rumors about his vices.

The leaders of the Spanish party, Judges Miguel Bataller and Guillermo Aguirre, were as uncertain about the events in Europe as the viceroy. They knew that their only hope for retaining control of the colony lay in recognizing any peninsular authority with the slightest appearance of legitimacy. They also recognized that their situation would be desperate indeed, under the circumstances, if the viceroy remained as the supreme authority in New Spain. Thus they saw the formation of the Junta of Seville as their salvation and attributed to it the legitimacy necessary to require obedience from the colonial officials. In this way they hoped to restore their influence and undermine that of the viceroy. Iturrigaray, by contrast, did not believe that the Junta of Seville enjoyed the authority his enemies attributed to it, because other juntas were also operating in other Spanish provinces. Later writers have often criticized the viceroy for not accepting the authority of the Seville junta. These authors have confused the Junta of Seville, one of many such juntas in Spain, with the Supreme Governing Junta that eventually came to represent the entire country. While it is true that the Supreme Governing Junta eventually met in Seville, it was not organized until September 25, 1808—after Iturrigaray had been overthrown.

It was not only on constitutional grounds that the viceroy refused to recognize the Seville junta. He also argued that if its authority were accepted, one of the junta's first acts would be to reestablish the Law of Consolidation. Similarly, he warned that the junta would replace the archbishop and other Spanish functionaries who had supported his administration.[117] To gain popular support, he assured the people that, following the precise letter of the Law of Consolidation, he would not send any funds to Spain without direct orders from the king, "even if he ran the risk of being held responsible and [being] forced to pay from [his own] pocket."[118]

While these events were taking place, the City Council of Mexico proposed the creation of a regional junta similar to those operating in Spain. The proposal argued that the Junta of Seville was merely one of many juntas in Spain and that therefore New Spain was not obliged to obey it. The city council's position was legally beyond reproach. If the Spanish throne were not occupied and if the inhabitants of Spain had formed various regional governing juntas, then the people of New Spain also had the right to form such bodies.[119] However, the proposal had grave implications, because the members of the city council were the leaders of the creole group. Iturrigaray tried to remain neutral, but he had to receive the city council's proposal. And since the formation of a regional junta did not preclude his participation, while recognition of the Seville junta would have meant his removal, the viceroy's motives were questioned by the Spaniards. The judges, as leaders of the Spanish party, concentrated on defeating the creole petition. Their attitude is understandable, not only because most of them feared that the creoles would not assist Spain, but also because they were about to lose their prestige and the great power they held in the colony.[120] Their problem was now complicated; in the future they would not only have to struggle against Iturrigaray, but also against the creoles.

The judges' position was greatly strengthened by the arrival of Juan Javat and Manuel Jáuregui, two envoys from the Seville junta, who had come to Mexico to win the colony's adherence to their junta. But before the judges could act, they had to resolve an internal disagreement. One of their group, the liberal Jacobo Villaurrutia, argued publicly that since there was no legitimate authority in Spain, a regional junta could be formed in the colony.[121] Because Villaurrutia had a following among liberal Spaniards in Veracruz, the judges sought to discredit him by having the *Gazeta de México* publish the rumor that Ferdinand VII had returned to the throne; such an event would have rendered Villaurrutia's arguments meaningless. Thus the judges hoped to regain the support of the Veracruz liberals.[122] Subsequently, they forced Villaurrutia to leave the colony.[123] The judges mounted a propaganda campaign designed to heighten public confusion and to hinder the viceroy's ability to act. They attempted to gain the support of those Spaniards who backed the viceroy and who believed he was acting in their own best interests. When Iturrigaray understood the purpose of these maneuvers, he suspended Judge Bataller from his post of supervisor of the *Gazeta de México* and reprimanded its editor, López Cancelada.[124] Iturrigaray, too, had learned the value of the press, and he tried to present an image of efficiency by frequently announcing in the papers all important civil and military appointments.[125] Since the viceroy seemed to be gaining the upper hand, the Spaniards decided that their only recourse was to depose him.

As the leaders of the Europeans, the judges were expected to direct the movement which was to become the first coup d'etat of the nineteenth century. However, Bataller, Aguirre, and the other judges did not dare carry out in public what they had planned in private.[126] Although their plans had the archbishop's approval, they lacked popular support. The judges, consequently, looked for a leader who both enjoyed the respect of the Spanish community and disliked the viceroy enough to carry out their plans. Gabriel de Yermo was such a man; he believed that the viceroy had impaired his honor and his wealth, and that unless Iturrigaray were removed, no man could be safe.[127] After seeking spiritual counsel, Yermo accepted the judges' mandate. He revealed the plans of the conspiracy to a small group of merchants and the heads of some of the leading families. The number actually involved in the conspiracy remains in doubt. Facundo Lizarza asserted that Yermo, "various members of the bench," and some merchants indebted to the pious works were the leaders.[128] Alamán added the archbishop, the inquisitor, and the majority of Spanish merchants and landowners, including all the merchants of Veracruz.[129] At midnight on Thursday, September 15, 1808, commanding three hundred employees of the city's Spanish merchants, Yermo captured the viceregal palace without much opposition. Most of the guards decided that Yermo represented more powerful interests than did the viceroy. The few who opposed the plot, such as Colonel Joaquín Coella and Major Martín Angel Michaus, were relieved of duty or sent away from the capital.[130] The following day, September 16, the *Gazeta de México* published the following statement: "Inhabitants of Mexico of all classes and circumstances: necessity is not subject to common laws. The People have taken custody of the person of His Excellency the Viceroy and have imperiously asked for his removal for reasons of utility and general convenience." The notice added that Pedro Garibay was assuming authority and asked the populace to remain calm and tranquil. The new viceroy made it clear that the people were in the hands of "a distinguished leader" and that they could be assured of the continued loyalty of the council of state, the archbishop, and the other officials.[131]

Meanwhile, the new authorities sent the viceroy and his family to Spain to face charges.[132] As soon as the viceroy was in custody, orders went out to detain those who were considered leaders of the movement for local autonomy, such as Primo de Verdad, Francisco Azcárate, Del Cristo, the Abbot Guadalupe, Francisco Cisneros, the Canon José Beristáin, and Father Melchor de Talamantes. The judges found them guilty of conspiring against the Crown, of working for independence, and of involving the viceroy in these causes. The judges used this tactic to demonstrate to the people their own great loyalty to the mother country. For the moment, they were successful; unfortunately for them, the struggle that they thought was finished was only beginning.

Pedro Garibay was about eighty when he took the reins of government from Iturrigaray. During his brief administration he satisfied the Spaniards who brought him to power by sending to Spain the contents of the viceregal treasury as well as 9 million pesos from the consolidation fund.[133] The new viceroy took the following measures to remove the economic barriers which had prevented the Spaniards from reaping great profits: (a) suspending the collection of annuities on ecclesiastical benefices; (b) abolishing a pension called the ecclesiastical subsidy; (c) approving the suspension of the Law of Consolidation which Iturrigaray had ordered; (d) removing restrictions from industry and agriculture; (e) suspending the sales tax of December 22, 1807, which Iturrigaray had authorized and which affected those who supplied meat to Mexico, like Yermo; and (f) reducing the taxes on sugar cane liquor. According to the Spaniards, these measures would eliminate the causes of the people's complaints.[134]

Although Spaniards of all classes appeared to be happy, Garibay feared that he would suffer his predecessor's fate.[135] The young Spaniards who had participated in Iturrigaray's overthrow, who had been determined to "exterminate evil men and protect good men," and who had been the pride of the merchants of Mexico City[136] later committed such outrages that they became intolerable. When Garibay was forced to call out the army to pacify them, the young men were so offended that, encouraged by their previous exploits, they attempted to depose the viceroy on October 30, 1808. However, he learned of the malcontents' plans in time to thwart them.[137]

The major complaint which had led to Iturrigaray's downfall was nullified by Spain during Garibay's administration. On January 14, 1809, after examining "with great care the representations of many institutions and individuals," the Regency—now the unified government of Spain—rescinded the Royal Law of Consolidation.[138] One might suppose that this act would restore the calm so desired by the Spaniards. However, Mexico's treasury was empty and Spain still required funds. The differences between Spaniards and creoles had increased, and to complicate matters, the Spaniards in Mexico were not united.

Once Garibay accomplished his mission, Archbishop Lizana replaced him. The new viceroy resolved the colony's financial crisis by obtaining voluntary loans from Spanish merchants and some wealthy creoles. Among the Spaniards who contributed were Gabriel Iturbe, Antonio Basoco, Tomás Domingo de Acha, Domingo de Lardizábal, Gabriel de Yermo, Antonio and Alonzo Terán, Sebastián de Heras, Eguía y Noriega, Diego de Agreda, the Tribunal of Chaplaincies, the ecclesiastical cabildo, and the *consulado*; each contributed more than fifty thousand pesos. Among the creoles who gave large sums were the marquis of Rayas, the marquis of Apartado, the marquis of Guardiola, the marquis of Santa Cruz de Iguanzo, and the count of Cortina. Numerous small gifts were also listed in the *Gazeta de México*.[139] In this way more than 3 million pesos were soon gathered.

The inhabitants of New Spain had earlier proposed this sort of cooperation, which they preferred to the Law of Consolidation. The success of the loan was due, in no small measure, to the willingness of those responsible for imprisoning Iturrigaray. They were certain that their loan would be repaid—as indeed it was. But the loan merely served to defray the cost of viceregal administration without resolving the colony's grave economic problems. Moreover, when the Spanish government learned that despite the millions sent to the peninsula from the consolidation fund, Mexico could still raise several millions for its own administration, the Regency asked New Spain for another loan of 20 million pesos. Such a request, at a time when the people of New Spain had not recovered from the effects of consolidation, once again provoked discontent in the colony. Abad y Queipo considered the request injudicious and detrimental to prosperity and to the interests of the treasury.[140] Bustamante believed that those who had made such demands "were either crazy or did not know our true situation."[141] But to a Spain overrun by French troops and fighting for its life, almost any demand made on the overseas empire seemed reasonable.

Instead of asking for a loan, Spain's most prudent course would have been to carry out fiscal reforms and to abolish the colonial monopolies which the Spanish merchants controlled. However, that would have meant returning the peninsulares to the position they had held during the Iturrigaray administration.[142] Any such reforms would be resisted by the Spanish merchants whose interests would be affected. Once more the political and economic crises of the monarchy provoked discontent in New Spain; new divisions appeared among the Spaniards in Mexico. The viceroy, Archbishop Lizana, took prudent action and calmed the fears of most Spaniards by ordering the confiscation of the properties of thirty-three Spaniards accused of favoring the French cause. But this was not enough. Lizana was a cautious but independent person; once the judges realized they could not make him their tool, they turned against him. In spite of his discretion, they believed him to be partial to the creoles, and given the climate of suspicion prevailing among the Spaniards, that was reason enough to oust him. Knowing that conspiracies were afoot, the viceroy ordered an investigation, which uncovered a group of plotters; including men who had overthrown Iturrigaray. Lizana believed that no purpose would be served by charging all who were involved, and punished only López de Cancelada and Judge Aguirre, exiling them from Mexico City.[144] Once exposed, the judges and merchants had no recourse but to demand that the authorities in Spain remove Lizana.

At this time Spain's highest authority, the Regency, resided in Cádiz and was influenced by the merchants of that city. The Spanish merchants in Mexico, therefore, had no difficulty in obtaining a hearing for their petition to remove Viceroy Lizana. The Regency ordered him dismissed and entrusted the government of New Spain to the Audiencia until it named a new viceroy.

The government had at last fallen into the hands of the judges, who had maintained a facade of loyalty as they conspired against Godoy, Iturrigaray, Garibay, Lizana, and the creoles. However, the judges did not agree upon the uses of their own power, and open discord broke out among them.[145] The Law of Consolidation had violently shattered the fragile unity of the Spanish elite. Although this was not the first time that New Spain had suffered political and economic crisis, the situation was unique because the mother country was now fighting for its life and could no longer serve as the final arbiter of colonial disputes. For the first time, the people saw clearly the corruption and ineptitude of the men who governed. The Audiencia ruled until August 25, 1810, when the new viceroy, Francisco Javier Venegas, arrived. By that time, however, the desire for home rule had grown too strong to contain.

NOTES

1. See the works of Earl J. Hamilton, especially his *War and Prices in Spain, 1651-1800* (Cambridge, 1947); Pierre Vilar, *Crecimiento y desarrollo. Economía e historia: reflexiones sobre el caso español* (Barcelona, 1964); and Richard Herr, *España y la revolución del siglo XVIII* (Madrid, 1964); hereafter cited as Herr, *España y la revolución*.

2. There are many works which describe this prosperity. In particular, see the commerce tables published by the Consulado of Veracruz for the first years of the nineteenth century in Lerdo de Tejada, *El Comercio esterior*, appendixes 16-21.

3. José María Luis Mora, *Méjico y sus revoluciones* (Paris, 1836), 1: 255, hereafter cited as Mora, *Méjico y sus revoluciones*; Luis Villoro, *El proceso ideológico de la revolución de independencia* (Mexico, 1967), pp. 17-18.

4. See the continuous lists of gifts which appear in the *Gazeta de México* for 1806, vols. 13 and 14, especially the months of July and August. Notice also how the gifts decline.

5. Alamán, *Historia*, 1: 123.

6. There have been few economic studies of the Church. Besides Mora's studies the most important work is Michael Costeloe, *Church Wealth in Mexico: A Study of the "Juzgado de Capellanías" in the Archbishopric of Mexico, 1800-1856* (Cambridge, 1967); hereafter cited as Costeloe, *Church Wealth*. See also Nancy M. Farriss, *Crown and Clergy in Colonial Mexico, 1759-1821* (London, 1968).

7. Manuel Abad y Queipo, "Representación sobre la inmunidad personal del clero, reducida por las leyes," in Hernández y Daválos, *Colección*, vol. 2, doc. 361, pp. 823-29.

8. Humboldt, *Ensayo político*, 2: 33; Representación de los vecinos de la ciudad de Valladolid y sus distritos, dueños de fincas rústicas y urbanas de 24 de octubre de 1805, AGN, BN, leg. 1667, exp. 19, cuaderno 7.

9. Ortiz de Ayala, *Resumen de la estadística*, p. 28.

10. Mora, *Obras Sueltas*, p. 210.

11. It has been generally held that the Law of Consolidation of 1798 did not hurt Spain because the property of the Church in Spain was of a different nature than its property in Mexico. It was alleged to have been held in mortmain, and thus the law forced it into the hands of those disposed to use it for the well-being of the nation.

However, the argument takes the complaints of those affected by the law's application in Mexico at face value. It further implies that there was no Tribunal of Chaplaincies, Testaments, and Pious Works in Spain or that it did not have the same function that it did in Mexico. This is all supposition. The few studies that exist on the subject suggest that the law was just as harmful to Spain as it would be to Mexico. See Antonio Domínguez Ortiz, *La sociedad española en el siglo XVIII* (Madrid, 1955), p. 166. For the agrarian question in Spain, see Gonzalo Anes, *Las crisis agrarias en la españa moderna* (Madrid, 1970). The law was applied to the Viceroyalty of New Granada in 1808 and does not appear to have been carried out. One of the very few studies of this subject in Mexico had been done by Masae Sugawara H. of the *Archivo General de la Nación* in his "Los antecedentes coloniales de la deuda pública de México," *Boletín del Archivo General de la Nación* 3 (1967): 131-402. Further documents are to appear in subsequent issues.

12. Costeloe, *Church Wealth*, pp. 46-65.

13. Ibid., pp. 47-48; Mora, *Méjico y sus revoluciones*, 1: 445-46.

14. Costeloe, *Church Wealth*, p. 85; Mora, *Méjico y sus revoluciones*, 1: 445-46.

15. Costeloe, *Church Wealth*, 67.

16. Such were the cases of Yermo and the Fagoagas.

17. Costeloe, *Church Wealth*, pp. 77-80.

18. Various copies of the Law of Consolidation may be found in AGN, BN, leg. 1,667, exp. 6.

19. *Real Cédula de Consolidación de Vales Reales y Real Instrucción que S.M. se ha servido aprobar para el cumplimiento del Real Decreto de enajenación de bienes pertenecientes a obras pías en los dominios de América y en las Filipinas* (Madrid, n.d.). This was found in AGN, RC, leg. 30, exp. 2.

20. See Enrique Florescano, *Precios del maíz y crisis agrícolas en México (1708-1810)* (Mexico, 1969).

21. Manuel Abad y Queipo, "Representación a nombre de los labradores y comerciantes de Valladolid de Michoacán en que se demuestran con claridad los inconvenientes de que se ejecute en las Américas la real cédula de 26 de diciembre de 1804, sobre enajenación de bienes raíces y cobro de capitales de capellanías y obras pías para la consolidación de vales," in Hernández y Dávalos, *Colección,* vol. 2, p. 856. See also, Representación del Cabildo Eclesiástico de Valladolid de 3 de octubre de 1805, AGN, BN, leg. 1,667, exp. 19, cuaderno 4, fols. 3-4. Hereafter cited as Representación del Cabildo Eclesiástico de Valladolid.

22. Representación del Real Tribunal de Minería, solicitando se suspenda el cumplimiento de lo resuelto por S. M. acerca de la venta de bienes de obras pías de 16 de septiembre de 1805, AGN, BN, exp. 19, cuaderno 8.

23. Representación del Ayuntamiento de la nobilísima ciudad de México, Archivo del Ex-Ayuntamiento de la ciudad de México, Actas del Cabildo, vol. 126, fols. 37-47. See also AGN, BN, leg. 1,667, exp. 19, cuaderno 3.

24. Representación del Cabildo Eclesiástico de Valladolid, fol. 4.

25. Representación del Real Tribunal de Minería, fol. 3.

26. Abad y Queipo, "Escrito presentado a D. Manuel Sixtos Espinosa del Consejo de Estado y director único del príncipe de la paz en asuntos de real hacienda, dirigido a fin de que suspendiese en las Américas la real cédula de 26 de diciembre de 1804 . . . ," in Hernández y Dávalos, *Colección*, vol. 2, pp, 866-67.

27. Representación del Ayuntamiento . . . de Mexico, fol. 38.

28. Representación de los labradores y comerciantes de Tehuacán, Puebla, enero de 1806, AGN, BN, leg. 1,667, exp. 19, cuaderno 6, fols. 1-2.

29. Representación de la ciudad de Pátzcuaro de 10 de enero de 1806, AGN, BN, leg. 1,667, exp. 19, cuaderno 7, fol. 3.

30. Among them were the marquis of San Miguel de Aguado, the Margués del Valle de la Colina, the Marshal Castilla, and Gabriel Yermo.

31. Representación de los labradores de México, fol. 13; Representación del Ayuntamiento de la ciudad de Puebla, 25 de octubre de 1805, AGN, BN, leg. 1,667, exp. 19, cuaderno 5, fol. 9.

32. Representación de los hacendados de México, fol. 14.

33. Representación del Ayuntamiento de la ciudad de Puebla, fols. 4-9.

34. Among its authors were the marquis of Santa Cruz de Iguanzo, Ignacio Iglesias, Francisco José de Urrutia, the marquis of Uluaba, Agustín de Rivero, Primo de Verdad y Ramos, Juan Francisco Azcárate, and Juan Francisco Sánchez de Tagle.

35. Representación del Ayuntamiento de la ciudad de México, fol. 20.

36. Representación del Real Tribunal de Minería, fol. 6.

37. Representación de los labradores de México, fol. 2; Representación del Ayuntamiento de Valladolid, 8 de octubre de 1805, AGN, BN, leg. 1,667, exp. 19, cuaderno 7, fol. 26.

38. Representación del Ayuntamiento de la ciudad de México, fol. 17; the Representación del Ayuntamiento de Valladolid estimated that between 10,000 and 12,000 families would be affected; the Representación del Ayuntamiento de la ciudad de Puebla estimated 16,000; the Representación del Cabildo Eclesiástico de Valladolid estimated 10,000; however, it also indicated that the pious funds in Michoacán were distributed among 2,300 persons; the Representación de los labradores y comerciantes de Valladolid put it at between 25,000 and 30,000 families.

39. Representación del Real Tribunal de Minería, fol. 19.

40. Representación de los labradores y comerciantes de Valladolid, in Hernández y Dávalos, *Colección*, vol. 2, p. 857.

41. Representación del Ayuntamiento de Valladolid, fol. 22.

42. Representación de los labradores de México, fol. 18.

43. Representación del Real Tribunal de Minería, fol. 7.

44. Representación del Ayuntamiento de la ciudad de Puebla, fol. 17.

45. Representación de los labradores y comerciantes de Tehuacán, Puebla, fol. 6; Representación de los hacenderos de México, fol. 19.

46. Representación del Cabildo Eclesiástico de Valladolid, fols. 9-15.

47. Representación del Ayuntamiento de la nobilísima ciudad de México, fol. 13.

48. According to the representatives of Mexico City, the outflow of coin exceeded the amount mined by 8 million pesos annually. According to the tables of commerce of the Consulado of Veracruz for the years 1802 and 1804, the outflow of gold and silver, not including that engraved or in powder, what was sent to Asia through trade, or the amount smuggled, reached 55,416,370 pesos. See also the tables of commerce in the Representación del Ayuntamiento de la ciudad de México, fol. 14.

49. Representación del Real Tribunal de Minería, fol. 15.

50. Representación de los labradores y comerciantes de Tehuacán, Puebla, fols. 14-15; Representación del Ayuntamiento de la ciudad de Puebla, fol. 13.

51. Representación de los labradores y comerciantes de Tehuacán, Puebla, fol. 27.

52. Representación del Ayuntamiento de la ciudad de Puebla, fol. 13.

53. Representación del Real Tribunal de Minería, fol. 15.

54. Representación de los labradores de México, fol. 27; Herr, *España y la revolución*, p. 372.

55. José de Iturrigaray to Ciudad de México and José de Iturrigaray to Tribunal de Minería, AGN, BN, leg. 1,667, exp. 19, cuaderno 2, fols. 1-4.

56. City of Mexico to Viceroy, October 31, 1805, AGN, BN, leg. 1,667, cuaderno 2. The representatives of the mining tribunal answered in more or less the same terms. They made it clear that far from "presuming that it would cause offense," they had the right to send "remonstrances to the king when they deemed it useful." They repeated that their statement had been sent to the Supreme Committee, and therefore they requested that it be forwarded to Spain for consideration (Tribunal de Minería to Iturrigaray, November 6, 1805, AGN, BN, leg. 1,667, exp. 19, cuaderno 3).

57. Bishop of Durango to Viceroy, August, 1805, AGN, BN, leg. 1,667, exp. 6.

58. The letter from the Consulado of Mexico to the viceroy was sent by the secretary, Soler (AGN, BN, leg. 1,667, exp. 19, cuaderno 2).

59. Iturrigaray to the judge commissioner of the Royal Acordada Tribunal, AGN, BN, leg. 1,667, exp. 19, cuaderno 8.

60. Juicio a Camilo Mesa por recolectar firmas, AGN, BN, leg. 1,667, exp. 9. In continuing the investigation, it was discovered that the idea of writing the representation came from the marquis of San Miguel de Aguayo (Juicio y declaración del licenciado Waldo Indalecio Bernal, AGN, BN, leg. 1,667, exp. 19, cuaderno 8).

61. Carta muy reservada del virrey al fiscal de lo civil sobre el recibo de las Representaciones . . . en donde se solicita la suspensión de la venta de bienes de obras pías, AGN, BN, leg. 1,667, exp. 19, cuaderno 2.

62. Informe muy reservado del fiscal de lo civil al virrey sobre las Representaciones recibidas de México, Puebla y Valladolid, AGN, BN, leg. 1,667, exp. 19, cuaderno 2.

63. Ibid.

64. Ibid.

65. Informe muy reservado del fiscal de lo civil al virrey; see also the Representación de los labradores y comerciantes de Valladolid.

66. Informe muy reservado del fiscal de Hacienda al virrey sobre las representaciones recibidas de México, Puebla y Valladolid, AGN, BN, leg. 1,667, exp. 19, cuaderno 2.

67. This reaction does not appear to have been made because of the Law of Consolidation of 1804. But it is important because, even though written in 1807, it argued against the law at a time when its effects could already be seen (Informe dado por el obispo y Cabildo de Puebla sobre las dificultades que se oponen a la erección de tres nuevos obispados, AGN, C, leg. 11, fols. 308-16).

68. Representación del Cabildo Eclesiástico de Valladolid, fol. 6.

69. Madolell was named to the post by the Supreme Committee of Consolidation in Spain and he arrived in Mexico to assume his duties in January, 1805 (AGN, BN, leg. 1,667, exp. 20, cuaderno 1).

70. Enrique Lafuente Ferrari, perhaps influenced by Father Mier, says in his book *El virrey Iturrigaray y los orígenes de la independencia en México* (Madrid, 1941), p. 43, that the Spaniards were the "ones most involved in the economic web of loans and debts," to the funds of pious works.

71. Mier, *Historia de la revolución de Nueva España*, p. xxvi.

72. *Diario de México*, vols. 6, 7, 8, and 9 for all of 1807 and from January to July of 1808.

73. This author consulted 600 decisions of the Subordinate Committee of Consolidation, AGN, BN, especially leg. 1,596, exp. 3 and 9; leg. 1,604, exp. 8, 14, and 47-50; all of leg. 1,667; leg. 1,802, exp. 21; and leg. 1,832.

74. They were guarantors as well as debtors in New Spain and in the Philippines (AGN, BN, leg. 1,667, exp. 8, 28; leg. 1,671, exp. 11, 16; leg. 1,802, exp. 2).

75. AGN, BN, leg. 1,667, exp. 8; leg. 1,832, exp. 6.

76. AGN, BN, leg. 1,667, exp. 28.

77. Ibid.

78. Ibid., exp. 29.

79. AGN, BN, leg. 1,777, exp. 104.

80. AGN, BN, leg. 352, exp. 21.

81. AGN, BN, leg. 1802, exp. 19.

82. Ibid., exp. 24.

83. AGN, BN, leg. 1,667, exp. 28.

84. AGN, BN, leg. 1,802, exp. 3.

85. He was the owner of the Temisco (Temixco) haciendas, San José (called Vista Hermosa), San Gabriel de Jalmolonga, and San Nicolás, which were together valued at more than 2 million pesos (Anastasio Zerecero, *Memorias para la historia de las revoluciones de México* [Mexico, 1869], p. 23).

86. Mier, *Historia de la revolución de Nueva España*, p. xxvi.

87. AGN, BN, leg. 1,802, exp. 27; leg. 1,832, exp. 3; leg. 1,671, exp. 21.

88. AGN, BN, leg. 1,814, exp. 20.

89. Ibid., exp. 14.

90. AGN, BN, leg. 1,667, exp. 28.

91. AGN, BN, leg. 1,596, exp. 21.

92. Alamán, *Historia*, 1: 137.

93. "Noticias de Nueva España en 1805," *Boletín de la Sociedad Mexicana de Geografía y Estadística* 2: 3-52.

94. The figures are located in various folders of volume 2 of AGN, Consolidación. See also *El Año Nuevo* (Mexico, 1865) and *Memoria de Hacienda, 1872*, appendix 20.

95. AGN, BN, leg. 1,667, exp. 1-2.

96. "Noticias de la Nueva España."

97. The funds were estimated at 301,429 pesos. The state attorney of the treasury placed them at 368,889 pesos (AGN, BN, leg. 1,667, exp. 19, cuaderno 2).

98. AGN, BN, leg. 1,667, exp. 1. However, through secret machination which included the cooperation of Britain—then the enemy—a sum in silver which may have been as high as 50 million dollars was taken from Mexico to France in 1807 on neutral United States ships. This was to pay Spain's subsidy to Napoleon. See Arthur P. Whitaker: *The United States and the Independence of Latin America, 1800-1830* (New York, 1964), pp. 17-22.

99. "Remisión de Caudales a España," *Gazeta de México* 15, no. 119, p. 832. .

100. AGN, BN, leg. 1,667, exp. 1.

101. Real Instrucción que S. M. se ha servido aprobar para el cumplimiento del Real Decreto de enajenación, art. 45.

102. Mora, *Méjico y sus revoluciones*, 1: 447-48.

103. AGN, RC, vol. 197, exp. 60, fol. 1.

104. Mier, *Historia de la revolución de Nueva España*, p. 27; Alamán, *Historia*, 1: 168; Mora, *Méjico y sus revoluciones*, 2: 263.

105. Lafuente Ferrari, *El Virrey Iturrigaray*, p. 27. For a work favorable to the viceroy, see Jack A. Haddick, "The Administration of Viceroy Iturrigaray," (Ph.D. diss., University of Texas, 1954).

106. Humboldt, *Ensayo político*, 4: 180.

107. *Jornal Económico Mercantil de Veracruz*, 1, no. 2, p. 6.

108. *Diario de México*, 4, no. 343, p. 46; also Haddick, "Iturrigaray."

109. El amigo y defensor de los buenos europeos, "Refutación al cuaderno intitulado *Verdadero origen, carácter, causas, resortes . . . ,*" in Hernández y Dávalos, *Colección*, vol. 1, p. 891.

110. Humboldt, *Ensayo político*, 4: 198. For a recent reevaluation of Godoy's administration, see Herr, *España y la revolución*, pp. 290-33. On the *afrancesados*, see Miguel Artola, *Los afrancesados* (Madrid, 1953).

111. Andrés Cavo, *Los tres siglos de México durante el gobierno español hasta la entrada del ejército trigarante . . . publícala con notas y suplementos, el lic. Carlos María Bustamante* (Mexico, 1836), vol. 2, pp. 244-45.

112. Mora, *Méjico y sus revoluciones*, 1: 164-65.

113. Humboldt, *Ensayo político*, 4: 33; Lafuente Ferrari notes that the merchants of Mexico City referred to those of Veracruz as smugglers (*El virrey Iturrigaray*, p. 49).

114. Mora, *Méjico y sus revoluciones*, 2: 261.

115. Ibid.

116. The decision was taken on July 22 with the agreement of the Supreme Committee of the Treasury (Alamán, *Historia*, 1: 168).

117. Alamán, *Historia*, 1: 192.

118. Juan López Cancelada, *Conducta del excelentísimo señor d. José de Iturrigaray durante su gobierno en Nueva España. Se contesta a la vindicación de don Facundo Lizarza . . .* (Cadiz, 1812), p. 38.

119. Lafuente Ferrari, *El virrey Iturrigaray*, p. 7. See the introduction to the book written by Ballesteros Beretta.

120. Mora, *Méjico y sus revoluciones*, 2: 277.

121. Jacobo Villaurrutia, *Voto que di en la junta general tenida en Méjico en treinta y uno de agosto de 1808, sobre si se había de reconocer por soberana a la junta supreme de Sevilla y papeles que escribí por las contestaciones ocurridas en la ley del nueve del siguiente septiembre sobre la necesidad de una junta de diputados del reyno y autoridad para convocarla* (Havana, 1814), p. 6.

122. Alamán, *Historia*, 1: 178.

123. Voto consultivo del Real Acuerdo para que se suspenda la Junta, Biblioteca Nacional de México, *Colección Lafragua*, vol. 315, fols. 1-5; Mora, *Méjico y sus revoluciones*, 2: 231.

124. López Cancelada, *Conducta del señor José Iturrigaray*, p. 42.

125. Viceroy Iturrigaray named Brigadier García Dávila as field marshal of the royal armies on September 13, and a day before his imprisonment he had made several appointments to the bureaucracy. See *Gazeta de México* and *Diario de México* of those dates.

126. Lafuente Ferrari, *El virrey Iturrigaray*, p. 242.

127. "Fragmentos de la defensa de Gabriel de Yermo," in Hernández y Dávalos, *Colección*, vol. 1, p. 761.

128. Facundo Lizarza, "Discurso que publica . . . vindicando al excelentísimo señor don José de Iturrigaray, de las falsas imputaciones de un cuaderno titulado por ironía *Verdad sabida y buena se guardada,"* in Hernández y Dávalos, *Colección*, vol. 1, p. 744.

129. Alamán, *Historia*, 1: 229.

130. Ibid., 1:244.

131. *Diario de México*, 2, no. 1,082, supplement; *Gazeta de México* 15, no. 97, p. 679.

132. AGN, H, vol. 442, fols. 39-49. Iturrigaray's captors paid for his passage to Spain; among them were Yermo and other prominent Spanish merchants. However, only Yermo seems to have been reimbursed.

133. Cavo, *Los tres siglos de México*, 3: 251-52; Alamán, *Historia*, 1: 267.

134. All this took place within a month after the viceroy had been deposed. See *Gazeta de México*, 15, no. 119, p. 813; Alamán, *Historia*, 1: 236.

135. Cavo, *Los tres siglos de México*, 2: 251.

136. *Gazeta de México*, 15, no. 98, p. 687-88.

137. Mora, *Méjico y sus revoluciones*, 2: 307.

138. AGN, RC, leg. 201, exp. 14, fol. 1.

139. *Gazeta de México*, 16, no. 144, p. 1,888; no. 147, p. 118.

140. Manuel Abad y Queipo, "Representación al arzobispo virrey contra la ejecución de la Real Cécula de 12 de marzo de 1809 sobre el préstamo de $20,000,000," in Hernández y Dávalos, *Colección*, vol. 2, p. 884.

141. Cavo, *Los tres siglos de México*, 3: 266.

142. Abad y Queipo proposed that the *alcabala* tax be increased, as well as taxes on sugar cane liquor and tobacco, and that free trade be established. See Abad y Queipo, "Representación al arzobispo virrey," in Hernández y Dávalos, *Colección*, vol. 2, pp. 884-85.

143. AGN, RC, vol. 201, exp. 14. fol. 2.

144. In Aguirre's case, however, he was unable to do it because "such was the outcry raised by the group, of which he was a member, that he was forced to have him return from Puebla," (Cavo, *Los tres siglos de México*, 3: 268).

145. Alamán, *Historia*, 1: 305-06.

THREE

The Spaniards during
the War of Independence

Only a relatively small portion of the population—the Spaniards, the creoles, and a minority of the mestizos—participated in the political and ideological struggles prior to 1810. At first the masses found it difficult to identify with the creole-led movement and only joined later when they saw the opportunity to avenge old grievances. The people's opportunity came on the morning of September 16, 1810, when Father Miguel Hidalgo called them to arms with the cry "Death to bad government." The rebel leaders had no clear-cut revolutionary program. They merely wished to remove the Spaniards and to establish local autonomy in replacing them. They did not favor separation from the monarchy; rather, they intended to save New Spain from the French until Ferdinand VII was freed. Therefore they refused to recognize the authority of any official appointed while Spain appeared to be under French domination.

The newly appointed viceroy, Francisco Javier Venegas, arrived in Mexico only two days before the Hidalgo movement erupted; and the rapid succession of events prevented him from forming his own opinion of the origins and development of the conflict he had inherited. As a result he was forced to rely upon the advice of the same group of Spaniards who had been responsible for the removal of his three predecessors. Venegas's principal concern was to preserve control of Mexico for himself, and to accomplish this he was willing to defend the privileges of the Spanish faction which supported him.

Although this study is not concerned with the details of the armed struggle, it is important to realize that the conflict was exceedingly bitter. Both sides acted brutally. For example, while insurgent "hordes" massacred their enemies in Guanajuato, the royalists

47

annihilated their adversaries elsewhere. The War of Independence crystallized the long-repressed conflict between the creoles and Spaniards. At first, due to the numerical disparity between the two groups, it appeared that the struggle would end rapidly. Matters were not that simple, however, for material interests as well as ideological questions complicated the situation. The creoles were divided and fought on both sides. Although the creole oligarchy opposed the rebels because they feared anarchy and the possible loss of their property, they were actually waiting for the right moment to assume control.[1]

Before the Spaniards could organize an effective opposition to the rebels, they had to unify the partisans of the Crown, particularly those interested in maintaining the status quo. This problem was not new. When the French invaded the peninsula in 1808, Viceroy Iturrigaray had attempted to unite the oligarchy by identifying the creoles with the fortunes of Spain.[2] He initiated a propaganda campaign with the argument that unlike the possessions of other colonial powers, the Spanish colonies were an integral part of the monarchy, and as a result, its inhabitants had the same rights as those of the peninsula.[3] Other writers also maintained that there were no differences between Europeans and Americans. One such pamphleteer asserted that Spaniards and creoles were united by ties of blood, common interests, and welfare.[4] Later, Dr. Florencio Pérez y Comoto sought to shame the creoles for rebelling by insisting that they had become wealthy only because they enjoyed the good fortune of being part of the Spanish empire.[5] Words failed to impress most of the creoles, who remained hostile. Their grievances against the Spaniards had deep roots and could not be eliminated by mere assertions of friendship and benevolence.

Although the Hidalgo revolt began as a creole movement to overthrow the Spanish oligarchy which had taken control of New Spain's government, neither the creoles, nor the Spaniards, nor the masses had committed themselves wholly to one side or the other. As the struggle progressed, both groups tried to win the loyalty of the undecided. Venegas waited impatiently for the moment when he could end the Indian tribute and thus gain new adherents for his government.[6] Miguel Hidalgo, also wishing to attract support, abolished slavery and eliminated some monopolies that affected creoles.[7] Both the royalist and insurgent armies were composed of mestizo and Indian groups and led by creole officers. Since many of the rebel leaders had defected from the ranks of the royalist army, the

Spaniards feared that desertions would further weaken their forces. Therefore they frequently begged Spain for trained troops.[8] The mother country, then fighting the French, could not respond immediately to these requests. However, in 1812 the merchants of Cádiz sent two battalions of troops, which arrived in Veracruz only to be stricken by disease in that unhealthy climate.[9]

The attitude of most Spaniards toward the War of Independence exasperated the authorities. They fled to the capital or to the coast and seemed more interested in protecting their riches than in defending the government. When the rebels approached Guadalajara, for example, the Europeans abandoned the city instead of fighting as Roque Abarca, the chief of the royalist army, advised. Led by the bishop, they went to San Blas and then to Acapulco, alleging that they were not soldiers and could not be expected to fight.[10] Besides the bishop and members of the Audiencia, many employees and "citizens of the highest distinction" from Guadalajara, Guanajuato, and Zacatecas participated in this "forced flight."[11] The commander of the royalist army, General Félix María Calleja, complained to the viceroy in 1811 that the Spaniards showed "little interest, lack of patriotism, and criminal indifference." He found this attitude incomprehensible, since he believed the aim of the rebels was the "extermination of the Europeans." Calleja was disgusted with the Spaniards' propensity to remain peaceful spectators in the struggle, which "affects them most of all," and to leave the defense of their lives in American hands. Those few who were inclined to serve in the army demanded "privileges and distinctions contrary to military discipline."[12] To make matters worse, a few Spaniards joined the cause of Mexican independence. Some were motivated by personal reasons, while others acted out of sympathy with the insurgents' liberal ideals.[13] More Europeans joined the rebels as the conflict progressed. Some Spaniards helped to plan the struggle, and a few took an active part in the fighting.[14]

The intensity of the contest forced both sides to take strong measures, particularly in order to finance their cause and to discipline their followers. The insurgents resorted to confiscating property belonging to Europeans and unfriendly creoles and taxing the towns they occupied. The royalists also found it difficult to obtain funds. At first they relied upon money appropriated from the treasury and the contributions of private individuals. Later they, too, confiscated the possessions of those creoles who actively opposed them or who were suspected of sympathizing with the rebels.[15]

The viceregal government was handicapped by its commitment to support Spain in its fight against France. Although Mexico had emptied its treasury in 1811, the Crown requested 20 million pesos to prosecute the war in Europe. Viceroy Venegas had no recourse other than loans or gifts from the creole and Spanish oligarchy. Spaniards and Spanish institutions in the colony bore the principal burden. Bishops, cathedral chapters, religious communities, the *consulados,* and those Spanish merchants who had financed the previous viceroys donated large sums. The creoles, however, contributed only under pressure; "what to the European was a generous and voluntary act was to the Mexican an odious extraction which, because of its constant repetition, became intolerable."[16] Spain's prolonged war in Europe and the viceregal government's inability to defeat the rebels in New Spain was beginning to tax the loyalty of most Spaniards. Hidalgo's defeat, furthermore, did not end the insurrection (as many had hoped), and the rebellion continued under a new leader, José María Morelos. Some questioned Spain's ability to survive and were doubtful about the desirability of maintaining ties with the mother country.[17]

Although Hidalgo's defeat enhanced Viceroy Venegas' reputation, it was the army which benefited most. In fact, since rebel resistance continued, the survival of civilian authority seemed to depend on the army. As a result, many came to believe that General Calleja, the army's renowned leader, was more important than the viceroy. Strong differences eventually arose between the civil and military authorities. Calleja became convinced that he was entitled to decide all military matters. Venegas disagreed, emphasizing that as commander-in-chief, the ultimate authority was his. After all, he had elevated Calleja to the position that officer now enjoyed. Morelos' activities exacerbated these divisions. A disagreement over whether to attack Morelos in Taxco, as the viceroy proposed, or to await a more opportune moment, as the chief of the army recommended, resulted in a profound enmity between them. In his correspondence, Calleja angrily asserted the army's supremacy over civil authority.[18]

As soon as the dispute among colonial authorities became evident, the Spanish oligarchy, which had overthrown Iturrigaray, intervened. They could have resolved the question themselves, but in order to maintain a semblance of legitimacy, they had decided to refer all such conflicts to Spain. The oligarchy supported Calleja because the viceroy had offended the merchants of Mexico City, Puebla, and Veracruz by demanding a loan of 2 million pesos to defray administrative expenses. To obtain those funds he demanded that the Church, as well as private individuals, turn in their gold and silver articles. Since they could not accuse Venegas of being partial to the creoles, the Spanish oligarchy sought to damage his reputation in Spain. As evidence of his incompetence, they pointed out that it had once occurred to him to "buy all the horses . . . in the country."[19] At the same time that the Spanish oligarchy was undermining Venegas, they described Calleja as the only man capable of succeeding the viceroy and suppressing the revolution.[20] A few Spaniards, like Abad y Queipo, however, were not so enthusiastic about Calleja and feared that he might become a partisan of independence.[21]

The pro-Calleja faction triumphed and Venegas fell from power. The new viceroy seemed to satisfy the Spaniards' desires: Calleja's interests were in the colony; he was familiar with the territory; and more important, he understood the character of the Mexicans. Calleja and his European backers understood each other from the beginning. The Spanish capitalists respected his decisions and quickly contributed the funds he demanded for fighting Morelos. Although Calleja was determined to destroy the insurgents, his new position created unexpected difficulties. As viceroy he needed political tact as well as military skill, particularly since the independence movement took two forms: "that of insurrection and that of parliamentary debate."[22]

The invitation to the subjects of New Spain to participate in the formation and organization of the Spanish Cortes and the experience that Mexicans acquired while electing their representatives to that body greatly changed the nature of the struggle for home rule. Earlier, the people had demonstrated their disgust with Spanish government by taking part in the armed revolt. The election of deputies to the Cortes provided the opportunity for them to express their discontent through the parliamentary process. Elections were held in the summer of 1810 with great enthusiasm and solemnity. The Regency in Spain, which had ordered the elections, forbade the participation of Europeans. Although they opposed the decision, the peninsulares did not obstruct the elections because they believed that they could control the viceroy and thus neutralize any liberal decrees which the Cortes might enact.

The Spaniards' exclusion was short-lived, because the Cortes rejected the proposal of the deputies from New Spain that only those born in the colony could be elected to represent it. After regaining their right to take part in elections, the Europeans used their influence to exclude the majority of the population from participation. They achieved this objective when the Cortes established residency and personal-property requirements for holding office. This assured the peninsulares that any elected deputy would oppose liberal measures which might be detrimental to the economic interests of the Spanish colonial oligarchy.[23]

Nevertheless, the fifteen Mexican deputies from New Spain played a very important role in the Cortes. They defended their constituents' interests and actively participated in the parliamentary debates. The work of the Cortes, which began on September 24, 1810, culminated on March 19, 1812, with the promulgation of the Political Constitution of the Spanish Monarchy. The Constitution of 1812 altered radically the structure of government in the Spanish world. Viceroyalties were abolished and divided into provinces governed by an official known as the political chief. As a result, the former viceroy became the political chief of the province of New Spain, one of five provinces created from the former Viceroyalty of New Spain, but he retained overall military authority as comander-in-chief of the army. Although the creoles were determined that the constitution should be obeyed, the liberal character of the new charter posed problems because it affected the economic interests of the Spaniards and the Church.[24]

Economic subjects, especially free trade, had provoked heated debate on both sides of the Atlantic. Interests for and against the measure were active in attempting to win the Cortes to their side. The Royal Consulado of Mexico, for example, opposed free trade because it "harms public law, insults the obligations of the Spanish throne, . . . impoverishes the nation, . . . retards progress, good customs, and tranquility, and precipitates division and anarchy."[25] Abad y Queipo, who opposed free trade even though he knew the creoles favored it, argued that "to abolish forever monopolies and the general restrictions which have existed up to now . . . would leave [New Spain] without agriculture, without art, without industry, without commerce, without a navy, without an army, without enlightenment, without glory, without honor."[26]

Although these two Spanish opinions are perhaps exaggerated, they reflect the issue's grave importance. To the creoles, free trade was necessary to further their political aspirations. The Spaniards, however, considered the monopoly they enjoyed to be a small repayment for the benefits and protection the creoles received from Spain. In this context, Deputy Mariano Mendiola Valverde's assertion that in Mexico commercial interests were "opposed to national interests"[27] gives some indication of the strength of the creoles' opinion.

The establishment of free trade, the removal of all restraints on agriculture, free distribution of mercury for mining, the elimination of ecclesiastical and military privilege, freedom of the press, and transformation of the office of the viceroy to that of political chief of the province of Mexico—only one of many provinces in New Spain—were all measures that the oligarchy had constantly opposed, but which the Cortes decreed.[28] Since the constitution attacked the very basis of the Spaniards' power, they attempted to nullify its effects in New Spain.

On September 9, 1812, Viceroy Venegas received three hundred copies of the constitution which he was to proclaim. However, he postponed publishing it and hesitated in distributing the copies to other officials. He also delayed conducting the popular elections for the city councils that the constitution had authorized.[29] Despite the viceroy's tactics, the people learned of the constitutional provision and held elections. The creoles' triumph was indisputable. Not a single Spaniard won a position, even though military and ecclesiastical authorities, like Calleja and the bishop of Mexico, intervened in an attempt to elect peninsulares.[30] Everywhere, the people had the opportunity to show their "hatred for the Europeans."[31] Venegas, who presided over the electoral committee of Mexico City, witnessed his compatriots' total defeat at the polls. Since there were allegations of voting irregularities, he suspended the election in Mexico City, but was unable to do the same in the rest of New Spain, which, for electoral purposes, had been divided into the provinces of Oaxaca, Puebla, Tlaxcala, Querétaro, Veracruz, Valladolid de Michoacán, Guanajuato, San Luis Potosí, and Mexico.[32]

That was the political situation that Calleja inherited when he took charge of the Province of New Spain on March 4, 1813. The constitution had introduced political changes which could not be ignored. The "parliamentary" creoles knew that the constitution favored them economically and politically, and they were determined to see it enforced. Besides placing restrictions on the government, the new freedoms also helped the insurgents, who attempted to provoke the authorities into violating the constitution and thus to win "parliamentary" creoles to their side.[33] Calleja decided to respect the constitution, trusting that the insurgents could be persuaded to do likewise. In this way he hoped to calm the fears of those royalists who had not yet decided to support it.[34] Calleja ordered that the elections which Venegas had suspended be held. He also accepted the limitations which the constitution imposed upon his power. As a result his authority was confined to Veracruz, Oaxaca, Puebla, Mexico, Michoacán, and Tlaxacala, putting him on an equal footing with the political chiefs of the other provinces.[35] He did, however, refuse to comply with one reform: freedom of the press. Calleja accepted the Audiencia's decision to restrict the press because of supposed abuses, including criticism of the Spanish government and support of the insurgents' cause.

Economic as well as political problems plagued Calleja. The government had a public debt of 30 million pesos; his treasury was so depleted that he could not pay the civil servants.[36] Like his predecessors, Calleja had to rely upon the European merchants for financial support. He did not hesitate to request their aid, always reminding them that such sacrifices were necessary to ensure their riches.[37] The Spanish oligarchy found his argument persuasive and always came to his assistance. The day he assumed office, for example, Calleja requested a loan of 1½ million pesos from the Consulado of Mexico. Although they had already contributed liberally, the Spanish merchants rapidly collected more than 1 million pesos.[38] They also accepted an increase in taxes. When voluntary loans did not provide the amount needed, Calleja resorted to forced loans.[39]

The problems resulting from the execution of the Spanish constitution soon ended. Upon returning to Spain on May 4, 1814, Ferdinand VII abolished the Cortes and nullified its laws, including the constitution. The king not only restored absolutism, but also imprisoned many liberal leaders, among them the Mexicans Miguel Ramos Arizpe and Joaquín Maniau. News of Ferdinand's actions reached New Spain in August, 1814. The judges, the merchants, and the clergy received it with "enthusiasm bordering on delirium."[40] In their happiness they were even willing to fraternize with the Mexicans. The European liberals and the proconstitutionalists, however, became so angry that Calleja was forced to take precautionary measures to prevent public protests similar to those which had

MEXICO IN 1814

Provinces

1. Provincias Internas de Occidente
2. Provincias Internas
3. Nueva Galicia
4. San Luis Potosí
5. Nueva España
6. Yucatán
7. Guatemala

México 5

occurred in Spain.[41] But there was no doubt that the majority of Spaniards considered the abolition of the constitution a great triumph. The absolutists insisted on consolidating their victory by restoring the Inquisition and imprisoning various Spanish and creole liberals, including José María Fagoaga and the marquis of Rayas.[43]

Ferdinand VII's return radicalized the insurgent movement and clearly defined the ideological differences of the colonials. The insurgents worked feverishly to attract discontented Europeans to their cause. Dr. José María Cos argued that Spain's well-being was lost with the overthrow of the constitution and invited the liberal Spaniards to join the independence movement. He promised that their lives and property would be respected.[44] This, he indicated, was guaranteed by the "Constitutional Decree for the Liberty of Mexican America," approved in Apatzingán on October 22, 1814. The decree expressed the insurgents' ideology and had its origins in the Congress of Anáhuac.[45] The appeal, however, fell on deaf ears. When Ferdinand restored Calleja's viceregal powers, the viceroy reestablished military efficiency and used it to defeat Morelos by the end of 1815.

Uncertain conditions in the colony and the restoration of peace in Spain together prompted the first large emigration of Europeans, with their capital, to the peninsula. A convoy of Europeans left Mexico City for Veracruz early in 1814, taking with them some 5 million pesos. Calleja tried unsuccessfully to stem the flow of emigrants at the end of October, 1814, by refusing to grant them passports. Among those leaving in October were soldiers, judges, prelates, merchants, and landowners, who took along approximately 7 million pesos.[46] The emigration of Spanish families continued throughout the entire period of the struggle for independence. Not all who left were "persons of means," as Alamán claimed; some were small shopkeepers. Most of them came from combat areas. In Oaxaca, for example, fifty-two of the city's eighty-two stores had been abandoned, and only three of those which remained open belonged to Europeans.[47] The authorities were preoccupied by the constant departure of Spaniards, but they were more disturbed by the flight of capital.[48] Quite possibly, native capitalists could have replaced the departing Europeans, but the colony's unstable situation did not allow time for an orderly transition.[49]

Although Calleja was concerned about the flight of people and capital, he was more disturbed by his inability to finance his administration. The viceregal government derived its income from the tobacco monopoly, the *alcabala,* and the tax on silver, all of which suffered as a result of the war. Calleja's financial requirements prompted him to issue copper money; he justified this extreme measure on the grounds that most of the specie had been exported to Spain.[50] Although the bureaucracy and the army had to accept the copper coinage, the merchants refused. The viceroy reacted to this by reducing the salaries of civil servants and by increasing the *alcabala* and property taxes by 10 percent. He also tried to establish a lottery and demanded a five hundred thousand-peso loan from the Consulado of Mexico; he received only three hundred thousand pesos.[51] Although the insurgents had suffered defeat—symbolized by the execution of Morelos in December, 1815—the viceroy was losing the Spaniards' support because of his economic policies.

Morelos's defeat had been achieved at great cost to the already precarious economy. Although the law protected Spanish merchants, events favored foreigners and creoles, who were displacing peninsulares in New Spain's trade. During the war years, foreigners captured more than 50 percent of Mexico's overseas trade. Commerce with Spain consisted of importing spirits, wines, paper, ribbons, and sundries, while the rest of Europe introduced manufactured products.[52] Internal trade required military protection, and that dependence led to notorious speculation involving the highest-ranking officers of the army. Royalist troops controlled the flow of trade by regulating access routes to ports and guarding merchandise in transport; this allowed them to engage in price speculation. Some officers, like La Madrid, Saturnino Samaniego, José Gabriel Armijo, José de la Cruz, Calleja, and Agustín de Iturbide, became indispensable to New Spain's internal commerce and acquired immense fortunes. Military participation in such a lucrative enterprise made Alamán suspect that "army commanders were in no hurry to crush the revolution because they were obtaining such great advantages from the present situation."[53]

Even though Calleja had put down the insurgents, the Spanish oligarchy chafed under his rule. His enemies began to undermine his prestige in the court of Ferdinand VII. Bishop Abad y Queipo informed the king that Calleja had been a favorite of Mexican liberals in 1812 and that he lacked the will and ability to pacify the colony.[54] Bishop Antonio Joaquín Pérez of Puebla withdrew his support from Calleja when he learned of the methods employed to repress the insurgents, charging that the viceroy's army had shed "much innocent blood, which could and should have been avoided."[55] He further alleged that under the guise of opposing the insurgents, many detestable robberies and murders had been committed. These criticisms and the reports of emigrating Europeans led to his removal.[56]

Juan Ruiz de Apodaca replaced Calleja on September 20, 1816. Thereafter, the Spanish government sought to pacify the colony by offering pardons to all those rebels who remained in the field. The new tactic proved successful because most insurgent leaders, lacking the resources to continue the struggle, accepted amnesty. Finally only Vicente Guerrero continued to fight in the south; Guadalupe Victoria, alone and without an army, was forced into hiding. The colony's calm was again broken in 1817 when the Spaniard Francisco Javier Mina attempted to restore the constitution. The liberal Spaniards of Veracruz, as well as some former insurgents, supported the movement. Mina failed, however, in his attempts to subvert the army by inducing liberal Spanish soldiers to revolt, and his short-lived invasion posed no danger to public order in New Spain.

By the beginning of 1820 the rebels had been virtually eliminated and no longer posed a threat to the government. But the colony's apparent calm was shattered when news arrived from Spain that the liberals had rebelled and forced Ferdinand VII to restore the constitution, and that the Cortes was once again in session. These were changes which the Spanish and creole oligarchies refused to accept because insurgency might be revived under the protection of the constitution.

Ten years of struggle had increased the number of Europeans who were ardent enemies of absolutism. Spanish liberals had introduced Masonry, which found many followers among the creoles. These developments forced the peninsular and creole oligarchy (a conservative aristocracy), the Church, and the army to change their minds about the political independence of New Spain. Above all, they wanted to maintain the status quo, but the new liberal government of Spain threatened their interests. Therefore they decided to lead the colony, under their strict control, toward independence. They chose Agustín de Iturbide to simulate a struggle against the rebels, while convincing them to accept the oligarchy's plan for independence—the Plan of Iguala, which established a Mexican empire. The oligarchy was successful and awaited the arrival of the last

Spanish governor, Juan O'Donojú, to negotiate an agreement. He proved amenable and agreed to sign the Treaty of Córdoba, which provided for Mexico's independence. Then the oligarchy attempted to force the people to accept the Plan of Iguala and the Treaty of Córdoba as solutions to all the colony's problems.

After long years of struggle, the true insurgents were frustrated and forced to accept political independence under principles very different from their own. Moreover, the future of the new government did not seem bright. The economy was in ruins, agriculture had been all but destroyed, the mines were abandoned, and commerce was paralyzed. Other nations, especially England and, to a lesser degree, the United States, were gaining control of the country's economic life. In the midst of these difficulties, the nascent monarchy began with only forty-two pesos in the treasury.

Although the Spaniards had severed New Spain from the mother country in order to retain the status quo, their situation changed substantially after independence. Thereafter, the creoles occupied a commanding position in the nation's politics. The peninsulares remained a tiny minority, but they neither enjoyed support in Spain nor wielded influence in the colony. The problems they faced after 1821 were very different from those they had previously overcome. Thereafter, they had no choice but to suffer the vicissitudes of national politics. They were now at the mercy of the creoles.[57]

NOTES

1. Manuel Abad y Queipo, "Informe dirigido a Fernando VII," in Alamán, *Historia,* 1: 609.

2. José de Iturrigaray, "Vivamos unidos si queremos ser invencibles," *Diario de México* 9, no. 1,063, pp. 239-41.

3. "Bando de 14 de abril de 1809," in Manuel Dublán and José María Lozano, *Legislación mexicana, o colección completa de las disposiciones legislativas expedidas desde la independencia de la República* (Mexico, 1876-1904), 1: 552-53; hereafter cited as Dublán and Lozano, *Legislación mexicana.*

4. Agustín Pomposo Fernández de San Salvador, *Memoria cristiana política sobre lo mucho que la Nueva España debe temer de su división en partidos, y las grandes ventajas que puede esperar de su unión y confraternidad* (Mexico, 1810), pp. 2-3.

5. Florencio Pérez y Comoto, *Discurso patriótico contra la rebelión que acaudilla el cura Hidalgo, y ventajas que ofrece la unión de todos los buenos ciudadanos* (Mexico, 1811), p. 14.

6. "Bando del virrey Francisco Javier Venegas publicando el de la Regencia de la Isla de León libertando de tributo a los indios," in Hernández y Dávalos, *Colección,* vol. 2, pp. 137-39.

7. "Bando del Sr. Hidalgo aboliendo la esclavitud, deroga las leyes relativas a tributos, impone alcabalas a los efectos nacionales y extranjeros, prohibe el uso de papel sellado y extingue el estanco del tabaco, pólvora, colores y otros," in Hernández y Dávalos, *Colección*, vol. 2, p. 243.

8. Manuel Abad y Queipo, "Representación sobre la necesidad de aumentar la fuerza armada para mantener la tranquilidad pública," in Hernández y Dávalos, *Colección*, vol. 2, pp. 880-83.

9. Mariano Torrente, *Historia de la independencia de México* (Madrid, 1918), p. 70; Alamán, *Historia*, 2: 437.

10. Alamán, *Historia*, 2: 16.

11. "El cabildo eclesiastico de Guadalajara manifiesta al virrey cual fue su conducta durante el tiempo que mandó el Sr. Hidalgo, y contestación del virrey," in Hernández y Dávalos *Colección*, vol. 2, p. 348.

12. Carlos María Bustamante, *Campañas del general D. Félix María Calleja, Comandante en gefe del ejército real de operaciones llamado del centro* (Mexico, 1828), p. 93. The letter was written in Guadalajara on January 28, 1811.

13. Mier, *Historia de la revolución de la Nueva España*, p. 15.

14. "Representación americana a las cortes de España, en 1 de agosto de 1811, con notas del editor inglés," in Hernández y Dávalos, *Colección*, vol. 3, p. 830.

15. "Bando sobre embargos de bienes europeos y que rindan cuentas los empleados de la real hacienda y de las iglesias," in Hernández y Dávalos, *Colección*, vol. 1, p. 272; "Exposición dirigida desde Zacatecas por Ignacio Rayón y D. José María Liceaga al general Calleja manifestando el motivo de la insurrección y proponiendo medios para terminarla," Alamán, *Historia*, 2: 583; "Decreto de Morelos," Alamán, *Historia*, 2: 589.

16. Alamán, *Historia*, 2: 226-27.

17. Manuel Abad y Queipo, "Edicto instructivo del obispo electo de Michoacán," in Hernández y Dávalos, *Colección*, vol. 3, pp. 914-18. See also Hamill, *The Hidalgo Revolt*, p. 165.

18. Alamán, *Historia*, 2: 449.

19. Ibid., 3: 135-36.

20. Ibid., 3: 510.

21. Abad y Queipo also believed that the propaganda against Venegas should have been attributed to those who sympathized with independence; see Manuel Abad y Queipo, "Representación a S. M.," cited by Neill Macauley, "The Army in New Spain and the Mexican Delegation to the Spanish Cortes," in Benson, *Mexico and the Spanish Cortes*, p. 140. It is true, however, that Venegas was already caught in a crossfire from the Spaniards as well as the creole liberals who attacked him for delaying the execution of the constitution.

22. Luis González y González, comp., *El Congreso de Anáhuac* (Mexico, 1963), p. 7.

23. David T. Garza, "Mexican Constitutional Expression in the Cortes of Cadiz," in Benson, *Mexico and the Spanish Cortes*, p. 53.

24. Luis Gonzaga Cuevas, *Porvenir de México, o juicio sobre su estado político en 1821 y 1851* (Mexico, 1851-57), p. 57.

25. Hernández y Dávalos, *Colección*, vol. 2, p. 500.

26. Manuel Abad y Queipo, "Representación a S. M. el 20 de junio de 1815 por el obispo electo de Michoacán . . . sobre la situación política de nuestras Américas," Latin American Collection, University of Texas, Austin, G. 360.

27. Alamán, *Historia*, 3: 81; John Hann, "The Role of the Mexican Deputies in the

Proposal and Enactment of Measures of Economic Reform Applicable to Mexico," in Benson, *Mexico and the Spanish Cortes*, pp. 175-76.

28. Dublán and Lozano, *Legislación mexicana*, 1: 96-437; Hernández y Dávalos, *Colección*, vol. 4, doc. 40; Nettie Lee Benson, *La diputación provincial y el federalismo mexicano* (Mexico, 1955), 21; hereafter cited as Benson, *La diputación provincial*.

29. Roger Cunniff, "Mexican Municipal Electoral Reform, 1810-1822," in Benson, *Mexico and the Spanish Cortes*, p. 77.

30. *Diario de México*, December 2, 1812, cited by Cunniff, ibid.

31. Alamán, *Historia*, 3: 273.

32. Cunniff, "Mexican Municipal Reform," pp. 27-73; Benson, "The Contested Election of 1812," *HAHR* 26 (August 1946): 336-80; Charles Berry, "The Election of the Mexican Deputies to the Spanish Cortes, 1810-1822," in Benson, *Mexico and the Spanish Cortes*, pp. 22-23.

33. Alamán, *Historia*, 3: 279.

34. Benson, *La diputación provincial*, p. 33.

35. Nettie L. Benson has demonstrated that the origin of Mexican federalism is to be found in the form of government established by the Constitution of 1812, particularly in the creation of the Provincial Deputations. See Benson, *La diputación provincial*, p. 21.

36. Alamán, *Historia*, 3: 364.

37. Ibid., p. 372.

38. Hernández y Dávalos, *Colección*, vol. 5, pp. 11-12; Alamán, *Historia*, 3: 373.

39. Alamán, *Historia*, 3: 400-402.

40. Anastasio Zerecero, *Memorias para la historia de las revoluciones de México*, p. 19.

41. Alamán, *Historia*, 3: 143, 147.

42. Carlos María Bustamante, *La Constitución de Apatzingán* (Mexico, 1960), p. 119.

43. Lorenzo de Zavala, *Ensayo histórico de las revoluciones de México, desde 1808 hasta 1830* (Paris, 1831-32), vol. 1, p. 81.

44. "Proclama de Cos a los españoles habitantes de América, 21 de Octubre de 1814," Hernández y Dávalos, *Colección*, vol. 3, p. 702; "Manifiesto de la nación americana a los europeos que habitan este continente" (1814), Colección Lafragua, National Library, Mexico, vol. 238, p. 29.

45. See Ernesto de la Torre Villar, *La Constitución de Apatzingán y los creadores del estado mexicano* (Mexico, 1964), and his *Estudios sobre el Decreto Constitucional de Apatzingán* (Mexico, 1964); also González y González, *El Congreso de Anáhuac*.

46. Alamán, *Historia*, 4: 210-12.

47. Hernández y Dávalos, *Colección*, 4: 853-55.

48. Mora, *Méjico y sus revoluciones*, 1: 448; Alamán, *Historia*, 4: 661.

49. Mora, *Méjico y sus revoluciones*, 1: 449.

50. Hernández y Dávalos, *Colección*, vol. 6, p. 1,049.

51. Alamán, *Historia*, 4: 204-8, 359-60.

52. The growing participation of foreigners in New Spain's trade can be seen in José María Quiros, "Balanzas del comercio marítimo de Veracruz, 1816-1819," in Lerdo de Tejada, *El Comercio esterior de México*, appendixes 26-29.

53. Bishop Antonio Joaquín Pérez of Puebla denounced the trade to Calleja in April, 1816. The viceroy replied, defending his actions and denying the charges. See

"Controversia entre el obispo de Puebla y el virrey Calleja," *Boletín del Archivo General de la Nación*, 4 (September-October 1937): 660-61; see also Alamán, *Historia*, 4: 48-49, 416-19.

54. Abad y Queipo, "Representación a S. M. . . . sobre la situación política de nuestras Américas."

55. "Controversia entre el obispo de Puebla y el virrey Calleja," *BAGN* 4: 658.

56. Ibid., pp. 658-59.

57. Alamán, *Historia*, 5: 811.

FOUR

Two Incompatible Guarantees: Union and Independence

The first independent government faced three problems which required its immediate attention; first, to secure the financial resources necessary to govern; second, to find the ideological means to sustain the form of government with which independence was begun; and third, to pacify the country by unifying its European and American citizens.

The imperial regime lacked revenues because war and political instability had virtually destroyed the economy. The War of Independence had already led to an extraordinary increase in taxes, most of which the people evaded. Furthermore, the old sources of revenue had declined. For example, the "income from the tobacco [monopoly], the most valuable and most productive of the old order," had diminished to a pittance; even so, the empire had been forced to mortgage it as collateral for its debts. It was impossible to continue the colonial system of administration and taxation because it was "ruinous, poorly organized, and contrary to public opinion and to the general welfare." On the other hand, to eliminate it completely would be unthinkable because the administration needed the bureaucracy, particularly for collecting funds for the increasing civil and military expenditures.[1] However, the government also needed money to pay the salaries of the civil servants if it expected to hold their loyalty.

The Plan of Iguala and the Treaty of Córdoba were the government's legal bases, and the three guarantees of "union, religion, and independence" contained in these documents were thought to be sufficient to establish the new regime on a firm foundation. However, while everyone accepted the idea of religious unity, there was less support for political union and for independence.

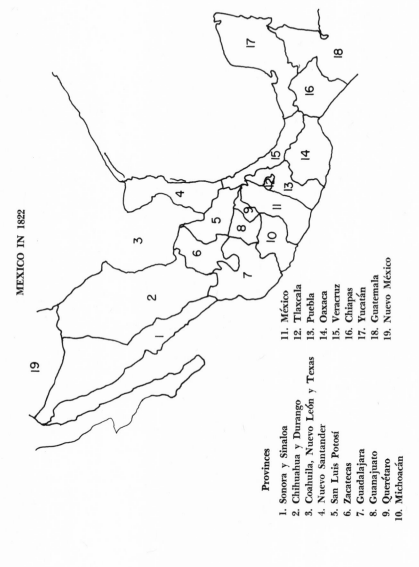

MEXICO IN 1822

Provinces

1. Sonora y Sinaloa
2. Chihuahua y Durango
3. Coahuila, Nuevo León y Texas
4. Nuevo Santander
5. San Luis Potosí
6. Zacatecas
7. Guadalajara
8. Guanajuato
9. Querétaro
10. Michoacán
11. México
12. Tlaxcala
13. Puebla
14. Oaxaca
15. Veracruz
16. Chiapas
17. Yucatán
18. Guatemala
19. Nuevo México

The preface of the Plan of Iguala praised Spain as "the most Catholic and pious, heroic, and magnanimous" of nations, while it criticized the Hidalgo movement as "the cause of so many misfortunes to . . . the nation because of the disorder, debauchery, and the multitude of vices" which had been engendered. The plan sought to convert the *peninsulares* to independence by calling for unity. "European Spaniards," it read, "your homeland is America because that is where you live; there you have your beloved wives, your young children, your lands, commerce, and goods." It appealed to the Americans with the question "Who among you can say that he is not a descendant of Spaniards?" thereby excluding the vast majority of the population, who lacked not only Spanish ancestors but the oligarchy's cultural and racial characteristics as well. Thus, the Plan of Iguala was hardly designed to further social homogeneity. The plan offered access to public office to all inhabitants, promising to protect every citizen's life and property and to preserve all the *fueros* and privileges of the regular and secular clergy. The document established "a committee to see that all the branches of government remain unchanged and that all religious, civil, and military employees continue to hold the same positions they previously occupied." Only those who were opposed to independence would be removed. Their places were to be taken by persons who had distinguished themselves for their "virtue and merit." Finally, the Plan of Iguala provided for the formation of "a protecting force to be called the Army of the Three Guarantees" to enforce its provisions.

The Treaty of Córdoba was signed eight months after the Plan of Iguala, despite the fact that Spanish troops continued to defend the last vestiges of royal power in Acapulco and Veracruz. The treaty ratified the Plan of Iguala, but it did not lead to domestic tranquility. Although the status quo was to be preserved and the government promised to safeguard ancient privileges, using the army, there could be no guarantee of undisturbed peace. At first, however, the entire population seemed to support Iturbide as the symbol of independence. The new government would be a monarchy. Until the Cortes of Spain ratified the Treaty of Córdoba and provided a Spanish prince to preside over the first Mexican empire, the throne remained vacant. A regency which included Iturbide and O'Donojú, and, upon the death of the latter, the bishop of Puebla would serve as the executive branch. The Sovereign Provisional Governing Committee of the Mexican empire served as the legislature until the first national congress convened. As president of the regency and commander-in-chief of the Army of the Three Guarantees, Iturbide acted as chief executive.

The generalissimo drew the members of his first cabinet from the conservative oligarchy in the hope that they would help him solve his administration's financial crisis. The new minister of finance, José Pérez Maldonado, was a man of advanced age and limited experience. Pérez, who had worked in the office of *alcabala* taxes before independence, unimaginatively sought to restore governmental solvency by floating another loan from the Spanish capitalists.[2] Such a solution was futile. There remained few Spanish subjects like those who once contributed three hundred thousand pesos to buy shoes for the Spanish army when it fought the invading French.[3] The small number who contributed to the new regime included high ecclesiastical authorities and some wealthy Spaniards and creoles. The Spaniard Manuel de Heras y Soto, a friend of Iturbide's, made the largest loan—forty thousand pesos. The creole capitalist Juan N. de Moncada y Berrio, the marquis of Jaral, and Juan Icaza each contributed a similar amount.[4] However, these contributions did not satisfy the administration's needs. The *Semanario Político y Literario de Méjico* suggested that the government drain flooded mines, establish free trade, and institute a direct tax. The latter should be accomplished, however, without placing excessive burdens on individuals and "without the spying and manipulation characteristic of the old internal revenue system." The paper believed that these changes would generate enough income to permit the empire to meet its obligations, reduce the debt substantially, and end the dependence on individual contributions.[5] The implementation of these reforms, however, was more complex in practice than in theory. The program required public and private cooperation, which in turn depended upon confidence in the government. Unfortunately, Iturbide did not inspire such trust. He seemed more concerned with ostentatious display in court than with sound fiscal policies. As a result, entrepreneurs lacked the assurance necessary to invest their capital.

The government, unable to raise the funds required to maintain "the honor and decorum of this opulent empire," turned to paper money.[6] Public employees were paid with currency, and the regime even attempted to meet some of its internal debts with it. In order to facilitate its acceptance, the minister of finance permitted merchants to pay up to one-sixth of their customs duties in paper.[7] Most people, however, lacked confidence in the new currency, and the Indians failed to comprehend it.[8] Some critics went so far as to predict that paper money would lead to the government's downfall.[9] The measure did fail and the government remained mired in its financial crisis. Yet no one really believed that the country was poor. On the contrary, everyone expected Mexico's legendary wealth to reach new levels now that the nation was no longer forced to support a decaying Spain.

Although the government was nearly bankrupt, its leaders remained optimistic. The Provisional Governing Committee authorized a salary of 120,000 pesos for Iturbide and a lifetime annual pension of 12,000 pesos for O'Donojú's widow.[10] In order to meet increasing government obligations, on January 2, 1822, the committee authorized the generalissimo to negotiate a loan of 1½ million pesos, using the customs revenues as security. Iturbide was reminded that some of the nation's income was already "affected by other debts" and that he could not promise the same future income for two different loans.[11]

It became increasingly apparent that the flight of the Spaniards had created a shortage of specie. Iturbide had permitted those Europeans who wished to leave to take with them whatever wealth they possessed. However, when the sovereign committee realized that defeated Spanish soldiers were returning home with large quantities of money, it limited the amount they could take according to their rank as of February 4, 1822.[12] It further instructed the regency to police the concession of "money permits" and to ascertain whether those requesting them intended to export large sums.[13] Although the ruling restricted commerce and violated Article 15 of the Treaty of Córdoba, it was intended to reduce the adverse flow of currency. But the order became impossible to enforce.

When the government could not otherwise obtain the necessary revenue, it turned to forced loans. In June, 1822, for example, the *consulados* were ordered to provide 600,000 pesos from their levies on internal trade.[14] Later the government demanded a loan of 2,800,000 pesos to cover daily expenditures for the remainder of the year. In both cases, Iturbide promised to repay the obligations as soon as he received the first contributions from the empire's inhabitants.[15] Joaquín Obregón, head of the Finance and Commerce Commission, admitted that these forced loans were in violation of "the principles of just taxation and political economy." He further disclosed that some citizens had been jailed for refusing to comply or because they lacked the funds demanded.[16] He therefore recommended that the government end the practice of forced loans and that a study be initiated to determine the true state of all government finances. If no other way could be found, then the regime should resolve its crisis by selling the property of the temporalities.

Iturbide was partially responsible for the administration's grave financial situation. In order to obtain the backing of the merchants and capitalists, he had reduced the *alcabala* tax from 16 to 6 percent, abolished taxes on spirits, mescal, and transportation, cancelled the 10 percent property and rent tax, and eliminated all the emergency taxes which the Spanish government had levied during the war. Since the government was not only short of funds but also operating with a deficit of 2 million pesos, the minister of finance proposed to resolve the financial crisis by allowing vacancies in the bureaucracy to remain unfilled, reducing the salaries of those who were well paid, abolishing departments which were not indispensable, drastically reducing the army to a force sufficient merely to maintain order, hastening the evacuation of the Spanish "expeditionaries," who were costing the nation 35,000 pesos a month, and, finally, imposing a moderate direct tax.[17] None of the suggestions were fully implemented because each of them adversely affected some important group or interest. The government, therefore, looked to other countries for a solution. On June 25, 1822, Congress capitulated, authorizing the regency to negotiate a loan of 25 to 30 million pesos from foreign financiers under "the least onerous conditions to the nation."[18]

The imperial government not only failed to correct its financial difficulties; it was also incapable of solving its political problems. Neither the Bourbon supporters of the Plan of Iguala nor the republican liberals were pleased with the new government; both, for different reasons, sought to undermine Iturbide's prestige. When the government announced that the Spanish Cortes had rejected the Treaty of Córdoba on February 13, 1822, the Spaniards began to wonder about their future and wasted no opportunity to attack the generalissimo.[19] The Mexicans were also dissatisfied with the government because the same powerful colonial groups—the Church, the army, and the oligarchy—still controlled it. Many Mexicans did not believe that they would be free as long as the peninsulares enjoyed the benefits of independence.[20] Determined to find positions for themselves in the bureaucracy, they directed their first efforts against the

Spanish, asking that they be removed from public employment. Europeans had occupied most of the administrative posts of importance until the War of Independence, when some peninsulares, fearful of popular reaction, resigned. By 1820 the viceregal government felt the pressure of Mexicans wanting government jobs. In order to remain impartial, it published notices of existing vacancies, especially in the department of finance, requiring only that applicants support the monarchy.[21] Once independence was achieved, the Spanish bureaucrats abandoned their provincial posts and gathered in the capital under very flimsy pretexts. The imperial government therefore ordered public employees either to return to their posts within eight days or forfeit their jobs.[22]

Although the Plan of Iguala guaranteed public employees their positions, the new situation required that others be appointed. Those who had collaborated in winning independence had to be placated; as one pamphlet maintained, society should be served by "the men of the hour."[23] So the sovereign committee published an order specifying that public employees would be chosen by lot from a list of all those persons "with sufficient merit."[24] Later, jobs were granted only to those who had sworn to uphold independence. Men who refused lost their salaries.[25] The number of vacancies in public jobs continued to increase as Spaniards resigned their posts throughout the country. Newspapers announced openings in intendencies, in the customs department, in the ministry of justice, for public scribes, within the tobacco monopoly, and for director general of *alcabalas*.[27] Owing to the rapid changes in the civil service, the government faced a serious problem with an undisciplined, discouraged, and ill-paid bureaucracy. Many employees lacked discretion, revealing government activities without regard to their impact even when they were of a sensitive nature.[28] As a result, the administration attempted to reform the system by abolishing many clumsy and abusive colonial regulations and by enforcing the rules against bureaucratic corruption, particularly embezzlement.[29] The government thus hoped to have a more disciplined bureaucracy, thereby saving money on salaries and increasing the efficiency of its tax collections.

The government, however, reflected the bitter divisions of the society. As Alamán described it:

> There were among the Europeans ignorant men with crude ideals who would be content only if they murdered all those who had been born in the country. Unfortunately, there were among the nation's sons those with

equally barbarous ideals who, if they could, would kill all Europeans in a single day. Both were motivated by no other purpose than to satiate their mutual hatreds.[30]

Even before independence, criticism of the Spaniards had become so bitter that a pamphlet entitled *The Ox Has Been Pricked So Much That It Will Attack* had been written to defend them. It condemned the fact that the Spaniards were considered the most wretched of men; that they were accused of being responsible for everything bad and charged with disobeying the laws and changing them to suit their interests; and that they were accused of living in a foreign land with the intention of exploiting it and then returning home to enjoy their spoils. The pamphlet concluded by asking for unity and requesting that the Spaniards give the Americans "proof of their love" for Mexico.[31] A second issue explained that Spaniards were needed in commerce because few "*indianos* [Mexicans] dare to ply the seas for commerce." The pamphlet denied that Spaniards dominated the bureaucracy because of favoritism; it was because they were nearer the seat of power and thus the most likely to receive appointments. The Spaniards' privileged position, it maintained, was the result of "the state of things and the nature of men."[32]

The amount of propaganda in favor of unity increased as other publications appeared. A European launched "a challenge of reconciliation."[33] A Mexican accepted the challenge, calling the Europeans his brothers and asserting that Christian charity had united them.[34] "The Lover of His Fellow Men" labeled rivalry "that infernal monster" and asked that "peace, concord, and unity" prevail.[35] Nicolás Bravo believed that it should not be necessary to invoke the principles of moderation and hospitality in order to build "our union with our Spanish brothers from Europe."[36] Someone even advocated that all writings opposed to unity be burned, so that "enmity, discord, rivalry, and the hated names *gachupín* and creole," would disappear forever, and men could "thereafter [call themselves], merely, brothers."[37]

But not everyone backed the drive for reconciliation. A Mexican recommended sarcastically that a fourth guarantee should consist of punishing the Spaniards.[38] Another maintained that the people should oppose the Spaniards because they continued to abuse their authority. He cited the cases of the intendant José María Septién and General José de la Cruz, who misused the power the Spanish government had given them and were now demanding privileges from city councils. The pamphleteer counseled that charges be brought against them and that the people remain vigilant to prevent such abuses in the future.[39]

The first major attack against the guarantee of unity, however, was by the Spaniard Francisco Lagranda, who believed that Iturbide's efforts to protect the Europeans would fail because the sovereign people did not approve. In a pamphlet, *Prudent Counsel about One of the Guarantees,* he maintained that the nation was now paying for the "despotism and pride" with which the Spaniards had once treated the Mexicans, when the Europeans had looked upon "the creole as the most wretched servant and the Indian as a miserable slave." Therefore, Lagranda insisted, it was necessary for the peninsulares to leave the country to save their lives and property; he further maintained that José Joaquín de Iturbide, the generalissimo's father, "should also depart for the public well-being" if his health and advanced age permitted it.[40]

Because it was considered a threat to the guarantee of unity, Lagranda's pamphlet elicited hostile reactions, especially in official quarters. Pedro Celestino Negrete, the Spanish general in charge of the imperial army, sent a statement to various parts of the country in which he declared that the pamphlet was a "malignant abortion that scandalized the empire."[41] The menace posed by the "incendiary pamphlet" led General Negrete to prevent the mail from leaving Mexico City so that the offending work would not be disseminated in the provinces. He also threatened the author or authors with "prompt, severe, exemplary, and comprehensive" punishment.[42] On the morning of December 12, 1821, the generalissimo censured the work, prevented its distribution, and "attempted to have the author charged and imprisoned by due process."[43] The charges of subversion were also extended to include the authors of the pamphlets and periodicals *Hombre Libre, El Fraile y su Pelahuejo, México Dormido, Cincuenta Preguntas del Pensador,* issue number 5 of *La Abeja de Chilpancingo,* and any others that supposedly attacked the basis of independence.[44] The arguments, however, continued.

In his *Fifty Questions,* José Joaquín Fernández de Lizardi, "the Mexican Thinker," asked the meaning of certain principles, particularly the guarantee of unity. Among the questions he propounded were:

26. Should the guarantee of unity be extended to those who abhor or hate our system?

27. Can anyone rationally offer any just reason for not accepting that question?

28. Will those 1,400 men who embarked in Cádiz last month with Veracruz as their destination and the two regiments of the line who are traveling to this empire come to swear allegiance to independence, or do they bring their little rifles to fire volleys of salute to the Army of the Three Guarantees?

29. Should we receive them with open arms, invite them to join the union, or prevent their landing at all costs?

30. If these soldiers fearlessly attempt to reduce us to our ancient slavery, will they succeed?

31. Is it convenient for them to enter this kingdom, mix with our troops, and wear our uniforms?[45]

"An ignorant woman" answered the Thinker's questions,[46] but the government responded more emphatically by placing him on the subversive list. Fernández de Lizardi wrote other pamphlets concerning the Europeans. In one he criticized some writers' attitudes toward the Spaniards, warning them that although many peninsulares would gladly return to the old despotism, they were not the only ones so inclined. Among Mexican women, he wrote, there are "infinite numbers" who support "chaquetismo" [the Spaniards], and if it were up to them, there would not be a single American who was not the slave of a [woman's] European husband or lover."[47] However, he did admit that there were some Spaniards who not only cared for Mexicans but who had also "braved danger" for them. From these he asked forgiveness for those who used the press to insult them.

Juan José Sivrob, the intendant of Guanajuato, counseled the Spaniards to act with caution because "Americans are docile, accommodating, and generous," but once their sensibilities are aroused, they would never hestitate "to be at your throats." Therefore, he recommended that the Europeans "live with circumspection" and unite with Iturbide.[49] Other publications emphasized the harm which the economy and society would suffer if the Spaniards left, not only because of "the incalculable exportation of wealth" which would affect commerce adversely, but also because of "the emigration of the majority of persons who sustain it." One writer maintained that the peninsulares would not be harmed and that they could consider their lives, well-being, and property free of any danger.[50] Another defended the Spaniards by assuring the Americans that, in general, the Europeans were good and that, as a result, their children—Mexicans—were also good. He asked: "Is it not true that we have lived united over the long period of three hundred years?"[51]

Because of the general uneasiness, Iturbide issued a proclamation guaranteeing that the Spaniards would live unmolested. He hoped to remove some of their doubts and fears by reminding them that his father, whom he venerated, was a European. His father had a wife whom he loved and children who were his delight.[52] The imperial government tried to foster unity by various means. During public festivals it had some Spanish women dress as Indians and some Indian women dress as Spaniards as a symbol of unity and observance of the third guarantee.[53] The regency requested that the Sovereign Constituent Congress approve a law which would prohibit the classification of citizens according to place of birth.[54] However, obtaining the necessary compliance and cooperation to guarantee solidarity was not an easy task. It was impossible to erase three centuries of disagreements and friction between Spaniards and creoles with plans, treaties, and official good will. No matter how hard he tried, Iturbide could not obtain unity. Furthermore, time was against him. The majority were not willing to tolerate indefinitely an independent nation in which the social and economic status quo remained as before. As a result, Iturbide's efforts to persuade Spaniards to remain in the country failed because he could not allay Mexican hostility.

The Spanish emigration, which began in 1814, continued at an increasing rate. Important civil and ecclesiastic functionaries, as well as members of the Spanish army who had not managed to put down roots in the colony, fled after refusing to swear allegiance to the independent government. The Consulado of Veracruz noted that despite the enormous sacrifices entailed, whole families escaped to the coast.[55] There they sought the protection of the Spanish army occupying the fortress of San Juan de Ulúa, which guarded the port of Veracruz. From the safety of the fortress, General Novella advised his compatriots to find security there.[56] However, the fortress commander thought the Spanish capitalists needed little urging to leave, because the imperial government had made them victims of arbitrary demands.[57] Juan José Espinosa de los Monteros, later Mexico's minister of foreign affairs, believed that the peninsulares were driven to flee because of feelings "born of terror and panic."[58] Such was the Spaniards' fear that some were even willing to indenture themselves to those who could help them return to Spain.[59] As a result, Iturbide was powerless to stop them.

When the number of emigrants increased dramatically, Iturbide's government became more alarmed and decided to impose obstacles to the issuance of passports, particularly to those who were taking large sums of money with them. It prohibited the exportation of money in January, 1822,[60] but was forced to retreat in March with the hope that confidence would be restored and that business would prosper once more.[61] It is impossible at present to estimate precisely the amount of capital lost as a result of Spanish emigration. Most contemporary sources refer vaguely to "great wealth,"[62] "powerful interests,"[63] and "currency." The Consulado of Veracruz calculated "the real estate, riches, and commercial goods" of the Spanish merchants at approximately 35 million pesos, but between 12 million and 15 million pesos were owned by merchants in the Veracruz trade who lived "overseas."[64] It is unlikely, however, that any of this capital left Mexico in 1822. The *Informes del Consulado de Veracruz* and the *Memorias de Hacienda* of the time demonstrate that peninsulares still dominated Mexican trade. It seems reasonable to conclude, therefore, that the capital Mexico lost was wealth belonging to the departing civil, clerical, and military officials.

In the prevailing atmosphere of fear and tension the army served as a bulwark in maintaining public order. But the loyalty of the military was an uncertain thing. Iturbide had appointed to the highest ranks many of those who fought with him in the royalist army. The army's senior officer, for example, was the Spanish General Pedro Celestino Negrete, Iturbide's ally. Except for Vicente Guerrero, who was named field marshal, men who fought with the insurgents received lower ranks.[65] Discontent was not limited to the generals. After independence it became necessary to reorganize the armed forces; soldiers were transferred to different battalions and regimental names were changed. The glory associated with the old royalist battalions disappeared along with these changes, and many old soldiers refused to serve in the new units. By 1821, desertions reduced the army, which had once numbered 8,308, to 1,802 officers and 3,161 enlisted men.[66] Furthermore, the regency's finances became so critical that the government appointed individuals to raise money through voluntary gifts in order to clothe the Army of the Three Guarantees.[67]

These circumstances made it impossible to predict the army's loyalty if an uprising should occur. Most people did not trust the Spanish soldiers who had capitulated and many believed that their presence was incompatible with independence.[68] The more violent suggested that they be executed.[69] To make matters worse, General José Dávila, commander of the Spanish forces at the fortress of San Juan de Ulúa, was known to be urging the European soldiers to rebel.[70] The Constituent Congress tried to prevent any disorders by offering to promote those Spanish officers who had voluntarily joined the Army of the Three Guarantees a month before independence had been achieved.[71] However, the situation remained tense throughout the country. Then a series of incidents occurred which, in addition to undermining the principle of unity, seemed to threaten independence itself.

The attitude of some Spanish soldiers in Toluca irritated the populace and even the generalissimo, who judged their conduct to be "contrary to what should be expected of grateful, moderate, and circumspect men." Some citizens complained that the soldiers had treated the people with contempt, had mocked the government, and had blasphemed against "God himself." In one instance a Spanish captain "insulted a young woman's honor" while in the process of closing a house of pleasure.[72] Spanish soldiers committed similar acts in other cities. One writer, "The Lover of Unity," maintained that the soldiers' attitude had only served to cause doubts about "peaceful Europeans" and that, as a result, they deserved to "have their weapons as well as their pants taken away from them and be given a beating of twenty-five lashes each." He regretted that the third guarantee prevented such punishment.[73] Uncertainty increased when, at the same time that many peninsulares were deserting the Army of the Three Guarantees, news arrived that 400 Spanish soldiers had landed in San Juan de Ulúa. Iturbide attempted to allay the peoples' fears by promising to punish any soldier who violated the law.

As tension heightened, the Spaniards began to react strongly. In Texcoco, for example, soldiers tried to flee to Veracruz to join their compatriots in the fortress, but the townspeople stopped them.[74] Amid this atmosphere of distrust the Spanish soldiers at Juchi rebelled. The imperial generals Anastasio Bustamante and José Antonio Echávarri, a Mexican and a European, respectively, quelled the insurrection and imprisoned the rebels, with a force of only 300 dragoons. The incident was minor, but the government hoped to prevent the rebellion from spreading to the other Spanish regiments—the Zaragoza, Castilla, and Zamora—which had surrendered and were awaiting repatriation.[75] Promising to punish the guilty and to protect those whose only connection with the revolt had been their birth in Spain, the regency denounced the conspiracy as "impotent in its means, imprudent in its organization, and senseless in its purpose."[76] With a sign of relief, *El Noticioso* declared that the country had been saved from a "sinister stroke which would have caused a general upheaval in a great and generous nation."[77] Iturbide tried to calm the citizens of the empire by accusing Dávila of being responsible for organizing the insurrection and by reminding the Spanish officers of their duty. Then he called for unity and declared that the crimes committed by a few Spaniards did not change his opinion of the other Europeans who he believed supported the government. As a result of the uprising, authorities ordered that the soldiers who had capitulated and who were being evacuated to Cuba be sent to Tampico instead of Veracruz in order to avoid incidents like the one in Juchi.[78]

The nation's tranquility was again shattered when news arrived on February 13, 1822, that the Spanish Cortes had rejected the Treaty of Córdoba. The crisis deepened in May when, as a result of military and popular support, Iturbide was crowned Agustín I, emperor of Mexico. The legitimists had no recourse but to join forces with the republicans in opposing the emperor. This naturally increased public confusion and accelerated distrust of the Spaniards. Everyone automatically assumed that Spain would send troops to reconquer its former possession. Newspapermen and pamphleteers either exaggerated or ignored the threat, depending on their persuasion, but the general atmosphere was one of fear. One writer suggested that it would be necessary to build a "strong [wall] throughout the entire nation," well equipped with weapons, men, munitions, and supplies, to defend against invasions. He added that in order for the wall to be effective, it would be necessary to have at least four hundred thousand men under arms and a military budget of 30 million pesos devoted solely to defense.[79]

The whole country concentrated its attention on the activities of the Spaniards stationed at San Juan de Ulúa. The government, under heavy popular pressure, tried to find new ways to drive the Europeans from the fortress, but without a navy it was an impossible task. The fortress overlooked the city of Veracruz and controlled entry to the port. Spanish troops frequently molested the townspeople and prevented Mexico from using its chief Atlantic port. Iturbide failed in his attempts to persuade Dávila to surrender the fortress because he tried to achieve national independence without severing diplomatic relations with Spain and even allowed Spanish ships and Spanish merchants to conduct business as they had done during the colonial years.[80] However, in view of his fruitless efforts, Congress instructed the emperor to prohibit the entry of Spanish ships into the Gulf of Mexico and authorized him to sever relations with Spain.[81] Most Mexicans believed they had to finish "skinning the tail" of the Spanish cat in order to be free. Otherwise there would always be European capitalists ready to help the forces of San Juan de Ulúa if General Dávila requested aid.[82] On the other hand, many Europeans believed that they would suffer if the fortress did not surrender. The Consulado of Veracruz declared that from a military point of view General Dávila's actions were excellent, but it doubted that he should continue them "at the expense of [the Spaniards'] tranquility, property, or lives."[83] Diego García and Manuel Torres, two leading Europeans, did not believe that Dávila's attitude deserved support from the Spanish government. They asserted that "reasonable Spaniards saw a need for independence," and they believed that if Dávila surrendered the fortress instead of promoting conflict, "the hateful distinctions between *gachupín* and creole" would disappear. They concluded that Dávila's presence in San Juan de Ulúa was interpreted as an act of bad faith on the part of Spain and the Spaniards, whereas if he gave up the fortress, the commander would be serving not only his fatherland but also the cause of humanity.[84] Such exhortations, however, were doomed to failure.

Since the government seemed unable to resolve the problem, some Mexicans took the task upon themselves. Antonio López de Santa Anna, charged with the defense of Veracruz, attempted to entice the Spanish army from the fortress on his own initiative. He failed, but his act unleashed a chain of events that led to the demise of the empire.

When Iturbide learned that Santa Anna had acted without orders, he lost confidence in his general and decided to remove him from command. Santa Anna, knowing that his position and prestige were in danger, allowed himself to be persuaded by the emperor's enemies—particularly Miguel de Santa María—to oppose Iturbide and proclaim a republic. On December 6, 1822, Santa Anna and General Guadalupe Victoria signed the Plan of Veracruz, which outlined the proposed new government. It repeated the Plan of Iguala's three guarantees; promised to protect the citizens' rights of liberty, equality,

and property; preserved clerical privilege; and transformed the Army of the Three Guarantees into the Army of Liberation. Finally, in order to win the support of those who sought public employment, it promised that in the consideration of future applications for government service, "the merit, talent, and public virtues" of the applicants would be taken into account.[85] Although Generals Santa Anna and Victoria proclaimed the Plan of Veracruz, it was written by Santa María, a native of Veracruz who was then Gran Colombia's ambassador to Mexico and who advocated the views of centralist republicans.[86]

General Dávila tried to take advantage of the situation by entering into negotiations with Santa Anna, but nothing resulted. Yet these talks were sufficient evidence for Iturbide to link Santa Anna to the Spaniards in a conspiracy against independence. Since some peninsulares also appeared to be plotting against him, the emperor reacted by issuing a decree requiring all Europeans, especially the Spanish soldiers who served in the royal army during the colonial period, to register with the magistrates of the provincial capitals. They were to report their political activities. Those who had favored Iturbide's government would be rewarded with some post where they would be of use to the nation. Anyone refusing to report would be apprehended and condemned to two years of forced labor in public works.[87] While the *bad* Spaniards were to be punished, Iturbide assured the *good* ones that they would be treated with equity, as the Plan of Iguala had promised.[88]

Various persons attempted to get Santa Anna to surrender. José María Tornel, for example, wrote him, explaining that the Spaniards were only concerned with exploiting the country and that many people looked upon them with scorn because they were leaving with the fruits of their "former plunderings."[89] This advice had no effect, and the emperor sent armies to destroy the rebels. The forces that attacked Santa Anna in defense of the emperor later decided to oppose Iturbide. However, the new opposition presented its own proposals, known as the Plan of Casa Mata. The plan is of particular importance because its author was the Spaniard Gregorio Arana, secretary and honor guard to the Spanish General Echávarri, then commander-in-chief of the army.[90] It appears that the Spaniards, having learned that Spain had rejected the Treaty of Córdoba, were once again attempting to take control of Mexico's government. Their plan consisted of eleven articles, which appeared, at least, to recognize the emperor, called for the meeting of a new congress, and granted administrative powers to the provinces so that they might govern themselves. Thus the plan was intended to satisfy long-held provincial desires for a larger role in national affairs. It also stated that the army would protect Iturbide.[91]

Once the plan was promulgated, nothing could stop the chain of events. By mid-March most provinces were already organizing their governments. Now that Iturbide had both the army and the people against him, his days in power were numbered. He had been unable either to achieve unity under the empire or to consolidate independence. At a nocturnal session of Congress on March 19, 1823, the emperor abdicated through an intermediary, Juan Gómez de Navarrete.[92] He declared that he had accepted the Crown against his will and admitted that his presence had been the cause of disturbances. He therefore charged Congress to assume the burdens of the nation and asked it to pay the debts he had contracted with various individuals, some of them his friends.[93]

NOTES

1. J. A. Castillón, ed., *República mexicana informes y manifiestos de los poderes ejecutivo y legislativo de 1821 a 1904* (Mexico, 1905), 1:10.

2. Zavala, *Umbral*, p. 129.

3. Alamán, *Historia*, 5:426.

4. Ibid., 5:427.

5. *Semanario Político y Literario de Méjico* 4, no. 1 (November 2, 1821): 16-17.

6. *Proyecto sobre el establecimiento de papel moneda* (Mexico, 1822), p. 1.

7. *Circular del ministro de hacienda, 30 de diciembre de 1822* (Mexico, 1823), articles 1-8.

8. *El Indio con la coscolina riñendo por el papel moneda* (Mexico, 1823), 1.

9. *Quejas del pueblo contra el papel moneda* (Mexico, 1823), p. 1.

10. Dublán and Lozano: *Legislación mexicana*, 1:552-53.

11. *Colección de los decretos y órdenes que ha expedido la Soberana Junta Provisional Gubernative del Imperio Mexicano, desde su instalación el 28 de septiembre de 1821, hasta 24 de febrero de 1822* (Mexico, 1822), pp. 155-56; hereafter cited as *Colección de decretos de la Soberana Junta.*

12. Ibid., pp. 219-21.

13. Alamán, *Historia*, 5:432.

14. *Colección de los decretos y órdenes del Soberano Congreso Mexicano, desde su instalación hasta el 30 de octubre de 1823, en que cesó* (Mexico, 1825), pp. 55-56; hereafter cited as *Collección de decretos del Soberano Congreso.*

15. *El Noticioso General de Méjico* 2, no. 135 (November 11, 1822): 1.

16. Mexico, Congreso, Comisiónes de Hacienda y Comercio, *Dictamen de las*

comisiones de hacienda y comercio reunidas sobre préstamo forzoso y arbitrios para subrogarlos (Mexico, 1822), pp. 3-4.

17. Mexico, Secretaría de Hacienda y Crédito Público, *Memoria de Hacienda . . . 1822* (Mexico, 1822), pp. 1-17.

18. Dublán and Lozano, *Legislación mexicana*, 1:617.

19. Agustín de Iturbide, *Manifiesto del general D. Agustín de Iturbide libertador de México* (Mexico, 1871), pp. 18-19.

20. Juan Suárez y Navarro, *Historia de México y del general Antonio López de Santa Anna . . .* (Mexico, 1850), p. 52; Lorenzo de Zavala: *Juicio imparcial sobre los acontecimientos de México en 1828-1829* (New York, 1830), p. 8, hereafter cited as *Zavala, Juicio.*

21. Dublán and Lozano, *Legislación mexicana*, 1:515.

22. *Gaceta Imperial de México* 1, no. 32 (December 1, 1821): 257.

23. *Provisión de empleos* (Mexico, 1821), [p. 4].

24. *Colección de decretos de la Soberana Junta*, p. 53.

25. Mexico, Secretaría de Relaciones Interiores y Exteriores, *Memoria . . . 1823* (Mexico, 1823), p. 6.

26. Joaquín Ramírez Sesma, comp., *Colección de decretos órdenes y circulares espedidas por los gobiernos nacionales de la federación mexicana desde el año de 1821, hasta el de 1826 . . .* (Mexico, 1827), p. 194; hereafter cited as Ramírez Sesma, *Colección de decretos.*

27. Cf. *Gaceta Imperial de México* 1, no. 15 (October 27, 1821): 107; 1, no. 21, November 8, 1821): 152; 1, no. 54 (January 19, 1822): 436; 1, no. 64 (February 9, 1822): 507-08; 1, no. 67 (February 16, 1822): 530; 1, no. 70 (February 23, 1822): 556; 1, no. 71 (February 26, 1822): 562; 2, no. 49 (May 4, 1822): 373; 2, no. 41 (May 21, 1822): 310; 2, no. 77 (August 6, 1822): 596; 2, no. 78 (August 8, 1822): 604; 2, no. 131 (November 28, 1822): 1,000.

28. Ramírez Sesma, *Colección de decretos*, 323.

29. *El Noticioso General de Méjico* 1 (November 27, 1822): 1-3.

30. Alamán, *Historia*, 5:125.

31. *Tanto le pican al buey hasta que embiste* (Mexico, 1820), pp. 1-7.

32. *Segunda parte de tanto le pican al buey hasta que embiste* (Mexico, 1820), 1-4.

33. El Amigo de Todos, *Desafío del europeo al americano* (Mexico, 1820), p. 2.

34. *Un americano por todos contra el europeo duelista y contestación al papel titulado desafío del europeo al americano* (Mexico, 1820), p. 4.

35. El Amante de sus Semejantes, *Ahora sí, ahora sí europeos y americanos se hermanaron ya* (Mexico, 1820), pp. 3-6.

36. Nicolás Bravo, *Carta de Nicolás Bravo, Tlaxcala, April 17, 1821,* Colección Lafragua, National Library, Mexico, vol. 393.

37. *La quema de los papeles contra la independencia, publicada por el anterior gobierno y por particulares es necesaria para mantener nuestra unión* (Mexico, 1821), p. 23.

38. L. E. *Una cuarta garantía muy necesaria al Estado* (Mexico, 1821), p. 1.

39. *Degradación que causa en los hombres la tiranía* (Mexico, 1821), p. 2. Later, some of these loans had to be repaid by the republic.

40. Francisco Lagranda, *Consejo prudente sobre una de las garantías* (Mexico, 1821), pp. 1-4.

41. Pedro Celestino Negrete, *D. José Antonio de Andrade y Baldomar . . . El exmo.*

sr. capitán general d. Pedro Celestino Negrete, se ha servido dirigirme . . . [*La*] *representación que los generales y gefes del ejército reunidos la noche del 11 del corriente en la junta presidida por el capitán general de la provincia, dirigieron a serenísimo señor almirante, para que S. A. tomase las providencias oportunas, a fin de proceder legalmente contra el autor del papel intitulado: "Consejo prudente sobre una de las garantías," y evitar los males que pudiese producir la circulación de tan escandaloso folleto* . . . (Guadalajara, 1821).

42. Ibid.

43. Ibid., "Agustín de Iturbide, Oficio de S. A. el sr. Generalísimo al Fiscal de Censura."

44. Ibid., "Agustín de Iturbide, Oficio de S. A. el sr. Generalísimo a la S. A. Regencia."

45. José Joaquín Fernández de Lizardi, *Cincuenta preguntas del Pensador a quien quiera responderlas* (Mexico, 1821), p. 5.

46. *Cincuenta respuestas de una muger ignorante a otras tantas preguntas del Pensador mexicano* (Mexico, 1821).

47. José Joaquín Fernández de Lizardi, *Ni están todos los que son ni son todos los que están o sea justa satisfacción que el Pensador mexicano da a los beneméritos europeos, agraviados sin razón por algunos incautos escritores. Especialmente se dirige a favor de los señores oficiales que han servido y actualmente sirven en el ejército imperial* (Mexico, 1821), p. 2.

48. Ibid., p. 3.

49. Juan José Sivrob, *Prevenciones a europeos descontentos* (Mexico, 1821), p. 2.

50. C. A. G., *Execusión de justicia contra los enemigos del estado o tercera garantía vindicada* (Mexico, 1821), pp. 5, 7.

51. Manuel Ramos, *Grito de un americano amante de sus compatriotas* (Guadalajara, 1821), p. 5.

52. Agustín de Iturbide: *Proclama, el primer gefe del ejército imperial de la tres garantías a los españoles europeos habitantes en esta América* (Mexico, 1821) pp. 2-3.

53. *Gaceta Imperial de México*, 2, no. 13 (March 28, 1822): 103.

54. Dublán and Lozano, *Legislación mexicana*, 1: 629.

55. *Oficios del Consulado de Veracruz al escmo. Ayuntamiento referentes al estado de la plaza y disposiciones del gobierno; con otras contestaciones ocurridas posteriormente* (Veracruz, 1821); hereafter cited as *Oficios del Consulado de Veracruz al escmo. Ayuntamiento*. See also AGN, Pasaportes, vols. 1 and 2.

56. *Don Antonio siempre el mismo se marcha a San Juan de Ulúa* (Mexico, 1822), p. 3.

57. El Cosmopolita, *Oficio del señor Lemaur al señor Echávarri* (Mexico, 1823), pp. 1-2.

58. Juan José Espinosa de los Monteros: *Documentos relativos al asunto pendiente sobre si se conceden pasaportes para salir del imperio* . . . (Mexico, 1822), p. 4.

59. *El Noticioso General de Méjico* 2, no. 114 (September 21, 1821): 4.

60. *Colección de decretos de la Soberana Junta*, pp. 168-70.

61. *Colección de decretos del Soberano Congreso*, pp. 15-16.

62. Mexico, Congreso, Comisión Ordinaria de Hacienda: *Dictamen de la comisión ordinaria de hacienda sobre la instancia que hacen los individuos de las secretarías de estado para que se les exhonere del descuento que sufren conforme al soberano decreto de 11 marzo último* (Mexico, 1822), pp. 1-3.

63. *Oficios del Consulado de Veracruz al escmo. Ayuntamiento,* p. 12.

64. Ibid., pp. 5, 13.

65. Zavala, *Umbral,* p. 143.

66. *Gaceta Imperial de México* 1, no. 14 (October 25, 1821): 101.

67. Alamán, *Historia,* 5: 448.

68. C. A. G., *Sentencia de muerte contra los capitulados o razones que justifican este procedimiento* (Mexico, 1822), p. 1.

69. *Los capitulados debían morir según la ley* (Mexico, 1822), p. 1.

70. Zavala, *Umbral,* p. 150.

71. Dublán and Lozano, *Legislación mexicana,* 1: 600.

72. Agustín de Iturbide: *El generalísimo almirante a los habitantes del imperio* (Mexico, 1822), p. 1.

73. El Amante de la Unión, *Hasta que se le vio una al sr. generalísimo* (Mexico, 1822), p. 1.

74. *Gaceta Imperial de México* 2, no. 17 (May 6, 1822): 130.

75. *El Noticioso General de Méjico* 2, no. 42 (May 8, 1822): 2.

76. *Gaceta Imperial de México* 2, no. 29 (April 27, 1822): 11.

77. *El Noticioso General de Méjico* 2 (April 8, 1822): 1.

78. Ibid., 2, no. 44 (April 15, 1822): 1.

79. A. F., *Ventajas de la independencia* (Mexico, 1821), pp. 1-3.

80. Ramírez Sesma, *Colección de decretos,* 111-19.

81. Ibid., p. 118.

82. J. M. de A.: *Somos libres pero aún nos falta el rabo por desollar* (Mexico, 1822), p. 2.

83. *Oficios del Consulado de Veracruz al escmo. Ayuntamiento,* p. 12.

84. Diego García Conde, et al., *Exposición de los europeos dirigida al general Dávila, pidiéndole la entrega del Castillo de San Juan de Ulúa* (Mexico, 1822), pp. 1-8.

85. Carlos María Bustamante, *Historia del emperador don Agustín de Iturbide, hasta su muerte, y sus consecuencias; y el establecimiento de la república popular federal* (Mexico, 1846), pp. 64-67; hereafter cited as Bustamante, *Historia del emperador.*

86. Ibid., p. 71.

87. *El Noticioso General de Méjico* 2, no. 151 (December 18, 1822): 2. See also José María Bocanegra; *Memorias para la historia de México independiente 1822-1846* (Mexico, 1892), 1: 167-71; hereafter cited as Bocanegra, *Memorias.*

88. *El Noticioso General de Méjico* 2, no. 151 (December 18, 1822): 2.

89. *Gaceta Imperial de México* 2, no. 146 (December 21, 1822): 2.

90. Nettie Lee Benson, "The Provincial Deputation in Mexico, Precursor of the Mexican Federal State," (PH.D. diss., University of Texas, 1949), pp. 140-41.

91. Nettie Lee Benson, "The Plan of Casa Mata," *HAHR* 25 (February 1945): 45-56.

92. Bustamante, *Historia del emperador,* pp. 114-15.

93. Ibid., p. 115.

FIVE

The Spaniards, the Bureaucracy, and the First Expulsion

Iturbide's abdication and departure from the country in May, 1823, increased the differences within the former colonial oligarchy. Once it had been united in the belief that monarchy was the best form of government for the nation: the Spaniards favored a Bourbon king, while the wealthy creoles supported Iturbide. The latter's rise to power pleased some creoles but alienated the Europeans. This division favored the republicans because many who supported legitimacy nevertheless preferred a republic to a creole monarch. After the emperor left, contending groups emerged around the issue of centralism versus federalism.

The prelates, the leading generals in the army, the wealthy merchants, the great landowners, and the wealthy Spaniards—all former partisans of the Bourbon dynasty—supported centralism. Through a strong central government the capitalist oligarchy of Mexico City and the surrounding area sought to control the provinces. Eventually Lucas Alamán would become the faction's outstanding spokesman. Leaderless, many of Iturbide's supporters were forced to join the partisans of a federal republic. Although the federalists were nationalists and generally anti-Spanish, they primarily defended the interests of the provinces rather than those of Mexico City. Their most prominent leaders, Miguel Ramos Arizpe, Lorenzo de Zavala, and Valentín Gómez Farías, represented three of the largest states.

The Plan of Casa Mata called for a new congress and granted the provinces adminstrative control of their affairs, thus establishing a de facto republic. The new executive branch was composed of a triumvirate representing discordant interests. They were Pedro Celestino Negrete, a Spaniard and a monarchist noted for his fierce opposition to the insurgents;[1] Nicolás Bravo, grand master of the

Scottish Rite Masonic Lodges, which were composed primarily of
Spaniards;[2] and Guadalupe Victoria, a former rebel insurgent and a
moderate advocate of federalism. The triumvirate was seldom complete because one or another of its members was often in the
provinces on special missions. Therefore three substitutes were named
from among former insurgents: Vicente Guerrero, Miguel
Domínguez, and José Mariano Michelena.

In spite of the great popular resentment against the Spaniards, who
seemed to invite the invasion and reconquest of Mexico by their
presence in high government posts, the government permitted two
commissioners from Spain to arrive early in 1823 to negotiate a peace
treaty. The men, Juan Ramón Osés and Santiago Irisarri, met with
the triumvirate's representative, Guadalupe Victoria, in Jalapa. The
Spaniards were authorized to enter into provisional commercial
agreements,[3] but the Mexican government was willing only to
negotiate recognition and the surrender of the fortress of San Juan de
Ulúa.[4] The talks were doomed from the start. The commissioners
represented shaky as well as "revolutionary" governments: a Spain
governed by a radical Cortes and a Mexico governed by a provisional triumvirate. In April, 1823, French armies again invaded
Spain, overthrowing the constitutional government and restoring
Ferdinand VII as an absolute monarch; therefore the Spanish
commissioners left Mexico the following month without reaching an
agreement. In spite of this, commercial relations between Mexico and
Spain were continued, while Spaniards in Mexico retained their trade
monopoly and close ties with the troops in San Juan de Ulúa.[5]

The new Mexican government not only faced the problem of
Spanish recognition, it also inherited a deepening financial crisis.
Minister of Finance Francisco de Arrillaga reported that the salaries
of public employees and the military were in arrears and that there
was little hope that they would be paid in the near future. The
country's economy was devastated; government revenues had decreased tremendously. The Veracruz customs, which had formerly
been the chief source of wealth, yielded only 20,000 to 30,000 pesos.
Income from the tobacco and powder monopolies was down to "a
little less than absolutely nothing"; both the mining industry and the
mint were paralyzed; the mails, the lottery, and other sources of
revenue had fallen upon a "brief decline"; and the *consulados,* because they were in the hands of foreigners, refused to lend any aid.[6]

Mexico City's budget alone was causing a deficiency of 144,000 pesos monthly, while the mint contributed a 94,000-peso deficit. Arrillaga maintained that 1 million pesos were needed merely to resolve the most immediate problems. Therefore he reluctantly recommended forced loans. To ensure their success, he also advised that the government meet its obligations to Spanish merchants who had previously made such loans. He asked particularly that the 1,220,894-peso forced loan which Iturbide had received from Veracruz prior to independence be paid, arguing that it was the most "pressing and important" national debt. Without such measures the finance minister could see no way in which the government could restore its credit.[7]

The triumvirate was unable to resolve the nation's financial crisis. At the end of 1823 the minister of finance reported to Congress that the treasury was in shambles, that public revenues were exhausted, and that involuntary loans on businesses had been "pressed to infinity." The government was nearly bankrupt and had accumulated a national debt of 44,714,563 pesos. However, he reminded them that this sum was small compared to the national debt of the United States.[8] The triumvirate admitted publicly that it had no funds and therefore asked Congress for permission to borrow from individuals.[9] But there was little that a caretaker government could do, and it was left to the first elected republican government to solve the monetary problem.

The triumvirate acted more forcefully on political issues. It denounced the Iturbide regime for corrupting the nation's morals and exposed the former emperor's sordid manipulations.[10] One of its first acts was to terminate the Plan of Iguala, the Treaty of Córdoba, and the law of February 24, 1822, which had supported the imperial government.[11] When it learned that Generals Luis Quintanar and Anastasio Bustamante appeared to be leading a pro-Iturbide movement in Guadalajara, the triumvirate forced Congress to approve strong measures against them. Congress decreed that if Iturbide returned to Mexico he would be declared an enemy of the state, and anyone who favored and assisted him would be guilty of treason.[12] The measure proved effective. When Iturbide did come back to Mexico the following year, he was apprehended, court-martialed, and executed. With Iturbide's death, the monarchist party lost all hope.

In this atmosphere of tension, the provinces, which had been converted into states upon ratification of the new constitution, proceeded to elect a president. Guadalupe Victoria and Nicolás Bravo became the first constitutional president and vice-president of the United States of Mexico. Victoria's triumph provided great satisfaction to the former insurgent liberals, since he, together with Guerrero, was a symbol of resistance in the colony. Furthermore, his personal prestige made the people certain that peace, tranquility, and prosperity would be assured. Victoria's administration inspired confidence because he attempted to heal the nation's divisions, asking the leaders of the contending factions to participate in his government. Thus both Lucas Alamán, leader of the conservatives, and Miguel Ramos Arizpe, representing the liberal federalists, occupied cabinet posts. Furthermore, after February, 1824, the government could pay its civil and military employees—by virtue of a loan of 3,200,000 pounds sterling which Francisco de Borja Migoni negotiated in London with Goldschmidt and Company.[13]

Nevertheless, political calm did not return. People were discontented not only because Spaniards still profited from the independent government, but also because the corruption identified with colonial administration seemed to continue. Everywhere people displayed such open hatred for Spaniards that the government was forced to act. The states generally took the lead; Jalisco passed laws disarming Spaniards and dismissing them from the army.[14] The former insurgent Vicente Gómez agitated in Puebla for similar laws.[15] In the state of Mexico, three military men, Antonio Aldama, Francisco Hernández, and Luis Pinzón, proposed that Spaniards be removed from all public employment. The City Council of Cuernavaca approved their plan in a nocturnal session on January 17, 1824, and recommended that only nationals be public employees because they deserved it by virtue of "natural and civil law."[16]

The first major anti-Spanish demonstration occurred on January 23, 1824, when General José María Lobato led a mutiny. Troops in the capital under the command of Lieutenant Colonel José Stáboli and Captains Barberi and Melgarejo also joined in the rebellion.[17] The rebels captured the Bethlemite convent and the Gallos barracks.[18] By the end of the day the only troops which had not joined them were two hundred soldiers under the command of Félix Merino.[19] The principal demand of the rebels was that all Spaniards be removed from the bureaucracy, at least until Spain recognized Mexico's independence. As an afterthought they also demanded the dismissal of anyone not supporting "the system of liberty."[20] The incident caused

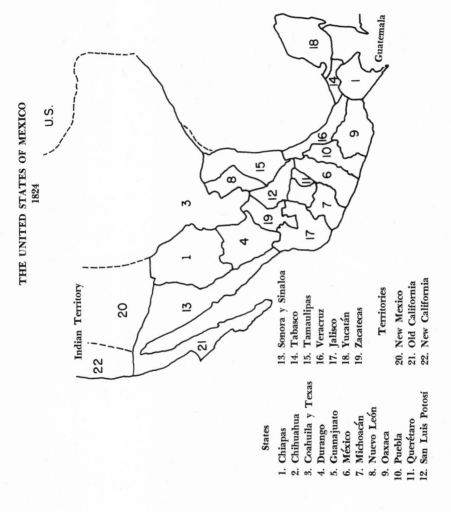

THE UNITED STATES OF MEXICO
1824

U.S.

Indian Territory

Guatemala

States

1. Chiapas
2. Chihuahua
3. Coahuila y Texas
4. Durango
5. Guanajuato
6. México
7. Michoacán
8. Nuevo León
9. Oaxaca
10. Puebla
11. Querétaro
12. San Luis Potosí

13. Sonora y Sinaloa
14. Tabasco
15. Tamaulipas
16. Veracruz
17. Jalisco
18. Yucatán
19. Zacatecas

Territories

20. New Mexico
21. Old California
22. New California

an uproar in Mexico City and threatened the stability of the government. The chief executive entered into negotiations with the insurgents, while Congress met in an extraordinary session at ten that night to try to resolve the matter.[21] The president denounced the insurrection and refused to consider Lobato's petition unless the latter surrendered.[22] Furthermore, he called upon all army officers to support the government, under pain of being declared outlaws.[23] General Vicente Guerrero joined in condemning the rebellion, although he recognized the growing public sentiment against Spaniards in government.[24] Faced with the government's strong reaction, General Lobato tried to justify his conduct, explaining in a proclamation published in the newspaper *El Aguila Mexicana* that his demands would ensure the nation's independence and happiness and that he had acted only to avoid another more dangerous upheaval.[25] Lobato capitulated eventually because of official pressure. Stáboli, Barberi, Rodríguez, and Melgarejo, however, continued to resist and had to be subdued by force. A court-martial found Stáboli guilty of a capital crime, but his sentence was commuted to perpetual exile under punishment of death should he return. The others received lesser sentences.[26]

Although the insurrection in Mexico City was rapidly resolved, anti-Spanish sentiment remained strong. Armed bands of Mexicans roamed the country attacking Spaniards. In Oaxaca, Antonio and Manuel León were determined to keep Lobato's cause alive; others, like Loreto Cataño, killed several peaceful Spaniards and looted their properties.[27] Attacks against Spaniards continued and many state legislatures were encouraged to pass laws against them. Authorities in Campeche, pressured by violent public demonstrations, declared war against Spain and supported the principles which Lobato had championed.[28] A bill was introduced in the Congress restricting Spaniards' rights because they were citizens of a country at war with Mexico.[29] News that Spain was preparing an invasion of Mexico made the already widespread xenophobia even more severe.

The fact that Spain and Mexico were technically at war served to intensify the public's demand that Spaniards be removed from the government. A commission was appointed by the government to resolve the delicate problem of the rights and obligations of Spaniards residing in Mexico. It began by redefining the situation in light of Spain's refusal to recognize Mexico's independence. Whereas Iturbide's government had emphasized unity, the new republic placed the greatest emphasis on independence. The commission declared that it was incorrect to consider the Spaniards subjects of Spain; once they had accepted independence, they automatically became Mexican citizens. To those who argued that the Spaniards should be punished because they opposed independence, the commission replied that justice would then require punishing the many creoles who had also fought the insurgents. The commission made it clear that Spain's obstinate refusal to recognize Mexican independence jeopardized the Spaniards, but it also noted that many peninsualres disapproved of Spain's attitude. Therefore, it recommended that the government should: (a) guarantee the persons, property, and other rights of Spaniards residing in Mexico; (b) consider the guarantee of unity dependent upon independence; (c) grant citizenship to those Spaniards who were living in Mexico when independence was declared, at the same time refusing it to those who had immigrated later; (d) give no government employment to Spaniards until Spain recognized Mexico; (e) forbid the export of capital belonging to Spaniards who were leaving the country; (f) remove suspicious Spaniards from their present civil or military appointments and provide them with money and passports to leave; and (g) allow the states and the federal government to pass such laws as they considered necessary in individual cases.[30]

Not all the members of the commission were in agreement, however. José Miguel Guridi y Alcocer and Ignacio Saldívar issued a minority report in which they argued that the Spaniards were citizens of Mexico with the same rights and obligations as any other citizens of the republic. Otherwise, the citizenship they had received would be merely an empty gesture; they would incur the obligations, like paying taxes, but would acquire none of the privileges. Thus, it would be unjust to exclude them from government employment. They further argued that by the guarantee of unity, the Spanish had gained Mexican citizenship and lost Spanish citizenship. As a result they could not be denied the former, since that would leave them "with neither an adoptive nor a natural fatherland."[31]

While the legal status of the Spaniards was being debated, Congress passed a series of laws in October, 1824, designed to reduce the power of the Spanish-controlled *consulados* in government affairs. In this way it hoped to destroy one of the strongest colonial institutions, which had most vigorously defended the interests of the monarchy. Despite these actions, the people continued to resent the

Spaniards; their wealth and position aroused Mexican cupidity. Those who worked for rich Spaniards believed that they had a right to their employers' property. Many felt that the Europeans were responsible for the poverty which existed, arguing that the Spaniards had acquired their wealth by means of privileges received from the colonial government.[32] Resentment of the Spaniards was widespread and was to become one of the most important political issues.

Naturally, rumors of a new Spanish invasion were exaggerated under these circumstances. News spread throughout the nation that an expedition under the command of former viceroy Apodaca was departing from Cádiz to invade Mexico.[33] Newspapers added to popular fears by overstating the danger. *El Sol* began a special column entitled "Daily Observations of the Enemy and the Horizon," which included detailed reports of Spanish activities at the fortress of San Juan de Ulúa. Other newspapers followed suit, so that the entire nation grew increasingly concerned about the Spanish-held fortress. The administration was influenced by the national hysteria and took measures which had the effect of endangering the floundering economy. After the first foreign loan was negotiated with Goldschmidt and Company, it arranged for a second loan with Barclay and Company, also of London. These loans allowed the government to allocate vast sums for defense. The ministry of war radically increased its budget to 16,011,990 pesos,[34] and the ministry of the navy allocated 2,943,553 for coastal defense. Most of these funds were spent in the acquisition of military equipment—including a submarine—and in paying 62,502 soldiers.[35]

The fortress remained a constant symbol of Spanish colonial despotism in the minds of most Mexicans, particularly because of the continual attacks on Veracruz by Spanish soldiers stationed in San Juan de Ulúa. Moreover, the fortress obstructed commerce and prevented the nation's chief seaport from being fully used. Trade suffered, because it had to be carried through the smaller and less accessible port of Alvarado; customs revenues also decreased. However, the most grievous affront to the nation's dignity was the repeated artillery bombardment of the city of Veracruz, which had to be evacuated after nearly two years of fighting.[36] During this time the commanders of the fortress, José Dávila, Francisco Lemaur, and José Copinger, maintained an almost constant cannonade which, as Zavala later asserted, was interrupted only by weariness or caprice. The Mexican commanders Miguel Barragán and Santa Anna made futile attempts to capture the fortress but never attempted a frontal attack.

The only way to take the fortress seemed to be a combined land and sea blockade, and this was not possible until a Mexican navy was created. Early in 1825, the Mexicans began to strengthen their blockade. At first only a small coast guard squadron performed the task, but later, as newly acquired Mexican warships began to arrive from England, the noose tightened. The shortage of supplies and the unhealthy climate began to take their toll inside the fortress. By August, Brigadier Copinger, now in command of the garrison (variously estimated at between four hundred[37] and eight hundred soldiers[38]), began to feel abandoned by his immediate superior in Havana. For nearly a year he and his men had received supplies irregularly, whenever Spanish ships could slip by Mexican forces. But beginning in July, the Mexican blockade was strengthened to such an extent that a Spanish squadron sent to relieve the troops in the fortress had to turn back.

When President Victoria learned of the Spaniards' situation, he sent Minister Ignacio Esteva to negotiate the capitulation of the fortress. The Spanish commander proposed that the Mexican commander of Veracruz, General Barragán, provision his troops for three days, and if within that time no Spanish fleet came to relieve them, he would surrender his forces.[39] No Spanish ships arrived, and the fortress surrendered on September 15, 1825. Mexico agreed to care for the sick and wounded and to arrange for the garrison's passage to Havana. Soldiers were to be treated with the honors of war and were allowed to retain their side arms; civilians who had taken refuge in the fortress were permitted to retain their properties and to go where they wished. The Spaniards released all prisoners and turned the fortress over intact to the Mexican authorities.[40]

The capital received the news of San Juan de Ulúa's surrender on November 23 at two o'clock in the afternoon, amid shouts of joy and grave assertions that now Mexico was truly free.[41] Indeed, the entire republic reacted in a similar fashion; everywhere the first strong stirrings of nationalism began. The president declared three days of national holidays to mark the solemn event. Now that San Juan de Ulúa was in Mexican hands, everyone expected the nations of Europe to establish relations with Mexico or, at the very least, to take the first steps toward official recognition.[42]

If the capitulation of the fortress brought joy to the nation, it did not improve the peninsulares' situation. Spain continued to refuse recognition to Mexico and still threatened to invade the country. For many Europeans, emigration seemed to be the only alternative. The higher clergy took the lead by abandoning their dioceses. The archbishop of Mexico, Pedro Fonte, returned to Spain because he refused to acknowledge Mexico's independence.[43] Similarly, all the Spanish bishops in Mexico, with the exception of the bishops of Yucatán and Oaxaca, abandoned Mexico for Spain.[44] The bishop of Puebla, a Mexican, remained in his post. The most important single group of Spaniards to remain were the merchants, who continued to dominate the nation's commerce by excluding foreigners and influencing the government through loans granted in times of crisis.[45] Some wealthy merchants gained such excessive control that fellow Spanish businessmen criticized them openly. Andrés María Nieto, for example, published a pamphlet entitled *Some Spaniards' Treason Exposed by One of Them,* in which he severely chided the wealthy merchant Antonio de Olarte. Nieto noted sarcastically that he was unaware of any services Olarte might have rendered the independence movement, unless the usurious loans that Olarte and other rich Spaniards made to the government counted as patriotism.[46] Most Mexicans agreed with Nieto's criticisms and looked forward to the day when the Spanish merchants' power over Mexico would be destroyed.

That day was hastened by the founding of York Rite Masonic Lodges in September, 1825, under the auspices of Father José María Alpuche e Infante and the United States minister to Mexico, Joel Poinsett. The new Masonic lodges attracted men of the moderate and radical left, including such important individuals as Minister of Finance José Ignacio Esteva and Minister of Justice Miguel Ramos Arizpe, and leading politicians like Lorenzo de Zavala. The new *yorkino* lodges had great popular appeal, and within a few months there were 130 throughout the nation.[47] At the same time, the more conservative *escocés,* or Scottish Rite lodges, declined in influence, as many of the more liberal members abandoned them for their new rivals. These secret societies served as places to organize political programs and to direct political opinion; members argued about the laws, the government, and government employees—questions which concerned everyone.

The radical wing of the *yorkinos* led the attack against Europeans in public service and revived the precepts of the earlier Lobato insurrection. They counted on the great wave of nationalist feeling aroused by the capitulation of San Juan de Ulúa to support them. Indeed, there were many Mexicans who wanted not only to oust the Spaniards from Mexico, but also to invade Cuba and sever the last chains of Spanish colonialism in America.[48] That feeling was actively fanned by Cuban exiles, who hoped Mexico would help them free their island nation. Anti-Spanish feelings increased despite repeated attempts by various groups to promote unity and discourage popular antipathy.[49] Pablo Villavicencio, writing under the pseudonym "El Payo del Rosario," noticed that a few foreign merchants were beginning to replace the Spaniards, but he still resented the latter's influence. In his opinion, there were only three kinds of Spaniards: "good, bad, and indifferent; the good were dead, the bad were alive, and the indifferent were in paintings."[50] Other more virulent critics damned the Spaniards and decried their presence in government jobs.[51] As criticism of the Spaniards by the public and the press grew, the government took several measures intended to restore tranquility. The military was prohibited from recruiting or promoting Europeans in either civil or military positions.[52] Later, in April, 1826, Spaniards were denied entry into any of the nation's ports, regardless of their point of departure, as long as a state of war existed between Mexico and Spain.[53]

Anti-Spanish rhetoric helped radical *yorkinos* win a series of local elections in 1826 and early 1827. While still fresh from their electoral victories, the *yorkinos* discovered a conspiracy initiated by Father Joaquín Arenas; exposure of the plot allowed them to justify extreme attacks against the peninsulares. José María Tornel y Mendivil, an eyewitness, described Arenas as an irresponsible, eccentric Spanish friar in the order of Saint James.[54] At one time Arenas had claimed to be an expert in dyeing textiles and had advertised his services in local papers.[55] On January 18, 1827, he approached General Ignacio Mora, military commander of the Federal District and the state of Mexico, with a plan to restore Spanish dominion over the nation. General Mora was extremely cautious; he invited Arenas to meet with him the next day, and then quickly informed President Victoria of the event. Given the sensitive nature of the situation, the administration moved with absolute discretion. The president appointed a commission to spy on the meeting and discover the nature of the conspiracy. Francisco Molinos del Campo, the governor of the Federal District, represented the *escoceses*, and José María Tornel, the president's

private secretary and a deputy from the state of Veracruz, represented the *yorkinos*.[56] The other members, Colonel Ignacio Falcón,
Captain Lauriano Muñoz, and Francisco Ruiz Fernández, were presumably neutral. The five men were to listen in on the second meeting from an adjoining room in General Mora's house.

When Father Arenas arrived the next day, Mora asked the priest to
describe his plan in detail. Arenas explained that it had originated in
Madrid and was intended to save the Catholic faith, which was being
attacked in Mexico by the press and by the free flow of heretical
books. A royal commissioner, who was already in the country, was to
lead Ferdinand VII's partisans in an uprising against the impious
republican government. The royal commissioner had full powers to
act as he saw fit, in the name of the king. Father Arenas maintained
that "various generals, canons, and many individuals had already
joined" the conspiracy, and he asked General Mora to do likewise.[57]
Mora tried, but failed, to elicit names of persons involved. Arenas
claimed that the conspiracy was so well organized that no one knew
more than was necessary, and he did not even know the identity of
the royal commissioner.[58] The discussion was interrupted when
Governor Molinos del Campo burst into the room, telling Arenas
that he had heard everything and reproaching the priest with such
vehemence that, according to Tornel, it provoked "a momentary feeling of compassion for the accused." Betrayed, Father Arenas refused
to implicate anyone else; he believed he had no recourse but to
become "a martyr for his faith and his country."[59]

The following day the *yorkino* newspaper *El Correo de la
Federación Mexicana* announced Father Arenas's arrest and exposed
his plan, which consisted of restoring the Roman Catholic Apostolic
religion to the purity it had enjoyed before 1808, declaring the nation
the property of Ferdinand VII, appointing a regency composed of
bishops and ecclesiastic cabildos to govern the country in the name of
the Spanish king, expelling foreign diplomats who refused to recognize the king's authority, restoring Spanish troops to their posts and
emoluments, and returning government employees to the positions
they had occupied in 1820.[60] The *escocés* newspaper *El Sol* succinctly
announced that Father Arenas had been arrested "for conspiracy,
according to authorities, on behalf of the Bourbons," adding that it
favored strict punishment if the priest were truly guilty.[61] The
conspiracy caused new speculation because of its notoriety and because it seemed "to implicate nearly all classes, especially the most

influential and most meritorious."[62] Lucas Alamán, who considered the conspiracy "a true act of madness," believed that its supporters could be found among the leaders of the government.[63] Others attributed the plot to United States Minister Poinsett, claiming that one of his letters had been located among the friar's papers.[64] Although many were accused, a judicial inquiry indicted only four persons, all Spaniards: the ecclesiastics Manuel Segura, Rafael Torres, and Francisco Martínez, and General Gregorio Arana, the author of the Plan of Casa Mata.[65]

Although it was never a threat to national security, the conspiracy was used as a political tool for partisan purposes. The newspapers kept the issue on the front page during the investigation and lengthy trial. For the *yorkinos* the Arenas trial served the double purpose of compromising the clergy's prestige and heightening the popular anti-Spanish sentiment. For the first time they had a basis for their anti-*gachupín* generalizations and sought to convince the incredulous that all Europeans were bad. The burden of defending the Spaniards fell on the *escoceses,* whom the *yorkinos* branded as guilty by association. At first the *escoceses* attempted only to minimize the affair, but since their enemies insisted on exaggerating it, they reacted by denying its existence. The *escoceses* accused the *yorkinos* of inventing the entire episode and suggested the possibility that Arenas would be murdered in his cell before he could expose the farce.[66] In their paper *El Sol* they published such articles as "The Friar's Friary" and "Tell me whom you associate with and I'll tell you who you are" in an attempt to discredit the priest and thereby to ridicule the conspiracy as well. They told the public that Arenas had arrived in Mexico in chains, "on his sturdy mule," during Viceroy Apodaca's administration, and they accused the friar of being "a huckster, a quack, and a blatantly liberal writer."[67] The *escoceses* explained that their political adversaries wanted to provoke mistrust and disunity by attacking the clergy and Spanish-born citizens as the enemies of reforms necessary for national prosperity.[68] *El Sol* cautioned its readers against accepting such a demonstratively false conspiracy as proof that the *yorkinos* were right. They argued that the results of the trial would prove the *escoceses,* rather than the *yorkinos,* to be the true patriots.

A military court composed of four colonels, three *yorkinos*—Juan Andrade, José Romero, and Juan Arango—and the *escocés* José Antonio Facio prosecuted the conspirators. The plot had been discovered accidentally because of the conspirators' lack of prudence.

Fanatical in their hatred of independence, the accused freely admitted their actions, but refused to implicate anyone else, despite the efforts of the tribunal to identify their accomplices.[69] The court found Arenas guilty and sentenced him to be shot in the back as "a seditious traitor."[70] General Arana suffered the same fate.

During the trial, public outrage against Europeans increased, and when rumors spread that Spanish generals would lead a rebellion against independence, the government was forced to act. Minister of War Manuel Gómez Pedraza decided to apprehend the two leading Spanish generals, Pedro Celestino Negrete and José Echávarri, on March 31, 1827. The former was confined to a fortress in Acapulco and the latter to the fortress of Perote. The administration hoped this would restore public tranquility and deprive the peninsulares of their most likely leaders. Negrete and Echávarri were exiled but were eventually absolved of any guilt. According to Zavala, these findings were appropriate for the generals and for the cause of justice;[71] but in fact, justice had already been violated, and both men died in exile, Negrete in the United States and Echávarri in Bordeaux.[72]

The hysteria caused by the Arenas conspiracy forced Congress to enact legislation against the Spaniards. A *yorkino* majority began the debate in the Chamber of Deputies by introducing a bill requiring the dismissal of Europeans from government service. Deputy Anastasio Zerecero recalled that General Lobato and the people had already demonstrated their attitudes; he believed that the Spaniards' perverse machinations necessitated congressional action.[73] According to Zerecero, the *yorkinos* had never threatened independence, but the Spaniards were guilty of repeated acts like the Arenas conspiracy. The deputy argued that since independence, Mexico had done nothing but defend itself against Spanish rebellions, such as the ones in Juchi, Zacapoaxtla, Toluca, Puebla, and Casa Mata.[74] Why should such men have government employment, he asked, while loyal and peaceful *yorkinos* did not?

Deputy José María Couto disagreed. Besides labeling the proposed measure "impolitic and unjust," he considered it unnecessary and dangerous.[75] Only a few Spanish employees worked for the government, and since "they would continue dying of old age day by day," it was foolish to dismiss them all at once.[76] Couto attributed the nation's ills not to the Spaniards, but to the government's transitional nature, poor administration, bad laws, and abuse of the freedom of the press. If there was any single cause for the nation's grievances, he continued, it was not the few Spanish government workers, but the passions aroused by political parties. The deputy concluded that even if the Spaniards were dismissed, as the *yorkinos* demanded, the treasury did not possess sufficient funds to pay their salaries.[77]

In his reply, Zerecero claimed that the Europeans responded to seven years of kindness with threats and conspiracies against the nation's independence. It was useless to attribute the country's difficulties to other causes—they were all conjectures. But one thing was not a conjecture: the Spaniards' notorious hatred of independence for Mexico. Zerecero was certain that the majority of Spaniards, with few exceptions, were corrupt and that this was sufficient to justify the proposed legislation. He maintained that, since the Lobato revolt, "a multitude of public employees" had agreed to cover the salaries of any Spaniards dismissed by the government, and therefore, the treasury needed no additional funds. The bill, he said, was "just, useful, and worthy," and he asked that it be passed.[78]

Francisco Sánchez de Tagle, however, considered it unjust. He argued that a nation should live up to its commitments or risk losing the respect of other countries. "What nation would trust us," he asked, "if it knew that we might say: 'Our agreement does not bind us any more, now that it is no longer convenient. Then we were afraid of you, now we are not.' "[79] But Manuel Crescencio Rejón replied that other nations' opinions should not frighten Mexicans or suppress their patriotism. He recalled that legislators had been trying unsuccessfully to dismiss the Spaniards from government employment since the first congress. He insisted that the administration had indeed allowed Spaniards to remain in places where they might injure the country, and concluded that the situation should be remedied immediately.[80]

Other arguments were heard in Congress, but these were the principal positions supporting and opposing the proposed law against the Spaniards. After months of debate, the bill was approved on May 10, 1827, by an overwhelming majority of forty-eight to eleven.[81] The law was as follows:

Article 1. No individual born in Spain may hold office or employment in any branch of the government, civil or military, until Spain recognizes the nation's independence.
Article 2. The previous article includes ecclesiastical offices or employment of secular and regular clergy insofar as they exercise economic, governing,

or judicial power in the Church. This does not include the reverend bishops.

Article 3. The government is authorized to remove, until the time referred to in Article 1, priests, ministers, and missionaries from the Federal District and federal territories.

Article 4. The previous articles do not include children of Mexicans who merely happen to have been born in Spain and who now reside in the republic.

Article 5. Employees removed from public service by this law shall continue to receive their salaries, and their seniority shall continue in their respective departments.

Article 6. Posts vacated by the law shall be filled on a provisional basis in accordance with the law.

Article 7. Priests removed by the government, under the authority of Article 3, shall continue to receive their emoluments under conditions similar to those before their removal; and their co-adjudicators or substitutes shall be paid by the treasury.[82]

By "complying with the demands of the multitude,"[83] the law brought a brief moment of calm. Although it created friction among Mexicans and undoubtedly caused some injustices, it did not harm the Spaniards, since they continued to receive their salaries. The law was merely intended to remove them from the political arena.

The peace was quickly disrupted by a series of upheavals which racked the nation in the months that followed. A few, like the friars Domingo de San José and Mateo in Xamiltepec, Oaxaca, sought to imitate Father Arenas and restore Spanish rule in Mexico.[84] Most conspiracies, however, were directed against the Spaniards. In Pátzcuaro, Cristóbal Mexic, a former companion of Vicente Gómez, led a group of thirty men in an attack against the Spanish shopkeeper Francisco Iturbe. In Acapulco, José María Gallardo raised the banner of rebellion and refused to lay it aside until all of General Lobato's aims had been achieved.[85] On October 23, 1827, the towns of Tarímbaro and Tiripito, near Valladolid, organized a militia, demanding that Congress expel all Spaniards from Mexico.[86] Faced with such discontent, the federal government argued that the problems resulted from Spain's intransigence in refusing to recognize Mexico's independence. Furthermore, it maintained that Spain's current attitude reflected the same mentality which had led to the atrocities of the conquest, had allowed three centuries of oppression through the erratic and idiotic actions of proud and despotic colonial officials, and had supported the furious and bloody struggle to prevent independence.[87]

The Arenas conspiracy served to polarize the political parties, providing an issue around which each faction could unite. Since the *escoceses* were the only ones who defended them, the Spaniards joined their ranks. But this association was a liability to the *escoceses,* as subsequent electoral defeats demonstrated. Frightened by what appeared to be growing radical power, and desperate to regain some of their former prestige, the *escoceses* committed a series of tactical blunders. The *yorkinos,* on the other hand, exploited the popular resentment against the Spaniards. They had known from the first years of independence that anti-Spanish feeling had mass appeal, and they courted it accordingly. It was the magic talisman that gave them a growing bloc in Congress. The legislation of May, 1827, was intended to cater to that sentiment. But when the law seemed to exacerbate the situation, the *yorkinos* were ready to follow public opinion further. Moderates had asked the public to distinguish between Spaniards who had abandoned their country to support the republic and deserved to be treated hospitably in Mexico, and those who opposed independence because they had made their fortunes during the colonial period and therefore favored reconquest.[88] However, the public did not care for such distinctions and openly demanded total expulsion. Radical *yorkinos* promised to pass such a law as soon as they had a majority in Congress.

Most people believed that the Spanish had to be kept under surveillance in order to protect independence and insure internal tranquility. The day after the federal government passed the May 10 law removing Europeans from their jobs, the state of Mexico passed a bill prohibiting Spaniards, as well as Mexicans who favored Spain, from bearing arms. All those who could prove their peaceful intentions and their loyalty to the republic were excluded. Moreover, the law allowed authorities to search places where they suspected weapons might be concealed.[89] The following month José María Tornel argued, in a speech published by the *Correo de la Federación Mexicana,* that the nation needed drastic measures to ensure its internal security. No Spaniard, he maintained, would ever abandon his loyalty to his native land, and such an attitude was contrary to Mexico's interests. He reminded his listeners that during the War of Independence *peninsulares* had gladly donated their most precious belongings to finance the mother country's struggle to retain her colony. "Did not a French writer assert," he asked, "that every

Spaniard in Mexico had lost an empire and that each one of us has thrown off the yoke of sixty thousand emperors?"[90] Tornel argued that Europeans would subordinate any interest to obtain government jobs, where they would serve "with loathing, cowardice, and discontent" unless they were "betraying the interests of their adopted country."[91] Only total expulsion, he concluded, would end the grave danger facing the nation.

Before long the capital was full of rumors that Congress would soon pass laws expelling the peninsulares. People often said that Deputy Zerecero had already proposed such a measure in secret session. But the deputy sent a letter to one of the papers in Mexico City explaining that the Spaniards were petty enemies who would not "cut their own throats" by plotting to end independence. He offered, however, to introduce an expulsion law, should it ever become necessary.[92] While national politicians temporized, some states took action. In September, 1827, the Jalisco legislature ordered all Spaniards to be out of the state within twenty days and forbade their return until Spain recognized Mexico's independence.[93]

Since discontent was growing throughout the nation and since other legislatures were considering similar action, the federal Congress was forced to investigate the matter. A constitutional commission appointed by the Chamber of Deputies to study the Jalisco law declared it unconstitutional because it infringed upon federal prerogatives. The commission added that such a law was a threat to all those born abroad and not merely to Spaniards. However, the matter was not settled so easily. Senator Valentín Gómez Farías maintained that pro-Spanish elements were trying to include all foreign-born citizens in the dispute to protect their Spanish friends.[94] The *yorkino* newspaper *Correo de la Federación Mexicana* reported that Jalisco was enjoying complete tranquility because everyone knew that its laws would be enforced regardless of the chamber's decision.[95] The pro-*escocés El Sol* ridiculed the law, saying that it would expel only thirty poor Spaniards, while the wealthy and powerful could get waivers. If any peninsulares were to be feared, said *El Sol*, it should be those who were exempted, since they alone had the motivation or the means to conspire against independence.[96] The paper concluded that the whole thing was merely a political farce.

The Constitutional Commission maintained that the Jalisco law was unconstitutional because states could not expel naturalized citizens; the federal Congress alone had the power to expel any for-

eigners, and then only if peace and public order required it.[97] Therefore, it argued, the states could only petition Congress to enact such
laws. Few were willing to accept such a decision. A general debate
ensued as to whether the state legislatures had the power to expel
Spaniards from their territories. Some maintained that such actions
were unjust and contrary to the public interest; others claimed that,
once naturalized, a person could not lose his citizenship. The anti-
Spanish *El Amigo del Pueblo* disagreed with the Constitutional
Commission, alleging that while it was true that Congress reserved for
itself the power to protect national independence and internal peace,
nothing could prevent the states from acting to preserve those same
interests.[98] Indeed, some states did not wait for congressional
approval.

Within days after the passage of the Jalisco law, the state of
Zacatecas removed all Spaniards from state government jobs until
Spain recognized Mexico's independence.[99] Shortly thereafter,
Santiago García, commander of the Tres Villas battalion, presented
the Oaxaca legislature with a petition signed by his officers, demanding that all Spaniards be expelled from the state and insisting that the
legislature request the federal government to issue them passports to
leave the country.[100] Similar events occurred in Izúcar, Chielta, San
Andrés Chalchicomula, and Puebla.[101]

Faced with such reactions, the *escoceses* had to prepare a good
defense for the Spaniards; José María Luis Mora became their leading spokesman, arguing that it was time to protect the countless
"innocent victims of the most unjust persecution," who were about to
be thrown mercilessly into "abandonment, orphanage, and misery."
He was defending, he said, not only the Spaniards, but also "all those
who owed their living to businesses belonging to the persecuted, as
well as all the republic's inhabitants." The nation, he added, would be
destroyed unless "an extraordinary and vigorous" effort were made to
quiet the many "despicable orators and the many nervous, uncon-
trollable disturbers of public tranquility."[102] Mora argued that the
Spaniards, like the Mexicans, paid taxes, helped develop national
wealth and prosperity, and had contributed money to the nation's
liberty and independence. They had made other contributions, but
these acts alone should have been sufficient, he said, to grant them
the right of citizenship.

According to Mora, the Spaniards were accused of two things:
their opposition to independence and their distaste for the new nation

once it had separated itself from the mother country. In reply to the
first accusation, he claimed that many Mexicans had opposed the
1810 insurrection, and indeed, many of them had fought in royalist
ranks. The second charge he considered libelous, particularly in view
of all that Generals Echávarri and Negrete had done to protect the
nation's integrity.[103] Moreover, Mora was certain that the Spaniards
had no real ties with their native land, since everything they loved was
in Mexico. But, the most important consideration was that the nation
and the peninsulares had entered into an agreement at independence
by which the latter accepted all the duties and obligations of Mexican
citizenship and in return received all the rights and privileges that
went with it. He argued that the contract was legally binding and
could not be abrogated unilaterally by one of the parties involved.
Furthermore, he considered expulsion, regardless of the pretext, to be
unjust, arbitrary and hateful.[104]

Mora warned that if the Spaniards were expelled, Mexico would
lose their wealth and support, gaining only their enmity and that of
their Mexican relatives. He argued that the country needed
population as well as capital, and any act to diminish one would
affect the other. Thus, the expulsion of ten or twelve thousand families would considerably weaken the nation. Mexico required capital
to develop her infant industry; to expel the Spaniards would be
tantamount to losing most of the needed funds. Mora maintained
that such an act would debilitate the nation in the same way that
Spain's expulsion of the Moors and the Jews weakened that country's economy. Finally, Mora made a special appeal to the authorities concerned, reminding them of the important consequences their
decision would have and concluding that "the nation's salvation or
ruin" depended on the outcome of their deliberations.[105]

In refutation of Mora's arguments, the replies of those who favored
expulsion were printed in *El Amigo del Pueblo*.[106] The writers
maintained that the Spaniards had not become Mexican citizens by
virtue of the Plan of Iguala, since they accepted the plan not because
of the three guarantees but because it established a monarchy under a
Bourbon prince. According to Article 19 of the Treaty of Córdoba,
Europeans living in New Spain as well as Americans residing in the
peninsula would "decide if they wished to remain, adopting this or
that country." In such a situation, if a Spaniard chose to remain in
Mexico, this was not sufficient reason to grant him citizenship.[107]
Furthermore, according to *El Amigo del Pueblo,* the February 24,

1822, decree which granted "equal civil rights to all free inhabitants of the empire, regardless of their origin in the four corners of the world," was not a basis either for confirming or denying Mexican citizenship. In any case, the law of April 8, 1823, had declared the Plan of Iguala, the Treaty of Córdoba, and the decree of February 24, 1822, null and void, so that the nation was absolutely free to constitute itself as it deemed convenient. Moreover, even though the three guarantees remained in effect "through the free will of the nation," this could not be construed to mean the conferral of citizenship upon the Spaniards.[108]

El Amigo del Pueblo declared that arguments for and against the Europeans must take into account their status, length of residence, property, public services, and political activities. When viewed in this light, most peninsulares had to be condemned; it was doubtful that any Spaniards had lived "without contradictions." Then, it asked, to what extent had they contributed to national well-being by cultivating the soil, investing their capital, paying taxes, marrying and having children, and making monetary contributions to keep the nation independent? Even assuming that the Europeans had contributed to Mexico in these ways, it would not be unjust to banish them from the republic if the security of the country demanded it.[109] Of course it was clear, *El Amigo del Pueblo* declared, that expulsion did not mean driving every Spaniard out; the Jalisco law had already shown that exceptions would be made. It only expelled Spanish soldiers who could not prove their commitment to the country, those who continued to fight against independence after the Treaty of Córdoba had been published, and those who had entered the nation illegally. Even among the latter group, a soldier would be exempted if he had a Mexican wife, if he was a widower with children, or if he was physically disabled. Therefore, declared *El Amigo del Pueblo,* Mora and the editors of *escocés* newspapers were in error when they assumed that Spaniards would be exiled indiscriminately.[110]

The paper did not reproach peninsulares because they had formerly opposed independence, but because they wanted to return to the days of the colony, favored monarchy and opposed the republic, and stood accused of "turbulence, sedition, and conspiracy."[111] Their open distaste for independence was not unreasonable, since it was obvious that they had been forced to accept it by "the well-known authority of public opinion and bayonets."[112] Further, the paper did not question the assistance granted by Echávarri and Negrete, as well as other

Spaniards, who "willingly or by force aided with their wealth and influence."[113] In fact, *El Amigo del Pueblo* pointed out, there had been no reason for them to oppose the independence proclaimed by the Plan of Iguala, since it preserved their privileges. In spite of that, the editors indicated, no one could ignore the insurrections like Toluca and Juchi, which occurred when the Plan of Iguala was in effect and when the first congress staunchly supported the three guarantees. Even the Plan of Casa Mata, they added, had no purpose for the Spaniards other than "to restore completely the Plan of Iguala."[114] The paper maintained that the peninsulares had been able to regain their influence over the government by favoring the federal republic. Thereafter, they used their positions to undermine the system at its foundations "by seducing with gold those who would attack it, by corrupting the opinion of simpletons, by hiding in the shadow of the Church, by discrediting . . . the chief executive as well as patriots most distinguished for their love of our liberties, and above all, by taking care that the conspirators not be discovered regardless of the tragedy that their enterprise might cause."[115]

Neither *El Amigo del Pueblo* nor any other radical *yorkino* newspaper was willing to concede that the Spaniards could be trusted. The Arenas conspiracy had increased everyone's doubts and led many to believe that the Europeans' loyalties were not to Mexico, as they claimed, but to Spain, where, in addition to the similarities of background, customs, and religion, they had even stronger ties of birth, blood, and friendship. How could anyone trust them, people asked, at a time when Mexico was at war with Spain and when the entire nation feared an invasion?[116] Former Spanish soldiers aroused the greatest suspicion because they had defended Spain until the very end. The terms of their surrender allowed them to settle in Mexico with full legal rights. However, the editors of *El Amigo del Pueblo* maintained that such agreements were not valid, and they supported this statement by citing Jeremy Bentham, "whose authority cannot be doubted by anyone, not even the most avid partisan of cosmopolitanism."[117] Bentham argued that utility was the only power which bound contracts; they could be dissolved when they became prejudicial.[118] The *yorkinos* who led the anti-Spanish movement advanced such arguments to further their cause and to refute the *escoceses*. However, the issue the *yorkinos* never discussed was the possible harm that the expulsion might cause the nation.[119]

Shortly after the Jalisco law was passed, the *yorkinos* introduced a

similar bill in the state legislature of Mexico. It allowed thirty days
for Spaniards being expelled to leave the state and granted compensa-
tion to those removed from state employment. Future meetings of
Spaniards would be under surveillance, and those who remained by
exemption would have to report to the authorities once a month.[120]
After heated debate the measure passed on October 6 by a vote of
eleven to ten.[121] Lieutenant Governor Manuel Reyes Veramendi, a
major figure in instigating the legislation, worked diligently with
other *yorkinos* for its passage. Their greatest support, however, came
from the series of anti-Spanish demonstrations in Tlalpan, Ajusco,
and Apam, particularly those led by Ramón Parrés and Pascual
Muñiz, which finally convinced the legislature to approve the expulsion law. Some, like Governor Lorenzo de Zavala, believed that
the lieutenant governor and the radical *yorkinos* in the legislature
were responsible for many of the public disturbances.[122] Zavala
apparently opposed the law, but he refrained from public criticism because the lieutenant governor and the legislature had approved it. Although he was one of the *yorkino* leaders, Zavala disagreed with the
radicals. Early in the debates, he circulated a manifesto in which he
argued against the proposed law because it violated the promises
made in the Plan of Iguala, the Treaty of Córdoba, and the
guarantees of the federal constitution itself. Furthermore, he declared
some would lose fortunes as a result of the expulsion law, others
would take their capital out of the country, and the republic would
lose "many millions [of pesos] and much useful and industrious
manpower."[123]

The wealthiest Spaniards in the country resided in the state of
Mexico, but after the law was published they fled to the Federal District in hope of protection. Within weeks the Constitutional
Commission of the Congress studied the state law and declared it
unconstitutional. Its report emphatically proclaimed that "any [state]
law which was directed exclusively against Spaniards" was null and
void. It reaffirmed its previous declaration that only the Federal Congress could pass measures protecting the nation's independence and
ensuring public order for the entire federation.[124] Nevertheless, it became imperative that Congress take some action, since no one was
obeying the Constitutional Commission's rulings. During the
following month the state of Michoacán passed laws expelling the
Spaniards from its territory;[125] a bill was introduced in the legislature
of the state of Coahuila y Texas recommending surveillance for all

young, healthy, and single Spaniards;[126] and the Guanajuato legislature passed a law expelling former Spanish soldiers.[127]

These laws affected a tiny minority of the population. Harold D.
Sims estimates that there were 6,015 peninsulares in Mexico in 1827,
comprising one-tenth of 1 percent of the total population. Of that
number, 22 percent lived in the Federal District, 12 percent in Puebla,
10 percent in Oaxaca, and 7.5 percent in Yucatán; the remaining 48.5
percent were scattered throughout the country. Sims has also
analyzed the occupations of 2,416 Spaniards, about 40 percent of the
total European population; 820 were merchants, 477 were retired
military men, 373 were priests, 110 were engaged in maritime
activities, 23 were unemployed, 39 were engaged in industrial enterprises, 11 were farm administrators, and 78 did not give their occupation.[128]

Although few in number, the Spaniards did have influence, and
their presence aroused deep passions among the people. It was only a
matter of time before the federal Congress was forced to consider the
question of expelling them. Given the virulent anti-Spanish sentiment of the masses, the press, and the *yorkinos,* who were now in the
majority, the outcome of these deliberations was a foregone conclu-
sion.[129] On November 26, 1827, Deputy José Sixto Berduzco introduced a bill in the Chamber of Deputies to banish the Spaniards. It
called for the ouster from the country, within sixty days, of the
following Europeans who had arrived since 1821: former soldiers who
had surrendered, regardless of the terms of their capitulation; clergymen (who were to pay their own expenses); bachelors, widowers without children, vagrants, and those who had no "marital life"; and any
peninsulares, regardless of when they arrived, who refused to swear
allegiance to independence. The bill further proposed that the government pay the transportation cost for those who could not afford it
and recommended that all those exempted inform Congress so that
they might receive the rights and privileges of Mexicans.[130]

On November 27, Senator José María Alpuche introduced a bill in
the Senate requiring the following Spaniards to leave the country: all
soldiers who surrendered, regardless of their present domicile; all
bachelors who had no visible means of support or who had resided in
the republic less than eight years; all secular and regular clergy living
in Mexico less than twenty-five years or who were younger than
seventy years of age; and all Spaniards who had arrived after 1821. It
also provided that those entitled to salaries would receive them if they

resided in a friendly nation. Any Spaniards exempted by this law were required to swear allegiance to independence within twenty days; thereafter they would be permitted to come and go as they wished. Mexico would pay the passage of those evicted Spaniards who did not have sufficient funds. Married men could not force their families to follow them, but had to provide adequate endowments for their support. Finally, the law would lapse whenever Spain should recognize the independence of Mexico.[131]

The press was impatient with the pace of congressional action. The *yorkino* paper *El Aguila Mexicana* questioned the intentions of the Congress and demanded that the legislature expel the peninsulares. It also warned that pro-Spanish papers, such as *El Observador,* were trying to incite disorder and mistrust when they argued that the Europeans were innocent or that the nation would suffer if it drove them out.[132] On November 30, *El Sol* published the report of the Congressional Commission on Public Security, which had been signed by thirty-two legislators and was being introduced in the Chamber. The report recommended that the administration be empowered to set the date the Spaniards would be exiled and that the government have the right to exclude the following groups from expulsion: those who were married to Mexicans; those who had non-Spanish children; widowers with children born in Mexico; those who suffered from some permanent physical impediment; those over seventy; and those soldiers who had been given the right to remain in Mexico by the terms of their capitulation.

The commission recommended that all Spaniards who had arrived after independence, with or without passports, clergymen who had not been included in the exceptions, and all those who opposed independence be forced to leave the country. Also included were Spaniards who had emigrated from Mexico during the independence struggle or shortly after the federal republic had been declared, those who were suspect because of the services they had rendered the Spanish government, those who favored a monarchy, and those who had been expelled by the states. Former government employees and former soldiers would have to pay their own passage. All could return to Mexico as soon as Spain established relations with the new nation. The commission recommended that any powers granted the executive branch be limited to a period of six months. And it concluded with the hope that once the law was passed, all public demonstrations against the Spaniards would be relegated to "perpetual oblivion."[133]

Although some congressmen hoped to gain time by proposing such measures, others grew impatient. The latter hoped to prod the legislature into action by discussing the rising tide of popular demonstrations against the Spaniards and by reading into the congressional record the many statements against Europeans. For example, the Veracruz state legislature passed a law on December 4 expelling the Spaniards; the following day Deputy Zerecero put the law into the congressional record.[134]

Congress hesitantly began to act. On December 5 the Chamber's Constitutional Commission, composed of Juan José Romero, José Manuel Herrera, Casimiro Liceaga, José María Tornel, Matías Quintana Roo, and Manuel Crescencio Rejón, presented its opinion on the proposal to "expel some Spaniards." The commission reported that although some of the clauses violated the principle of individual rights, they were necessary to preserve Mexico's independence and well-being. Anti-Spanish demonstrations had occurred all over the republic, and the states of Jalisco, Mexico, Guanajuato, Coahuila y Texas, and Oaxaca had passed legislation against the Europeans. Therefore, the commission argued, it was necessary for the second federal Congress to deal with the elements of discord that presently threatened the country. After some spirited debate the report was approved in principle by a vote of forty-two to thirteen. Still, Congress was not ready to pass the desired legislation.[135]

The Chamber was inclined to discuss the issue in great detail, but it was pressured into action by demonstrations in Toluca, Atenco, San Agustín de las Cuevas, Xochimilco, and Ajusco, all favoring an expulsion law. Professional agitators were constantly in contact with politicians in the capital who instructed them to arouse the public against the Spaniards.[136] *El Sol,* which opposed banishment, maintained ironically that those Europeans who were exempt from the law would be the first to leave. They were fleeing all the states, the paper stated, and those living in ports or near the coast would "leave rather than move inland." The "expellables" understood well that the exceptions might be temporary, since the laws followed fashion rather than justice.[137]

Public unrest forced Governor Zavala to go to Ajusco in person to quell the demonstrations.[138] Responding to the pressure of the times, the Chamber passed the expulsion bill and forwarded it to the Senate. There the debate was much more dignified and disturbances were limited to "some feigned coughing, applause, and other signs of approval or disapproval."[139] By December 19 *El Amigo del Pueblo* was certain that the expulsion law would be passed; it answered those who criticized the legislation's exceptions by observing that they were necessary in a law which governed all Spaniards.[140] The next day both houses approved the following expulsion law:

1. Former Spanish soldiers and other Spaniards referred to in Article 16 of the Treaty of Córdoba will leave the republic's territory within a period of time stipulated by the government, not to exceed six months.

2. The government may exclude the following from the previous article: first, those married and living with Mexicans; second, those with non-Spanish children; third, those over seventy years of age; fourth, those suffering from a permanent physical disability.

3. Any Spaniards having arrived in the republic after the year 1821, with or without a passport, will leave within a period of time stipulated by the government, not to exceed six months.

4. The exceptions contained in Article 2 will apply to those who entered the country legally after 1821.

5. Spanish members of the regular clergy will also leave the republic, but the government may make exceptions for those who are included in the third and fourth parts of Article 2.

6. Bachelors having no recognized home for a period of two years, as well as those classified as vagrants by the laws of that part of the republic where they may reside, are subject to the stipulations of Articles 1, 3, and 5.

7. The government may exempt from the expulsion those Spaniards who have rendered distinguished service to the independence movement and have shown their affection for our institutions; it may also exempt their children, provided they support their fathers' patriotic actions. Professional men working in some important and useful science, art, or industry, if they are not suspected of subversion by the government, may also be exempted.

8. The president, in consultation with the cabinet, shall execute the previous article after having received a report from the governor of the state where the Spaniard resides.

9. He will in a similar fashion determine the danger to the republic which might be caused by any Spaniards not included in the previous articles, and he will order the expulsion of those he deems dangerous.

10. The powers granted to the government by Articles 7 and 9 shall end within six months after the law is published.

11. The administration will give Congress a monthly report concerning the execution of the law, and Congress may extend the period of time stipulated in the previous article.

12. The federal treasury shall pay the transportation cost of Spanish civil servants with a salary of less than 1,500 pesos, and those who, in the government's opinion, are indigent, to the closest port in Spain or in the United States of the North, as they choose, always maintaining the strictest economy according to the individual's class and rank.

13. In a similar fashion, the federal treasury shall pay the transportation cost of clergymen who lack the funds necessary or whose province or convent cannot provide it for them.

14. Government employees who are forced by this law to leave and who choose to reside in a friendly country shall have their salaries paid at a location in the republic chosen by the government.

15. The removal of Spaniards from the republic's territory shall only be in force while Spain does not recognize our independence.

16. Spaniards who, in accordance with the law, remain in the republic will take an oath of allegiance with whatever solemnities the government may deem necessary to maintain the independence of Mexico, its popular, representative, and federal form of government, its constitution and laws, and the constitution and laws of the state, district, or territory where they may reside.

17. Any Spaniards who refuse to take the aforementioned oath must leave the nation's territory immediately.

18. Articles 2 and 3 of the law of April 25, 1826, are abolished. Article 1, which prohibits the entry of those born in Spain or subjects of its government into any of the nation's ports, remains in effect.

19. Spaniards who remain in the republic may not establish their residence on the coast, and those who presently reside there may be required by the government to move inland, should it fear an invasion by enemy troops.

20. Any person who has participated in public demonstrations in behalf of expelling the Spaniards is hereby granted amnesty from federal prosecution. This amnesty does not deny the states their right to prosecute any infringement of their laws.

21. The amnesty granted does not include those demonstrators who also attempted to change the popular, representative, and federal form of government which Mexico has adopted.

Because of congressional reluctance to act harshly, the new federal expulsion law was weak and laced with defects. The many exceptions, written into the law against its sponsors' wishes, allowed the Spaniards countless loopholes. One observer said that the peninsulares had nothing to fear, since they were all excepted.[141] Many influential persons intervened on behalf of certain individuals, while others tried to conceal the number of Spaniards affected by the law.

The Europeans themselves did not demonstrate their disapproval, hoping that their good conduct would serve to minimize the danger they faced.[142] Nevertheless, many Spaniards left the country. Zavala asserted that nearly ten thousand families were directly or indirectly affected by the expulsion,[143] and that Mexico suffered "an enormous loss of capital and labor."[144] Lucas Alamán added that it was the capitalists who left, "taking not only the capital they could, about 12 million pesos, but also the much greater value of their industry."[145] Rich merchants from Veracruz, Mexico, Oaxaca, Guadalajara, Valladolid, Puebla, and other places left the country, along with shopkeepers, artisans, and many former soldiers—"people who generally did not have the means to pay their expenses and thus collected a fourth of their passage."[146]

According to official sources, 27 Spaniards entered Mexico in 1827, while 559 left. Of the 27 who arrived, 8 were merchants and the remainder were listed as private citizens. Of the 559 who departed, 207 were men, of whom 14 were private citizens, 84 were landowners, capitalists, or entrepreneurs, and the remainder were merchants. There were 102 members of the regular clergy and 11 seculars, 186 women, and 53 servants. Most of those leaving were from the Federal District and most of them left in December.[147] Their departures were voluntary, since the expulsion law of December 20, 1827, could not be implemented until the following year. Of the 6,015 Spaniards calculated by Sims to have been in Mexico in 1827, 2,749 were affected by the law. However, only 772 were to be expelled—352 under provisions of Article 9 and 420 under other sections of the law. Exceptions were granted to 1,977; 1,454 were declared to be excluded under the categories of the law by the states in which they resided, while 523 were granted exceptions by executive action (see Table 5). During 1828, 885 Spaniards and 53 of their servants obtained passports to leave Mexico; 393 requested them only for a limited time, but the remainder did not specify how long they would be gone.[148] Thus, if one includes among those who were lost to the nation the 492 who received passports without stating whether or when they would return, and if one further assumes that the 772 not granted exceptions were actually expelled, then one must conclude that a little over 1,000 Spaniards actually left Mexico because of the 1827 law.

Although some important Spanish merchants left, it should be noted that the wealthiest and most powerful businessmen, whose fortunes were invested in Mexican commerce or in loans to the govern-

TABLE 5

Number of Spaniards Expelled and Exempted by the 1827 Law

States	Expelled under the Law	Expelled by Article 9	Exempted by States	Exempted by Article 7
Chiapas	26	—	37	6
Chihuahua	42	18	89	13
Coahuila-Texas	—	—	—	1
Durango	56	6	127	14
Guanajuato	—	1	—	89
Mexico	—	17	—	24
Michoacán	12	15	95	7
Nuevo León	8	1	50	4
Oaxaca	53	—	224	84
Puebla	—	7	—	39
Querétaro	24	2	145	10
San Luis Potosí	86	32	147	19
Sonora-Sinaloa	37	7	65	51
Tabasco	6	—	69	—
Tamaulipas	—	1	—	3
Veracruz	—	210	—	3
Jalisco	—	2	—	6
Yucatán	54	6	388	5
Zacatecas	—	—	—	30
Federal District	—	27	—	114
Territories				
Colima	3	—	5	—
Nuevo México	7	—	5	—
Tlaxcala	6	—	8	1
Totals	420	352	1,454	523

Source: Primera Secretaría de Estado, Departamento del Interior, Sección Primera, *Informe* (Mexico, 1828).

NOTE: The blank spaces in the second and fourth columns indicate that no one fit that category. The blank spaces in the first and third columns indicate that the federal government did not receive the necessary information from the state governments as required by the law. No information on the subject is available for the California territories.

ment, remained. Among the most important were Antonio Olarte, Antonio Terán, Ramón Martínez Arellano, Gregorio Mier, Francisco Gámez, José García, Ramón Pardo, and Esteban Vélez Escalante.[149] Furthermore, those Spaniards owning "any sort of industry which employed Mexicans," as well as those born in Cuba and Puerto Rico, were allowed to stay. As a result, according to the minister of foreign affairs, the enforcement of the law was consistent with "demands of national security, justice, humanity, and public convenience."[150] Of the 1,500 Spanish clergy, about 265 were affected by the law, including members of the following orders: San Camilo, Saint Dominic, Saint Francis, Saint James, Saint Augustine, Carmelite, Mercedarian, Saint Ferdinand, Saint John, and Bethlemite; students of the apostolic colleges; and Hospitalers.[151] However, 97 received exceptions, 6 were ill and could not leave, 5 remained because of "important responsibilities," and 43 had their cases pending as of December, 1829. Presumably, the other 124 were expelled.[152]

It is impossible to know exactly how many Spaniards were expelled. Figures for the state of Mexico, where the wealthiest Spaniards lived, indicate that of the approximately 339 who lived there in 1828, 12 left voluntarily and 94 were expelled.[153] According to the official figures, which must be accepted with great caution, one out of every three Spaniards was affected by the law. However, this does not mean that they were actually expelled, since more than half were granted exemptions. One out of six Spaniards, or about one thousand, were officially required to leave the country. But there is little evidence to indicate that even that small number actually left. For example, Guanajuato, Durango, Guadalajara, Oaxaca, Puebla, Querétaro, San Luis Potosí, Tabasco, Veracruz, and Zacatecas requested that the federal treasury cover 32,344 pesos spent in expelling Spaniards from their areas.[154] Considering the fact that most of the Spaniards expelled were poor, the small sum spent on expulsion seems to indicate that few were actually forced to leave.

The expulsion law was approved in the hope that public tranquility would return. Indeed, four days after its passage, *El Sol* reported that groups demonstrating against the Spaniards had disbanded. The apparent calm proved illusory, however, because the masses soon realized that the law did not really oust the Spaniards. *El Sol* made its enforcement more difficult when it reported in January, 1828, that Spain had recognized several of its former colonies, including Mexico. These reports led many to believe that the Spaniards were capable of any subterfuge to defend their interests. It was rumored that many were bribing public officials to allow them to stay; Gabriel Yermo, for example, was supposed to have been given an exemption in return for five hundred ounces of gold.[155] Although an expulsion law had been passed, it seemed that none of the real issues had been settled.

NOTES

1. Zavala, *Umbral,* p. 145.
2. Ibid., p. 144.
3. México, Secretaría de Relaciones Interiores y Exteriores, *Memoria . . . 1823* (Mexico, 1823), p. 6; J. M. Miguel i Vergés, *La diplomacia española en México, 1822-1823* (Mexico, 1956); Carlos Bosch García, *Problemas diplomáticos del México independiente* (Mexico, 1947).
4. Ibid., p. 7.
5. Zavala, *Albores,* p. 16.
6. México, Secretaría de Hacienda y Crédito Público, *Memoria provisional de hacienda del 2 de junio de 1823* (Mexico, 1923), pp. 1-8.
7. Ibid., pp. 9-11.
8. México, Secretaría de Hacienda y Crédito Público, *Memoria de Hacienda, 12 de noviembre de 1823* (Mexico, 1823), pp. 1-2.
9. *Manifiesto del supremo poder ejecutivo a la nación* (Mexico, 1823), pp. 4-5.
10. *Gaceta del Supremo Gobierno de México,* no. 43 (March 23, 1824): 161.
11. Dublán and Lozano, *Legislación mexicana,* 1: 634; *Gaceta del Supremo Gobierno de México,* no. 58 (May 1, 1823): 218.
12. Dublán and Lozano, *Legislación mexicana,* 1: 705.
13. Zavala, *Albores,* p. 33; Jaime E. Rodríguez O., "Rocafuerte y el empréstito a Colombia," *Historia mexicana* 18 (April-June, 1969): 485-94; Jan Bazant, *Historia de la deuda exterior de México, 1823-1946* (Mexico, 1968), pp. 21-40.
14. Bocanegra, *Memorias,* 1: 291.
15. Ibid.
16. *Gaceta del Supremo Gobierno de México* 2, no. 13 (January 20, 1824): 46-49.
17. Zavala, *Albores,* p. 24; Bocanegra, *Memorias,* 1: 23.
18. Bocanegra, *Memorias,* 1: 291.
19. Zavala, *Albores,* p. 25.
20. Bocanegra, *Memorias,* 1: 337.
21. *El Aguila Mexicana,* no. 185 (January 24, 1824): 4.
22. Dublán and Lozano, *Legislación mexicana,* 1: 692.
23. Ibid.
24. Zavala, *Albores,* p. 26.
25. *El Aguila mexicana,* no. 293 (February 1, 1824): 4.
26. *Gaceta del Supremo Gobierno de México* 3, no. 22 (February 3, 1824): 75.
27. Bocanegra, *Memorias,* 1: 300-301.
28. Ibid., p. 295.
29. Ibid., p. 294.
30. *Dictamen de la comisión especial nombrada para regularizar los derechos y*

deberes de los españoles europeos residentes en el territorio de la federación . . .
(Mexico, 1824), pp. 1-20.

31. Ibid., pp. 11-14.

32. Zavala, *Juicio,* pp. 8-9.

33. Bocanegra, *Memorias,* 1: 300.

34. México, Secretaría de Hacienda y Crédito Público, *Memoria de enero de 1825* (Mexico, 1825), p. 29.

35. Ibid., p. 33.

36. Zavala, *Albores,* p. 80.

37. Ibid., p. 83.

38. Manuel María Gimenez, *Memorias del coronel Manuel María Gimenez, ayudante de campo del general Antonio López de Santa Anna, 1798-1878* (Mexico, 1911), p. 26.

39. Ibid., p. 27.

40. Bocanegra, *Memorias,* 1: 570-73.

41. *El Sol,* no. 835 (November 24, 1825): 652.

42. Ibid., no. 840 (November 29, 1825): 668.

43. México, Secretaría de Justicia y Negocios Eclesiásticos: *Memoria del 7 de enero de 1825* (Mexico, 1825), 13.

44. México, Secretaría de Justicia y Negocios Eclesiásticos, *Memoria del 7 de enero de 1826* (Mexico, 1826).

45. Luis Espino, *Barata de empleos consignada a las calaveras y muertos desenterrados* (Mexico, 1825), p. 7.

46. Andrés María Nieto, *Traición de unos gachupines sabida por uno de ellos* (Mexico, 1825), pp. 2-5; Andrés María Nieto, *Segunda parte en la traición de unos gachupines* (Mexico, 1825), pp. 1-3. These were answered by José de Ocariz, *Declaración legal de la inocencia del ciudadano Antonio de Olarte, acusado calumniosamente de conspiración contra la patria por Andrés María Segismundo Nieto* (Mexico, 1826).

47. Zavala, *Albores,* p. 92.

48. Ibid., p. 141.

49. Unos insurgentes, *Nuestro mote es religión, independencia y unión* (Mexico, 1826). Five issues appeared with the same title.

50. Pablo Villavicencio, *Los coyotes de España vendrán pero los de la casa nos la pagarán* (Mexico, 1826), p. 2; Pablo Villavicencio published a second part under the title *Si vienen los godos nos cuelgan a todos* (Mexico, 1826).

51. *Malditos sean los gachupines que vinieron a este suelo y tanto daño han causado con su presencia* (Mexico, 1826), pp. 7-8.

52. Ramírez Sesma, *Colección de decretos,* p. 178.

53. Ibid., 177-78.

54. José María Tornel y Mendivil, *Breve reseña histórica de los acontecimientos más notables de la nación mexicana desde el año de 1821 hasta nuestros días* . . . (Mexico, 1852), p. 86; hereafter cited as Tornel, *Breve reseña.*

55. *El Sol,* no. 511 (November 5, 1824): 616.

56. Tornel, *Breve reseña,* p. 86; Zavala, *Albores,* p. 150; Bocanegra, *Memorias,* 1: 418.

57. Tornel, *Breve reseña,* p. 87.

58. Zavala, *Albores,* p. 151.

59. Tornel, *Breve reseña*, p. 88.
60. *Correo de la Federación Mexicana*, no. 81 (January 20, 1827): 41.
61. *El Sol*, no. 1,314 (January 20, 1827): 2,342.
62. Bocanegra, *Memorias*, 1: 326.
63. Alamán, *Historia*, 5: 826.
64. *El Sol*, no. 1,317 (January 23, 1827): 2,354.
65. Tornel adds José Amat, Father Hidalgo, and a certain "David from Puebla" to this group. Cf. Tornel, *Breve reseña*, p. 88.
66. *El Sol*, no. 1,316 (January 22, 1827): 2,346.
67. Ibid., no. 1,317 (January 23, 1827): 2,354.
68. Ibid., no. 1,318 (January 24, 1827): 2,358.
69. Zavala, *Albores*, p. 152.
70. *Repertorio Mexicana*, no. 1 (June 2, 1827): 5-6; *El Sol*, no. 1,350 (February 25, 1827): 2,485-86; Bocanegra, *Memorias*, 1: 610-771.
71. Zavala, *Albores*, p. 176.
72. Alamán, *Historia*, 5: 837.
73. *Correo de la Federación Mexicana* 2, no. 176 (April 25, 1827): 3.
74. Ibid.
75. *El Sol*, no. 1,452 (May 28, 1827): 2,950.
76. Ibid., p. 2,951.
77. Ibid.
78. Ibid., no. 1,453 (May 29, 1827): 2,954-55.
79. Ibid., no. 1,454 (May 30, 1827): 2,957.
80. Ibid., no. 1,456 (June 1, 1827): 2,965.
81. *Voz de la Patria* 2: no. 22 (April 7, 1830): 1.
82. Dublán and Lozano, *Legislación mexicana*, 2: 12.
83. Tornel, *Breve reseña*, 167.
84. *Correo de la Federación Mexicana*, no. 305 (September 2, 1827): 2.
85. Ibid., no. 23 (April 13, 1830): 6.
86. *Voz de la Patria* 2, no. 24 (April 17, 1830): 5.
87. México, Secretaría de Relaciones Interiores y Exteriores, *Memoria de 1828* (Mexico, 1828), pp. 8-10.
88. *Correo de la Federación Mexicana*, no. 1 (November 1, 1826): 2-3.
89. Ibid., no. 191 (May 11, 1827): 2.
90. Ibid., no. 194 (May 14, 1827): 1.
91. Ibid., p. 2.
92. Ibid., no. 83 (January 22, 1827): 4.
93. *El Sol*, no. 1, 569 (September 24, 1827): 3,423.
94. Ibid.
95. *Correo de la Federación Mexicana*, no. 328 (August 25, 1827): 4.
96. *El Sol*, no. 1,578 (October 3, 1827): 3,463.
97. *El Sol*, no. 1,611 (October 26, 1827): 3,553-54.
98. *El Amigo del Pueblo* 1: no. 9 (September 26, 1827): 8-13.
99. *Correo de la Federación Mexicana*, no. 326 (September 23, 1827): 2.
100. *Voz de la Patria* 2, no. 26 (April 28, 1830): 4-5.
101. Ibid., no. 30 (May 1, 1830): 1.
102. *El Sol*, no. 1,560 (September 14, 1827): 3,383; José María Luis Mora, *Obras sueltas* (Mexico, 1963), p. 538.

103. *El Sol,* no. 1,560 (September 14, 1827): 3,383.

104. Ibid., p. 3,385.

105. Mora, *Obras sueltas,* pp. 547-48.

106. *El Amigo del Pueblo* 1, no. 13 (October 14, 1827): 9-10.

107. Ibid., p. 6.

108. Ibid., pp. 6-9.

109. Ibid., pp. 10-11.

110. Ibid., 1, no. 14 (November 7, 1827): 1.

111. Ibid., p. 8.

112. Ibid.

113. Ibid., pp. 8-9.

114. Ibid., pp. 9-10.

115. Ibid., pp. 11-12.

116. Ibid., p. 14.

117. Ibid. 2, no. 3 (November 21, 1827): 67.

118. Ibid., p. 71.

119. Ibid. 1, no. 13 (October 24, 1827): 14.

120. *El Sol,* no. 1,586 (October 11, 1827): 3,495.

121. Zavala, *Albores,* p. 170.

122. Ibid.

123. Ibid., p. 167.

124. *El Sol,* no. 1,634 (November 18, 1827): 3,654.

125. Ibid., no. 1,637 (November 21, 1827): 3,663.

126. Ibid., no. 1,641 (November 24, 1827): 3,676.

127. Ibid., no. 1,643 (November 27, 1827): 3,687.

128. Harold Dana Sims, "The Expulsion of the Spaniards from Mexico, 1827-1828" (Ph.D. diss., University of Florida, 1968).

129. Tornel, *Breve reseña,* p. 166.

130. *El Sol,* no. 1,645 (November 29, 1827): 3,693.

131. Ibid., no. 1,644 (November 28, 1827): 3,690-91.

132. *El Aguila Mexicana,* no. 333 (November 29, 1827): 4.

133. *El Sol,* no. 1,646 (November 30, 1827): 3,698-99.

134. Juan A. Mateos, *Historia parlamentaria de los congresos mexicanos de 1821 a 1857* (Mexico, 1877-86), 4: 340-42.

135. *El Sol,* no. 1,653 (December 7, 1830): 3,726.

136. *Voz de la Patria,* 2, no. 28 (May 5, 1830): 4.

137. *El Sol,* no. 1,657 (December 11, 1827): 3,745.

138. *El Aguila Mexicana,* no. 352 (December 13, 1827): 4.

139. Ibid.

140. *El Amigo del Pueblo* 2, no. 7 (December 19, 1827): 196-97.

141. Luis Gonzaga Cuevas, *Porvenir de México, o juicio sobre su estado político en 1821-1851* (Mexico, 1857), p. 470.

142. Ibid., p. 448.

143. México (Estado), Gobernador, *Memoria del gobierno del estado de México, . . . 1829* (Mexico, 1829), p. 19; hereafter cited as *Memoria del estado de México, 1829.*

144. Zavala, *Albores,* p. 161.

145. Alamán, *Historia,* 5: 845.

146. Eugenio de Aviraneta e Ibargoyen, *Mis memorias íntimas, 1825-1829* (Mexico,

1906), p. 69; hereafter cited as Aviraneta, *Mis memorias.*

147. México, Secretaría de Relaciones Interiores y Exteriores, *Memoria . . . 1828* (Mexico, 1828), Appendix 3.

148. México, Secretaría de Relaciones Interiores y Exteriores, *Memoria . . . 1829* (Mexico, 1829), Appendix A; hereafter cited as *Memoria de Relaciones, 1829.*

149. *Razón de los préstamos que ha negociado el supremo gobierno de la federación, en virtud de la autorización concedida por los decretos del congreso general de 21 de noviembre y 24 de diciembre de 1827 . . .* (Mexico, 1829); Lista de los españoles exceptuados publicada por órdenes de José Joaquín de Herrera, general de brigada y gobernador del Distrito Federal, 23 de enero de 1833, Biblioteca Nacional, Colección Lafragua, vol. 395.

150. *Memoria de Relaciones, 1829,* pp. 9-10.

151. AGN, JE, vol. 83-2, leg. 26.

152. México, Secretaría de Justicia y Negocios Eclesiásticos, *Memoria . . . , 1829* (Mexico, 1829), appendix 21.

153. *Memoria del estado de México, 1829,* pp. 18-19.

154. México, Secretaría de Hacienda y Crédito Público, *Memoria . . . , 1829* (Mexico, 1829), doc. 40.

155. *Voz de la Patria* 3, no. 1 (June 2, 1830): 1.

SIX

Yorkino Nationalism and the Second Expulsion

The Law of Expulsion of December 20, 1827, did not satisfy either of the contending groups. Those favoring expulsion were frustrated by the law's many exemptions, while those opposing it would have preferred no expulsions. Nevertheless, the passage of the law was a *yorkino* triumph which discouraged the *escoceses* but did not end their resistance. Rather, it drove them to take extreme measures. Realizing that they could not protect their interests in Congress, the *escoceses* resorted to an armed insurrection known as the Montaño Revolt.

On December 23, three days after passage of the law expelling the Spaniards, J. Manuel Montaño rebelled, demanding the abolition of all secret societies, the restructuring of the cabinet, the banishment of United States Minister Joel Poinsett, and the implementation of the constitution and existing laws.[1] The last demand was designed to protect the Spaniards and prevent their expulsion. Important *escocés* leaders like Vice-president Nicolás Bravo, Generals José Francisco Verdejo and Miguel Barragán, and Colonels José Antonio Facio, Luis Correa, and Antonio Gutiérrez soon assumed control of the Montaño movement. According to Alamán, the revolt was to begin in Veracruz, since the rebels hoped to obtain support from the many Spaniards living there. However, they were outmaneuvered by President Victoria, who won the city's loyalty by appointing José Ignacio Esteva, an influential gentleman from Veracruz, as minister of finance.[2]

The real objectives of the insurrection remain unclear, since even contemporary observers were in complete disagreement. The chief executive declared that the rebels planned to destroy federalism and

116

charged the Spaniards with abusing "the innocence of the people of Mexico in order to corrupt them."[3] Zavala did not hesitate to accuse the Spaniards, "whose guilt was unquestionable, since they provided the gold necessary . . . to foment the coup."[4] Not everyone blamed the peninsulares, however. Carlos María Bustamante maintained that many Mexicans, including General Barragán, opposed the government and supported the rebellion. Indeed, Bustamante argued that in Jalapa, the news from Veracruz that Montaño had rebelled was received with great enthusiasm.[5]

The government moved rapidly and decisively to crush the rebels. Although various generals, including Manuel de Mier y Terán and Santa Anna, offered their services, the administration sent General Guerrero with six thousand troops, who defeated the five hundred insurgents led by Vice-president Nicolás Bravo and took the leaders prisoner.[6]

The public and the press were hostile toward Bravo and the rebels. Luis Espino accused the vice-president of being an egotist and of subordinating public interest to his "personal tastes."[7] Villavicencio charged that Bravo, who had been indifferent during the public debate about expelling the Spaniards, made "dangerous concessions" by joining the Montaño Revolt after the expulsion law had been approved. He recommended that the vice-president change his policies if he wanted to regain his former prestige as a hero of independence.[8]

The leaders of the rebellion were guilty of lèse majesté and, by law, could receive the death sentence. Public opinion, inflamed by radical *yorkinos,* demanded that the insurrectionists be treated severely. Nevertheless, many congressmen, hoping to heal the nation's wounds, recommended clemency. President Victoria proposed that the leaders of the movement be exiled temporarily to reduce the danger to the republic. Congress agreed, sentencing the rebel leaders to exile for a maximum of six years and awarding them a pension sufficient to support them abroad.

The two most important leaders, Generals Bravo and Barragán, chose exile in Colombia. Before departing, the former vice-president urged his countrymen to avoid the temptation to persecute the defeated, to heal the nation's divisions, and to let him and his companions be the last to be sacrificed in fratricidal struggles.[9] There was good reason to believe that political harmony could be restored, since the *yorkino* triumph had discredited the pro-Spanish *escoceses.* One of the *yorkino* leaders, Lorenzo de Zavala, exulted, "Never has there been a more complete or less costly triumph."[10]

Although the *escoceses* were removed as a political threat, the *yorkinos* split into two factions over the 1828 elections. Those who supported a radical program which included extending the expulsion law and instituting other important reforms chose Vicente Guerrero as their candidate because, like Guadalupe Victoria, he was a symbol of resistance to Spain during the War of Independence. The other faction, which believed that the existing expulsion law was adequate and favored gradual and moderate reforms, supported the candidacy of the Minister of War Manuel Gómez Pedraza, a former constitutional monarchist who had supported Iturbide's empire.

The candidates' ideological posture, however, played a secondary role in the electoral campaign. The personality, education, and physical appearance of the two aspirants became the principal issues. Gómez Pedraza, respectable, well educated, and a good orator, had extensive administrative experience and moved easily in Mexican high society. Guerrero, on the other hand, enjoyed widespread public support but was despised by the upper classes, who considered him their social inferior. The former insurgent leader's greatest liability was that leading civil and military bureaucrats believed that he lacked the "ability to direct large numbers and the education necessary to lead the nation."

When elections were conducted in September, Gómez Pedraza won, carrying eleven states to Guerrero's nine. As a result, Gómez Pedraza was to be president and Guerrero vice-president. However, the latter's partisans refused to accept the results, accusing the government of having intervened to elect the minister of war. More ominous still, Guerrero himself did not accept the electoral verdict.[11]

President Guadalupe Victoria and his ministers were accused of preventing Guerrero's election in order to protect the Europeans. To some, Gómez Pedraza's election was tantamount to a pro-Spanish victory. Talk of antigovernment rebellions spread. On September 7, 1828, rumors that General Santa Anna was about to rebel in Veracruz reached the capital. Shortly thereafter, on September 12, Santa Anna declared his opposition to the government,[12] and, with eight hundred men, captured the fortress of Perote.[13] In a brief manifesto he stated that the people and the army were annulling the presidential election, demanded the total expulsion of the peninsulares, supported Guerrero's election, and requested that the states conduct new elections to save the country from civil war.[14] The government reacted immediately; it sent an army of three thousand men under the command of General Manuel Rincón to quell the insurrection, declaring Santa Anna an outlaw if he did not surrender. Rincón had no difficulty in forcing Santa Anna from Perote and later sent him under guard to Oaxaca.[15]

Santa Anna was not alone in rebelling against the government. Manuel Reyes Veramendi led an uprising on September 21, supporting Santa Anna and demanding the total banishment of the Spaniards.[16] There were other similar movements, but the most important occurred in Mexico City on the night of November 30. Colonel Santiago García and José María Cadena, with two hundred soldiers and three hundred civic militia, barricaded themselves in the building of the Acordada.[17] The insurgents demanded the complete expulsion of the Europeans and announced their opposition to Gómez Pedraza. Although they were in agreement regarding the Spaniards, they were not so unanimous in their attitudes toward the president-elect. Eventually José María Cadena, who wanted to banish all Europeans but did not oppose Gómez Pedraza, withdrew from the movement because the others insisted on annulling the election.[18] Later General José María Lobato and Lorenzo de Zavala joined the remaining rebels.

When it became apparent that the movement had powerful support among the masses, the regime tried to negotiate. It sent the radical *yorkinos* José María Tornel and Ramón Rayón to persuade the dissidents to end their resistance, but the emissaries were unsuccessful. The longer the Victoria administration temporized, the more popular support the rebels seemed to gain. Finally, on December 2, fighting began between the insurgents and government forces. The following day Vicente Guerrero, the army's leading general and the defeated presidential candidate of the radicals, joined the uprising. Seeing that the balance of power had shifted in favor of the rebels and that a bloody civil war appeared imminent, President-elect Manuel Gómez Pedraza renounced his electoral victory on December 4 and left Mexico.[19] The radicals were victorious, and the moderates, deprived of their candidate, seemed to be completely defeated.

The following day, masses demonstrating in support of the victory of the Acordada movement marched in the direction of the Parián market, where most of the Spanish merchants had their shops. The

Parián was a large building which Guillermo Prieto once described as "a stylish emporium, the golden dream of the famous *cotorronas,* the beautiful ideal of coquettes and *catrinas,* as the good-looking girls of the time were called." The people who worked there retained Spanish traditions meticulously.[20] To the masses, the Parián was one of the most vivid surviving symbols of colonial domination. They arrived at its gates shouting demands that the Europeans be exiled. What may have originally been intended as a political demonstration rapidly degenerated into looting. Most rioters had no idea of the value of the things they ruined or stole. As a result, looters destroyed shops and stores indiscriminately, taking things they later sold for a pittance. Many shop owners lost all their possessions, and the damage was estimated at three million pesos.[21]

The masses did not understand the reasons for the Acordada revolt. All they knew was that President Victoria backed Gómez Pedraza, while Zavala and Lobato wanted "the Negro Guerrero to lead us."[22] The rebel leaders insisted that they had been forced to arms because of the Spaniards, who were responsible for all the republic's ills and who now threatened Mexico's federal union.[23] Although the movement was anti-Spanish, its principal short-term goal was to prevent Gómez Pedraza from taking office; this was accomplished when the president-elect left the country.

It was the responsibility of Congress to validate the election. Because Gómez Pedraza had left Mexico and the people had opposed him in the December demonstrations, Congress decided on January 9, 1829, that his election victory was invalid. But at the same time it declared that the votes Guerrero had received were valid. Therefore, Congress called for a run-off election between Generals Guerrero and Anastasio Bustamante for president; other candidates, for vice-president, were Ignacio Rayón, José Ignacio Godoy, and Melchor Múzquiz.[24] Three days later, the states chose Guerrero as president and Bustamante as vice-president.[25] Although many hoped that this compromise would restore order and tranquility, the new vice-president, representing a conservative faction, soon came into conflict with the president's radical group.

The political crisis exacerbated the country's economic difficulties. The minister of finance expected the 1828 budget of 14,200,000 pesos to result in a deficit of 1,500,000 pesos. Others argued that the deficit would be even greater because the army, which absorbed 80 percent of government expenditures, had received increased allotments. The problem was complicated by an economic depression resulting from the political situation; few were willing to risk their capital by investing it during such unstable times. To make matters worse, the states were not remitting their share of the tax revenue to the federal government. International factors made Mexico's economic situation even worse. A world-wide financial crisis bankrupted Mexico's bankers in London, depriving the government of the use of funds deposited there. But Mexico still had the obligation to repay the loans floated by British bankers. In fact, the repayment of the foreign debt became one of the greatest burdens on government finances. When Mexico stopped payment, the debt became one of its worst international liabilities.[26] Bad harvests and an epidemic further weakened the economy, reduced government revenues, and aggravated political tensions. There were no simple solutions to these problems, and most people looked for someone to blame. The Europeans became a convenient scapegoat for all the nation's ills.

Public antipathy toward the Spaniards was strong at the end of 1828. Manuel Reyes Veramendi, who had been extremely active in promoting the first expulsion law, led an insurrection on September 27, 1828, demanding the total expulsion of all peninsulares.[27] Later the anti-Spanish riots of the Parián stirred the people's hatred of the Europeans. These and other antipeninsular manifestations compelled Congress to reconsider the fate of the remaining Spaniards.

On January 9, 1829, the Commission on Public Security presented a new proposal to the Chamber of Deputies for expelling the peninsulares. The commission maintained that a new law was necessary to "secure the lives and property of the Spaniards." Such legislation, it believed, would calm the masses and end the demonstrations "which occur daily in the republic." The law would also have the salutary effect of revitalizing commerce and restoring public confidence and the prosperity of the nation. The commissioners were certain that their proposal would prevent future convulsions and would be the most effective remedy for the ills which had long afflicted Mexican society.

The members of the commission explained that they had considered and rejected the inclusion of exemptions because "the public resists them, since experience has shown that such clauses are sufficient to nullify the effects of the law." The proposed legislation would close the loopholes of the 1827 law. Article 1 required that all Spaniards leave the republic in the following fashion: (1) those living in the internal states and the territories of Upper and Lower California and New Mexico should leave their residences within a month after the law was published locally and quit the republic within three months; (2) those residing in the intermediate states and territories were to leave their homes within a month and the republic within two months; and (3) those residing in the Atlantic coast states would quit the country within a month of the publication of the law. Article 2 defined Spaniards as those born in the lands dominated by the king of Spain, including any sons born at sea, but not those born in Cuba, Puerto Rico, and the Philippines. Article 3 provided a six-month jail term and the forcible expulsion of those who did not comply with Article 1. Spaniards who returned as long as a state of war existed with Spain would suffer the same punishment. Article 4 levied a fine of five hundred to one thousand pesos on anyone hiding peninsulares. Article 6 prohibited Europeans from leaving the country with goods belonging to their Mexican wives and also obliged them to leave a third of their property with their spouses and their children. It further stipulated that they could take only a third of their belongings in specie; the remainder had to consist of Mexican goods. Article 7 specified that salaries or pensions would be paid to those entitled to them on the condition that they settled in a friendly nation. Finally, it allowed the states to make free use of any funds they received through fines, but territories and the Federal District would have to have congressional approval for use of such funds.[28]

While Congress was debating the bill, political tension was growing. Deputy Basadre informed the Chamber that pro-Spanish *escoceses* had seized control of the state of Veracruz, imprisoning those who had opposed them. Once in power, they had voted for Gómez Pedraza even though the popular vote favored Guerrero. Basadre proposed that the federal government intervene to annul the actions of the Veracruz legislature.[29]

Debates in the press became heated. Partisans of a new expulsion law argued that all Spaniards, especially the capitalists, were exploiting the nation. They maintained that people like Antonio Terán had done nothing for the country but "lend money to the established government without ever becoming its supporters," and that "the Regency [was no better to such peninsulares] than the Spanish government, nor was the federal republic better than the empire."[30] Some, like Carlos María Bustamante, disagreed, lamenting the loss of so much wealth and talent as a result of the first expulsion law. To illustrate, Bustamante reported that the peninsulares who had emigrated to Bordeaux were such a great asset to their community that they had already founded three theaters. The radicals, however, were not convinced. The Spaniards who live in France, declared *Correo de la Federación,* are "as ordinary and inconspicuous as the majority of those who live among us." Furthermore, the paper asserted, the Europeans were so uncultured that only three or four families supported the theater in Mexico City. Other writers for the *Correo* reported on the activities and meetings of various former Spanish soldiers, all of whom were supposed to have been expelled by the 1827 law. Why, the writers asked, were they still living in Mexico? Was it because of their "lack of fear, great indifference, or little confidence," in the nation's laws?[31] Some writers simply demanded that "that damned race of Goths" be exiled; as long as they remained, the country would suffer more convulsions, because the Spaniards would always try to restore their traditional dominion over the Mexicans.[32]

The moderates also utilized the press. Carlos María Bustamante's *Voz de la Patria* argued that any further expulsion was against the national interest. He reported that there were persistent rumors that Spain was preparing to reconquer Mexico. The Republic could hardly defend itself if it were torn by internal divisions. According to Bustamante, too many important Spaniards had already left. He calculated that 4,600 passports had been granted to Europeans by January, 1829.[33] Furthermore, the *Voz de la Patria* warned that enormous sums, as much as 34,000,000 pesos, were leaving for France, not to mention the vast amounts smuggled to Spain, England, and the United States. In view of such a dangerous flight of men and capital, Carlos María Bustamante considered a second expulsion law both criminal and treasonous.[34]

Andrés Quintana Roo also criticized the commission's proposal. He questioned whether it was in the public interest, since the majority of the people were not in favor of the bill and considered the actions against the Spaniards an attack on property. Moreover, he declared, the peninsulares had given ample proof of their submission, obedience, and fidelity to Mexico's laws. It was silly to argue that Spaniards had rebelled at Juchi and Toluca, when it was General José Dávila, then commander of San Juan de Ulúa, who was responsible for those actions. He pointed out that no one maintained that all Europeans had defended the Republic. But if all peninsulares were to

be held responsible for the actions of a few, by the same logic all
Spaniards should be rewarded for the acts of men like General
Echávarri, who loved Mexico and had ended the menace of the
fortress of San Juan de Ulúa.[35] Quintana Roo further asserted that
the proposed law was "cruel and tyrannical" and would deprive
Mexico of half her population.[36] He therefore requested that
Congress defeat the new expulsion bill.

Such arguments evoked vehement replies. In response to
Bustamante, Deputy Isidro Reyes stated that he could not see how
expelling the Spaniards would endanger the country. On the other
hand, the peninsulares would be an internal threat in case of a foreign
invasion.[37] *El Correo de la Federación* sought to refute Quintana Roo
by arguing that it was "morally impossible" to tolerate the nation's
enemies. While admitting that some Mexicans were "as bad, if not
worse" than the Spaniards on certain political issues, the paper
attributed their attitudes to Spanish money or to old patterns of tra-
ditionalism.[38].

The long and heated congressional debates on the proposed expulsion law reflected the division of opinion among the people. Some,
like José María Gil, vigorously opposed the legislation.[39] José Sotero
Castañeda, on the other hand, wanted the exceptions included so the
law would not be "atrocious, unjust, and inhuman."[40] However, most
deputies seemed to believe, as did José Sixto Berduzco, that ninety-
nine out of every one hundred Mexicans supported such a measure.[41]
Joaquín Bazó argued that a new expulsion was necessary for "the
welfare of the republic and the consolidation of the present form of
government."[42] Juan Pablo Bermúdez considered the law "the only
salvation our beloved fatherland" has.[43] Deputy Zerecero argued that
the bill must be passed because public opinion demanded it.[44] After
more than a month of debate the Chamber approved the proposed
law and forwarded it to the Senate for consideration.

The people followed the lengthy debate with keen interest and generally seemed to favor granting special exemptions. Some believed
that former viceroy Iturrigaray's sons were worthy of such "a distinction."[45] Others argued that liberal Spaniards like the brothers
Ramón and Juan José Ceruti deserved to be protected, especially if
they had fought for independence. After all, they had been granted
citizenship. Although Ramón Ceruti had once favored the constitutional government of Spain, he was opposed to its present absolutist
regime. He considered himself a Mexican, declaring that he would

obey the law and would sacrifice himself once more for liberty since, as he stated, political ideals must not be changed to suit one's own interests.[46] However, some segments of the public were not at all tolerant. In Oaxaca, Spaniards were being expelled indiscriminately, and the city council even passed a law requiring all peninsulares to evacuate the city within eight days.[47]

In the midst of such public controversy the Senate began to discuss the new expulsion law on February 25.[48] Unlike the Chamber, a majority of the Senate favored a law with exemptions. Pedro Lanuza criticized the proposed law on the grounds that it was not based on reliable information. He recommended that the bill be returned to the commission with the instructions that it determine how many Spaniards resided in Mexico, who their families were, and what their relationships were to the public and private interests of the country. Manuel Crescencio Rejón proposed that, at the very least, more exceptions should be made. Other Senators agreed, suggesting that the following be exempted: the aged; those suffering from a grave physical impediment, as long as it lasted; those who had served the cause of Mexican independence from 1810 to 1821; those married and still living with their Mexican wives; and widowers with Mexican children.[49]

Senate critics argued that if such exemptions were passed, the law should not be called an expulsion law, but the law of "security for all the natural enemies of Mexico who wish to reside and conspire in the republic's bosom." Moreover, they claimed that the exemptions would encourage those who had already been expelled to return to Mexico by claiming citizenship in the United States, England, France, or Holland.[50] But in the end, those favoring more exemptions prevailed.

On March 12, 1829, Senator Ramón Pacheco Leal presented to the Chamber of Deputies the exemptions the Senate had passed and asked that the Chamber approve them. According to Carlos María Bustamante, the Chamber examined the exemptions briefly, but, after an hour, upheld its own earlier version.[51] The bill went back to the Senate for reconsideration, but that body was unwilling to approve it without exemptions. The upper chamber was strongly criticized for its "intolerable delays in treating matters of great importance to the fatherland."[52] On March 17th the Senate voted once again to request exemptions, and the following day Senator Berduzco returned the bill to the Chamber, asking that a second reading be waived and that the deputies approve the Senate's changes.[53] The Chamber hesitated for a day, but then capitulated. The second expulsion law was finally approved on March 20; it read as follows:

1. All Spaniards residing in the interior states and territories and the territories of Upper and Lower California and New Mexico shall leave their place of residence within a month after publication of the law and shall leave the republic within three months; those residing in the intermediate states and territories, including the Federal District, shall leave their residences within one month and the republic within two; and those residing in the Atlantic seaboard states and territories shall leave the republic within one month following the publication of the law.

2. All those born in lands dominated by the king of Spain as well as Spaniards' sons born at sea are considered Spanish. The only exceptions are those born in Cuba, Puerto Rico, and the Philippines.

3. The following are exempted from Article 1: (a) those suffering from a physical impediment, as long as the handicap lasts, and (b) the sons of Americans.

4. Those covered by the preceding article will bring to the Foreign Ministry, either personally or through an intermediary, the documents necessary to establish their status.

5. Spaniards who do not leave within the time specified by Article 1 shall be sentenced to six months in jail and then deported; those returning to the republic's territory as long as a state of war exists with Spain shall receive the same fate.

6. The executive branch will give Congress monthly reports concerning the expulsion.

7. The treasury, always maintaining the strictest economy, will pay the transportation costs to the nearest port in the United States of the North for those who, in the government's opinion, cannot afford to pay.

8. In a similar fashion, the federal treasury shall pay the cost of transporting clergymen who lack the necessary funds or whose province or convent cannot provide them.

9. The government will issue the necessary documents to those who may remain in the federal union but may not thereafter reside near the coast. The government shall have the necessary authority to require those presently living in coastal areas to move inland if it fears an invasion by enemy troops.

10. Any Spaniard entitled to income from the Union or from an ecclesiastical benefice shall receive whatever is due him under the law, provided he resides in a friendly nation and informs the Mexican consul of his whereabouts. Anyone residing in territories under the control of the king of Spain shall forfeit all such rights.

11. The law of December 20, 1827, is hereby abrogated, with the

exception of Article 18, which prohibits Spaniards and subjects of that government from entering the federal republic.

On March 22, *El Correo de la Federación* voiced its joyful approval of the new law congratulating the deputies of the Chamber for contributing to peace and unity. The new law was based on the same principles as the first; it differed in that it clearly specified those affected and provided for their punishment if they should fail to comply. It was not as vague as the much-criticized 1827 law and was therefore easier to apply; it had very few exemptions and seemed to be inflexible. Nevertheless, the implementation of this legislation did not live up to the expectations of many radicals.

The political and economic situation of the nation hampered those who would carry out the law. Indeed, its very authors were among the first to undermine it because many of them were related by blood or by marriage to Spaniards. They had no intention of expelling their relatives and quickly granted them exemptions. It was even difficult to expel the poor; more than forty wives with children visited the Chamber of Deputies on April 9 to present a petition protesting the proposed expulsion of their relatives and friends.[54] By noon on April 15, the Chamber of Deputies had granted approximately one hundred exemptions.[55]

The Church also defended its members. The ecclesiastical *cabildo* of Mexico City sent a petition to the minister of internal and foreign affairs explaining that the number of clergy had declined from 1,300 to about 400 and that, given such a shortage, the expulsion of 30 Spanish priests would cause the archdiocese great harm. Besides, 26 of the priests were too old, and for them, deportation was synonymous with death.[56] The petition was referred to the minister of justice, who replied that the government had "considered it necessary to the public interest" not to grant exemptions. But since the request concerned individuals of advanced age, the *cabildo* could file for an exemption "with the certainty that the government would grant the justice which the circumstances demand."[57] The minister received similar petitions from the *cabildo* of Puebla and other Church bodies; all got the same response as the *cabildo* of Mexico.

José María Bocanegra, then minister of internal and foreign affairs, later asserted that because of their nature and quantity, the exclusions virtually nullified the law.[58] By April 24, *El Correo de la Federación* reported that any Spaniard not related to a congressman suffered because the legislators were granting exemptions to their

relatives and friends. So many people received exemptions that
Congress was forced to pass an additional law stating that anyone
exempted by either chamber before April 22 was not affected by the
second expulsion law.[59] Immediately there was a noticeable increase
in the number of "cripples," and within four days Congress appointed
a committee of seven to verify the existence of such physical defects
and to determine if they were temporary or permanent.[60] However,
the judgment of the committee members was not above suspicion,
since they were believed to be unprincipled *yorkinos* who certified
"sick men well and healthy ones ill," depending on the amount their
patients paid them.[61]

As a result of these and other difficulties, President Guerrero had
to be lenient in carrying out the law. Moreover, since spring and
summer were unhealthy seasons in the coastal lowlands, the Senate
voted to postpone enforcement of the law until December.[62] The
delay would also give the regime more time to secure the funds
necessary to implement the deportations. The Chamber of Deputies
was not eager to agree, but after heated debate it voted thirty to
twenty-five in favor of temporarily suspending the law.[63] Thus, for the
moment at least, a compromise was reached.

It is difficult to determine the number of Spaniards who actually
left Mexico because of the second expulsion law. Some authors have
asserted that "thousands" left the republic, depriving it of much-
needed talent. Some states claimed that only a few Spaniards
remained; Chihuahua reported only 15 Europeans left within its bor-
ders.[64] Other states gave more detailed accounts. Guanajuato indicated that 137 Spaniards left with passports and 16 without them, 58
were granted exemptions because of ill health, 6 received exemptions
from the federal Congress, and 2 had cases pending.[65] Most of those
deported went either to New Orleans, if poor, or to Bordeaux, if
wealthy. Francisco Paula de Arrangoiz stated that Spaniards "with
means" went to Bordeaux, but few returned to Spain.[66]

The legislators were primarily interested in protecting Spaniards
whose services were needed and expelling those soldiers, bureaucrats,
and clergymen whose activities were considered dangerous. Most of
the deportees were former soldiers who had remained in the country
under the guarantee of their capitulation; they were the ones who
emigrated to New Orleans. It is very difficult to believe that the law
deprived the nation of much trained talent, since the majority of those
expelled were poor. On the other hand, 2,706 were exempted: 73 by

the Chamber of Deputies, 353 by the Senate, 1,491 because of permanent handicaps, 664 by temporary ailments, 11 because they were sons of Americans, and 14 by extraordinary executive clemency.[67] How many escaped detention or evaded the law in some other way, no one knows. Thus, if one assumes that there were about 5,000 Spaniards in Mexico in 1829, it is clear that nearly three-fifths remained.

Historians agree that the expulsion law was unjust, unnecessary, and absurd. They have said that the nation suffered "the most grievous harm," that "the economic consequences were terrible," that "nearly all capital disappeared," and that "countless bankruptcies occurred and wealth vanished."[68] These assertions are unfounded. Even before the expulsion laws were passed, H. G. Ward wrote that foreign investment and income from the silver mines were not sufficient to replace the capital which the "Old Spaniards" were sending to Europe.[69] Many Spanish merchants left Mexico long before the laws of expulsion were considered. Some of them, including Antonio Basoco, Tomás Domingo Acha, and Diego Agreda, were ably represented by leading politicians like Andrés Quintana Roo and continued to do business in Mexico from abroad.[70] Many Spanish merchant capitalists remained in the republic and escaped the expulsion laws because they made loans to a desperate government. One critic observed that "they saw that they could gain 300 percent in a few days, without fear of losing their money or running afoul of the law, and [therefore] without worrying about the consequences to the nation, they invested money in usurious loans to the government."[71] Such men as Antonio Olarte, Antonio Alonso Terán, Ramón Martínez Arellano, Francisco Gámez, José García, Ramón Pardo, Esteban Vélez Escalante, Gregorio Mier, Francisco Escalera, Manuel Gargollo, Florentino Martínez, Venecio Estanillo, Juan Estanillo, Juan Monasterio, José María Fagoaga, Antonio Ramón Landa, José María Rico, José Miguel Garibay, Pedro Jorrín, Ignacio Cortina Chávez, Francisco Ondovilla, and Francisco Arrillaga were needed by the penurious government and were readily exempted.[72]

Another supposedly bad consequence of the expulsion law was that Spanish merchants were replaced by French, English, and North American businessmen. This process, however, had begun earlier. Spanish merchants and capitalists withdrew from the Mexican market during and after the War of Independence to avoid losing their capital. While some peninsulares withheld their money from all

investment, many preferred to lend it to the government at high
interest rates. As a result, foreign merchants soon filled the vacuum
left by the Spaniards.[73] Some foreign firms were also in the lucrative
business of making short-term loans and loans with tremendously
high interest rates to the government.[74] Since this had occurred prior
to the passage of the expulsion laws, it is impossible to blame that
legislation for the situation. When these considerations are taken into account, it is hard to see the laws expelling the Spaniards as anything other than political ploys. The leaders of all sides knew that the
results would be negligible, but they also knew that the issue had
great political value and they exploited it accordingly.

NOTES

1. Alamán, *Historia,* 5: 835; Bocanegra, *Memorias,* 1: 441; *El Sol,* no. 676
(December 29, 1827): 3,816.

2. Alamán, *Historia,* 5: 385.

3. Guadalupe Victoria, *Mensaje del presidente de los Estados Unidos Mexicanos a
sus conciudadanos* (Monterrey, 1828), p. 1.

4. Zavala, *Albores,* p. 179. On the following page, he adds that the prisoners had a
large number of bags of gold which the Spaniards had given them.

5. *Voz de la Patria* 2 (January 26, 1828): 5.

6. *El Sol,* no. 1,831 (January 7, 1828): 3,863.

7. Luis Espino, *O muere Bravo en el palo, o mueren los del Congreso* (Mexico,
1828), p. 2.

8. Pablo Villavicencio, *Carta del Payo del Rosario al general Bravo, vicepresidente
de los Estados Unidos Mexicanos* (Puebla, 1828), 4-5.

9. Nicolás Bravo, *A los estados y a todos los habitantes de la Federación Mexicana*
(Mexico, 1828), p. 26.

10. Zavala, *Albores,* p. 184.

11. Ibid., p. 214.

12. *Pronunciamiento de Perote por el general Antonio López de Santa Anna, y
sucesos de su campaña hasta la derogación de la ley que lo proscribió . . .* (Mexico,
1829), p. 11.

13. Ibid., p. 11, states that the force was composed of "five hundred soldiers from
the third battalion, eighty dragoons of the second regiment, and two artillery pieces";
Zavala, *Albores,* p. 216, mentions eight hundred men; Bocanegra, *Memorias,* 1: 473,
states that Santa Anna rebelled with "a small force composed of an infantry battalion."

14. Bocanegra, *Memorias,* 1: 473.

15. Dublán and Lozano, *Legislación mexicana,* 2: 79-80.

16. *El Sol,* no. 1,937 (October 2, 1828): 7,634.

17. Zavala, *Juicio,* p. 19.

18. Zavala, *Albores,* p. 243.

19. Zerecero, *Memoria para la historia,* p. 109, claims to have been responsible for
the Acordada revolt, saying that he "organized it, directed it, and brought it about."

Later he "confessed before God and man that he had done wrong because it ended in the looting of the Parián, which had not been foreseen." Carlos María Bustamante claims that "no one can doubt that Zavala was responsible for the Acordada rebellion" *(Voz de la Patria* 3, no. 11 [July 17, 1830]: 4); see also Zavala, *Albores,* pp. 242-55.

20. Guillermo Prieto, *Memorias de mis tiempos* (Mexico, 1958), pp. 33-34; hereafter cited as Prieto, *Memorias.*

21. *Correo de la Federación,* no. 422 (July 30, 1828): 1.

22. Prieto, *Memorias,* p. 32.

23. *Voz de la Patria* 3, no. 10 (July 10, 1830): 7.

24. *Correo de la Federación,* no. 223 (January 10, 1829): 3.

25. Dublán and Lozano, *Legislación mexicana,* 2: 90.

26. Secretaría de Hacienda y Crédito Público, *Memoria de Hacienda . . . 1828* (Mexico, 1828), pp. 8-9; Rodríguez, "Rocafuerte y el empréstito," pp. 503-10.

27. *El Sol,* no. 1, 937 (October 2, 1828): 7,634.

28. *Correo de la Federación,* no. 223 (January 10, 1829): 2.

29. Ibid., no. 227 (January 14, 1829): 1.

30. Ibid., no. 236 (January 23, 1829): 3; Antonio Terán was a Spaniard whose name continued to appear in the list of government lenders, especially during the Anastasio Bustamante administration. Cf. Juan Antonio de Unzueta, *Informe presentado al Exmo. señor presidente de los Estados Unidos Mexicanos por el contador mayor gefe de la oficina de rezagos . . . en años 1830, 1831, y 1832* (Mexico, 1833), appendixes 1, 2, and 5.

31. *Correo de la Federación,* no. 237 (January 24, 1829): 3.

32. Ibid., no. 240 (January 27, 1829): 1.

33. *Voz de la Patria* 1, no. 4 (January 18, 1829): 3-4.

34. *Voz de la Patria* 1, no. 4 (January 18, 1829): 4; *Correo de la Federación,* no. 256 (February 12, 1829): 1.

35. *Correo de la Federación,* no. 251 (February 7, 1829): 1; no. 252 (February 8, 1829): 1.

36. Ibid., no. 253 (February 9, 1829): 1.

37. Ibid., no. 250 (February 6, 1829): 1.

38. Ibid., no. 243 (January 30, 1829): 4.

39. Ibid., no. 261 (February 17, 1829): 1.

40. Ibid., no. 262 (February 18, 1829): 1.

41. Ibid., no. 255 (February 11, 1829): 1.

42. Ibid., no. 264 (February 20, 1829): 1.

43. Ibid.

44. Ibid., no. 261 (February 17, 1829): 1.

45. Ibid., no. 244 (January 31, 1829): 2.

46. Ibid., no. 245 (February 1, 1829): 3.

47. Ibid., no. 255 (February 11, 1829): 2.

48. Ibid., no. 269 (February 25, 1829): 3.

49. Ibid., no. 268 (February 24, 1829): 2-3.

50. Ibid., no. 277 (March 5, 1829): 3.

51. *Voz de la Patria* 3, no. 20 (August 21, 1829): 6.

52. *Correo de la Federación,* no. 280 (March 15, 1829): 3.

53. *Voz de la Patria* 3, no. 21 (August 25, 1830): 1-3.

54. Ibid. 1, no. 15 (April 9, 1829): 1.

55. Ibid. 3, no. 23 (September 1, 1830): 1.

56. AGN, JE, vol. 84-B, exp. 28, fols. 105-9.

57. Ibid., fols. 110-12.

58. Bocanegra, *Memorias*, 1: 521.

59. Dublán and Lozano, *Legislación mexicana*, 2: 102.

60. Ibid.

61. Carlos María Bustamante, *Continuación del cuadro histórico de la revolución mexicana* (Mexico, 1953), 3: 237.

62. Francisco de Paula de Arrangoiz, *Méjico desde 1808 hasta 1867: Relación de los principales acontecimientos políticos que han tenido lugar desde la prisión del virrey Iturrigaray hasta la caída del segundo imperio* . . . (Madrid, 1872), p. 172; hereafter cited as Arrangoiz, *Méjico.*

63. *Voz de la Patria* 3, no. 23 (September 1, 1830).

64. Chihuahua (Estado), Gobernador, *Memoria presentada al congreso de Chihuahua* . . . (Chihuahua, 1829), p. 3.

65. Guanajuato (Estado), Gobernador, *Memoria que presenta el gobernador de Guanajuato de su administración pública* . . . *de 1829* (Guanajuato, 1830), p. 13.

66. Arrangoiz, *México*, p. 193; Aviraneta, *Mis memorias*, pp. 120-21.

67. Dublán and Lozano, *Legislación mexicana*, 2: 477.

68. Ernesto de la Torre Villar, ed., *Correspondencia diplomática franco-mexicana, 1808-1839* (Mexico, 1957), p. 239.

69. Henry G. Ward, *Mexico in 1827* (London, 1828), 1: xi.

70. Andrés Quintana Roo, *Informe del apoderado de los acreedores a los fondos del establecimiento de minería en un recurso dirigido al supremo gobierno por los responsables a las cuentas del aquel ramo, y algunos otros sobre el nombramiento de una comisión interventora* (Mexico, 1834); *Reflecsiones sobre las leyes de españoles* (Mexico, 1833), p. 4; Spanish capitalists and merchants abandoned Mexico after free trade was established because they were "disgusted by the prospect of such an encroachment upon their former monopoly, and discouraged, too, by the aspect of affairs" (Ward, *Mexico in 1827,* pp. 429, 441-42).

71. *Reflecsiones sobre las leyes de españoles,* p. 5.

72. José Joaquín de Herrera, *Lista de los españoles exceptuados; Lista de gachupines con sus nombres y apellidos, que deben salir de México luego que se publique la ley; Razón de los préstamos que ha negociado el supremo gobierno* (Mexico, 1827); Cristóbal de Urbe, *Declaran los gachupines la guerra contra los insurgentes* (Mexico, 1826) (I am indebted for these two works to Doris Ladd); Quintana Roo, *Informe del apoderado;* José Basilio Guerra, *Representación que el comercio nacional y estrangero de esta capital dirige al supremo gobierno* . . . (Mexico, 1831); *Estado que manifiesta el ingreso y egreso de caudales que ha tenido la tesorería general del ejército* (Mexico, 1823); Unzeuta, *Informe; Reflecsiones sobre las leyes de españoles.*

73. Guerra, *Representación que el comercio,* p. 17. Among the foreign commercial houses operating in Mexico at the beginning of 1829, the most important were: McCalmont Geaves and Co.; Manning and Marshall; Holdsworth, Fletcher and Co.; Robert Staples; Jaime Chabat and Son; the German India Co. (Prussian); J. P. Penny and Co.; Guillermo de Drusina; Laguerenne and Boudel; Dickson, Gordon and Co.; Stanley and George Black and Co.; Cross Mauntgre and Co.; Sugrud and Briandas; Gustavo Scheeder; Gustavo Uhde; Fernández and Verges; Eiveroll and Son; Peña

Brothers; Edward Wilson; Gustavo Sehenenheyda and Charles Vhde.

74. *Razón de los préstamos que ha negociando el supremo gobierno;* Ward, *Mexico in 1827,* 1: 66-68. Among them were Robert Staples; Manning and Marshall; Edward Wilson; Levenger and Co.; the German India Co.; Gustavo Schneider; Adouc and Plantevigne; and Gustavo Sehenenheyda and Charles Vhde.

SEVEN

Reconquest: The Spaniards' Trump Card

President Vicente Guerrero, who assumed office eleven days after the passage of the second expulsion law, became responsible for its implementation. This seemed appropriate to many observers because Guerrero was the leader of the *yorkino* faction most responsible for its passage. In addition, the government was in terrible financial difficulty when the new president took office. Former president Guadalupe Victoria had enjoyed a measure of stability because he had at his disposal substantial funds from the loans negotiated in London in 1824 and 1825. Initially, the treasury had been able simply to write checks on Mexico's London bankers, Goldschmidt and Company and Barclay and Company. All this came to an end in 1826, when the international financial market suffered a worldwide crisis. Many investors declared bankruptcy, including Mexico's bankers. By 1828, the government could not meet its quarterly interest payments. The resulting decline of Mexico's credit and the financial depression in England curtailed British investments in Mexico.[1]

According to Lorenzo de Zavala, Guerrero's minister of the treasury, the state of federal finances was "miserable." Few states could pay either their national taxes or the revenues from the federal tobacco monopoly. By 1829, customs receipts had dropped to half their 1826 and 1827 totals. Even the remainder, Zavala lamented, was "mortgaged to pay debts" which the government incurred in loans negotiated at 30 or 40 percent of face value. The profitable tobacco trade with the United States was also tied up in debts.[2] Under these circumstances, the treasury faced nearly impossible tasks. Earlier, the minister of finance, José Ignacio Esteva, had proposed that Congress authorize the sale of the right to collect customs taxes. In return, the "tax farmers" would be required to pay two-thirds the value of the duty in cash and the remainder in credits.[3] The tax farmers would receive a lion's share of the spoils from such a scheme because they would make a profit of 400 to 500 percent in return for advancing specie to the government.[4] Congress, however, rejected the plan.

Unable to resolve the financial crisis, Esteva resigned in 1827 and was replaced by Tomás Salgado, then by Francisco García, and finally by José Ignacio Pavón, all within the same year. None of the ministers were able to improve the situation. All they could accomplish was to negotiate short-term loans to pay the salaries of the bureaucrats and military men whose support was necessary to keep the regime in power. Such expedients, however, increased the nation's problems in the long run.

The government's heaviest financial burden was defense. In January, 1829, the War and Marine Ministry received 11,182,566 pesos from a total budget of 15,624,005 pesos.[5] Such vast expenditures were believed necessary because the republic feared a Spanish invasion. Everyone knew that Spain was willing to lose all its other colonies if it could regain Mexico. According to Jaime Delgado, rich Spaniards supported and encouraged Ferdinand VII's dreams of reconquering Mexico. Among the more important plans for reconquest listed by Delgado were those of Pascual de Churruca in June, 1824; Francisco Xavier de Cevérez in August, 1824; Francisco de Viado in October, 1828; Miguel Berueta y Abarca in 1828; and Joaquín de Miranda y Madariaga in April, 1829.[6] The dates indicate that most of these proposals were drawn up by Spaniards who left Mexico after Iturbide's downfall or the passage of the expulsion laws.

Although talk about a possible reconquest of Mexico had gone on for a long time, some Veracruz merchants began to consider it seriously in 1829. They reasoned that the country was ripe for invasion because the government lacked funds, commerce was paralyzed, foreign investors were leaving, and, most important, the people were restless. Furthermore, President Guerrero did not enjoy the support of the oligarchy, the army seemed capable of backing anyone who could satisfy its wishes, the clergy was openly undermining public morale, and the press was increasing tension with its scurrilous attacks against individuals and institutions. The Spaniards in Veracruz were in communication with the exiled merchants in France, who assured them of support in any proposed invasion.[7] Both groups of Europeans agreed that all peninsulares in Mexico would rebel against the government of "a few hundred loud-mouthed, anti-religious, and rebellious creoles."[8] Therefore they began to formulate plans for the invasion. According to Eugenio Aviraneta, one of the conspirators, it would not be necessary to restore a monarchy. Instead they would organize a "crusade" to provoke a race war against the creoles. Priests, like Father Miguel Bringas, would start the holy war from San Antonio de Béjar by inviting the Indians and castes to join the Spaniards in a struggle against the impious creoles. They were certain that they would receive the support of exiled Spanish soldiers then residing in New Orleans and Havana.[9] Besides the funds provided by the wealthy emigrés in France, they also would obtain funds from other Spaniards exiled to the United States and Cuba.[10] Finally, Ferdinand VII was persuaded to authorize an invasion organized and financed by Spanish merchants within and outside Mexico. In June, General Isidro Barradas arrived in Cuba commanding an army which was to reconquer Mexico.

Although they had been expecting it, the people of the United States of Mexico were surprised when the invasion finally began to materialize. At first *el Correo de la Federación* maintained in its July 4 issue that the whole episode was simply designed to discredit Mexico and that an invasion of the country would follow at a later date. But on July 8 it reported that the invasion was imminent and that it was led by Francisco Laborde, who believed he would encounter no resistance. Others disputed the report, claiming that Crown Prince Francisco de Paula himself was leading the invasion.[11] Some, like Mariano Arista, eagerly awaited the arrival of "the slaves of the tyrant of Madrid" so that they could show them that freedom was indestructible.[12] The public also argued about the merits of the defense preparations. *El Sol,* for example, was opposed to having former president Guadalupe Victoria in charge of the defense.[13] A few Mexicans, however, remained skeptical.[14] Carlos María Bustamante was sure that the entire invasion scare was a government ploy to obtain favorable legislation, a position he held until after the Spaniards had actually landed.[15]

Most Mexicans were sure that the invading force would leave Havana in July, but no one knew where it would land. In mid-July, French frigates reported sighting the Spanish fleet sailing toward Mexico. On July 21, *El Sol* called for unity in the face of such danger, and *El Correo de la Federación* reported that the Spaniards had landed in Sisal, twelve leagues from Mérida (Yucatán). The following day, the paper reported that General Santa Anna had asked the government's permission to attack the invader in the state of Yucatán. On the twenty-third, *El Sol* announced that patriotic groups were collecting funds in Veracruz to meet war expenses. The next day it reported that the people of Campeche were ready to defend themselves against the Spaniards. Contradictory rumors abounded, increasing the general confusion. On July 28, *Correo* announced that General Santa Anna, who was in charge of the defenses at Veracruz, had ordered Spaniards residing in Mexico to turn in their weapons. A subsequent editorial sought to calm the nation by arguing that the republic had never enjoyed such unlimited freedom, "nor offered a more complete picture of internal tranquility." While *Correo* did not know where the Spaniards were going, readers were reassured with the suggestion that they were headed for Central America. *El Sol* appeared less optimistic as it printed a speech by José María Tornel exhorting the people to defend their nation because, at that very moment, "the enemy cannon were firing off the coast of Yucatán."

While Mexicans speculated about the invasion, on July 27, 1829, General Barradas landed with four thousand men at Cabo Rojo, twelve leagues from Tampico. Since he was expected to land further south, the Spanish general faced no opposition, and was able to take the small towns near his beachhead, even capturing the city of Tampico. A few days later, he defeated a small Mexican force in Altamira led by General Felipe de la Garza. As planned, Father Miguel Bringas exhorted the faithful to join the holy cause. "The wars, pestilence, banditry, murder, and the many other plagues which afflict this modern Egypt," he said, were God's punishment for having abandoned his holy faith. Therefore, Father Bringas asked the Mexicans to support His Most Catholic Majesty, Ferdinand VII. Few people were won by this crusading appeal, and General Barradas, a realist, offered to pay for the horses, chickens, and other supplies which his army needed. In this way he hoped to alienate as few Mexicans as possible during the course of the reconquest.[16]

News of the actual invasion prompted a wave of patriotism in which everyone rushed to contribute to national defense. President Guerrero announced that he would give half his salary to the war effort.[17] Others immediately declared that they would do the same—his cabinet, many high-ranking public officials, some important ecclesiastic *cabildos,* like those of Mexico and Monterrey,[18] and some prominent Spaniards, including O'Donojú's widow.[19] In emergency sessions, Congress decreed that properties belonging to Spaniards residing in foreign countries would be expropriated and sold. It approved the auction of national lands in order to obtain funds rapidly and authorized the administration to demand forced loans from the states.[20] Furthermore, it granted double pay for soldiers in combat areas[21] and permitted all those who had been deported for the Montaño Revolt to return if they wished to join in the defense of Mexico.[22] In its search for additional troops, Congress abolished slavery and exhorted the former slaves to defend their country.

Congress also took measures to increase internal security. Spanish residents of Mexico and those who had been exiled previously were to be summarily executed if captured while fighting against the republic.[23] Later it passed a law expelling all Spaniards remaining in Mexico within one week of the publication of the legislation. Finally, it invested the president with extraordinary powers so that he might take whatever measures were necessary to defend the nation and to preserve public tranquility.[24]

Once the invasion was confirmed, all those who had been skeptical hastened to demonstrate their patriotism. Indeed, strong feelings of nationalism led to widespread feelings of xenophobia. Some, like Francisco Ibar, were certain that the Anglo-Americans were really behind the invasion.[25] Most Mexicans, however, grew increasingly anti-Spanish. *Correo de la Federación* rejoiced in the latest expulsion law, declaring, "While it is true that there are fewer capitalists, there are also fewer enemies; and if there are shortages, we have less fears; and even though our credit has declined, we remain free."[26] Most commentators agreed that Europeans residing in Mexico were responsible for the invasion because it would have been "ridiculously quixotic" for the Spanish to invade Mexico without some hope of internal support. Everyone believed that Ferdinand VII had committed a grave error in trusting the exiled Spaniards, since Spain was about to suffer one more crushing defeat.[27]

Such visions of a rapid victory, however, failed to take into account the wretched condition of the Mexican army and the grave logistical problems it faced. Since it was difficult to transfer units to the unhealthy lowlands of Veracruz, General Santa Anna had to bear the brunt of the defense. Although his army was poorly fed and in rags,[28] Santa Anna attempted to frighten the enemy with a show of strength. The Mexican commander announced that he was moving against the

Spaniards with an army of twenty thousand men who would give the invaders no quarter.[29] Being a humanitarian, however, he offered them a chance to surrender with honor. Meanwhile, the Mexican government organized two more armies, one under the command of General Mier y Terán and another held in reserve, commanded by the vice-president, General Anastasio Bustamante. While General Mier y Terán marched to the coast, Bustamante's army of three thousand men was deployed in the highland cities of Jalapa, Córdoba, and Orizaba. There they would be protected from the unhealthy lowlands climate but would remain within easy reach of the coast should the Spaniards attempt to land a second force.

Fortunately for Mexico, the invaders were singularly unsuccessful. A storm separated five hundred men from the main body of troops, leaving them lost and at the mercy of Mexican guerrillas. Although two hundred exiled Europeans arrived with the invading forces, only three more Spaniards joined them after they landed.[30] The would-be conquerors soon faced starvation, since they could not purchase food from a hostile population.[31] The Spaniards' worst enemy, however, was the unhealthy climate. Even before they fought the first battle, the invaders suffered heavy losses to yellow fever and other tropical diseases. Within a few weeks after landing, their camp "had been converted into a vast hospital."[32] By the end of August, the Mexican armies of Generals Santa Anna and Mier y Terán began to close in on their helpless enemy. Finally, on September 11, 1829, General Barradas surrendered to General Mier y Terán. The Spaniards turned their weapons over to the Mexicans, swore never again to attack the republic, and agreed to pay all maintenance costs until they were repatriated to Cuba. The Mexican government promised to care for the sick and wounded and to protect the Spanish from outraged Mexican citizens.[33]

The results were a disaster for Ferdinand VII. Unable to finance the expedition himself, he had allowed the exiled Spaniards to carry it out for him. Contrary to expectations, they found no support; instead, they lost 1,500 lives and 1½ million pesos.[34] The people of Mexico had clearly demonstrated that they no longer wanted any ties with Spain.[35] But in spite of the laws and the invasion, some Europeans still remained in Mexico—a situation that would pose further divisions in the future.

News of the surrender reached Mexico City on September 20, 1829. Joy, relief, and pride were momentarily complete. *El Sol* praised Generals Mier y Terán and Santa Anna for bringing glory to the nation. The invaders, it said, "came as soldiers and left disarmed, came dressed and left naked."[36] Two days later *El Correo de la Federación* described the rejoicing Mexicans: "The ringing bells, the volleys, the rockets in the air, and the shouts of *viva* replaced the somber silence" of yesterday. But best of all, *Correo* stated, the nation had endured the invasion without resorting to internal restrictions.[37] This comment failed to consider the treatment accorded the Spaniards.

Despite the extraordinary powers Congress had granted, President Vicente Guerrero's government was extremely restricted because his political enemies were unusually hostile to him and his cabinet, particularly to Lorenzo de Zavala, his chief advisor. Mexican high society and even middle-class bureaucrats considered the president unfit to govern because of his alleged lower-class origins and lack of education. Many contemptuously referred to him as a Negro, an Indian, or a half-breed. Zavala said that Guerrero's political creed could be reduced to the following: "A love of independence, the federal republic, popular representation, and a leveling of the classes of society, as well as a hatred of monarchy and a strong belief in the expulsion of the Spaniards from Mexico."[38] Most of these attitudes were in conflict with the oligarchy's desires.

As a result of extreme hostility, Guerrero's government began to disintegrate shortly after the invasion. Zavala resigned on October 1, 1829, because of the severe criticisms and personal insults he was subjected to as Guerrero's chief advisor. A month later, on November 5, a procentralist rebellion occurred in Campeche. Ignacio Roca, commander of the city of Campeche, and José Segundo Carvajal, commander of the national troops in Yucatán, demanded the overthrow of the federal system and establishment of a strong centralized national government.[39] Although he still retained the extraordinary powers which Congress had granted him during the Spanish invasion, Guerrero tried to persuade the rebels to give up without a struggle. His efforts failed, and on December 4, the vice-president, General Bustamante, proclaimed the Plan of Jalapa, which called for a return to order, and led his reserve army in rebellion against the national government. Most of the army joined the vice-president, who called himself "the protector of the Constitution and the laws." Guerrero was the second president to face a revolt led by the vice-president. Both were conservative, pro-Spanish movements.

President Guerrero could find no support in Mexico City. Therefore, after renouncing his extraordinary powers, he personally led an army against the rebels. Upon his departure, Congress named the minister of foreign affairs, José María Bocanegra, as the acting chief executive. However, the Mexico City garrison, who supported the rebels, imprisoned Bocanegra and named Pedro Vélez to head a caretaker government. When Guerrero learned of the events in the capital, he ordered his army to return, but they refused. Betrayed by the army, the president fled to the mountains in the south to continue the struggle. Anastasio Bustamante entered Mexico City in triumph and organized a new government in January, 1830.

NOTES

1. Alamán, *Historia*, 5: 812; Rodríguez, "Rocafuerte y el empréstito," pp. 493-55.
2. México, Secretaría de Relaciones Interiores y Exteriores, *Exposición del despacho de hacienda . . . 1829* (Mexico, 1829), p. 6.
3. Zavala, *Albores*, pp. 193-95.
4. Alamán, *Historia*, 5: 835; Zavala, *Albores*, p. 195.
5. México, Secretaría de Hacienda: *Memoria . . . 1829* (Mexico, 1829), pp. 9-10.
6. Jaime Delgado, *España y México en el siglo XIX, 1820-1830*, 3 vols. (Madrid, 1950), 1: 429-70.
7. Aviraneta, *Mis memorias*, pp. 120-21.
8. Ibid., p. 75.
9. Ibid., p. 76.
10. Ibid., p. 77.
11. *Correo de la Federación*, no. 401 (August 8, 1829): 1.
12. Ibid., no. 398 (August 5, 1829): 3.
13. *El Sol*, no. 6 (July 6, 1829): 21.
14. *Correo de la Federación*, no. 412 (July 19, 1829): 3.
15. *Voz de la Patria* 2, no. 29 (May 8, 1830): 4.
16. *El Sol*, no. 37 (August 6, 1829): 146; *Correo de la Federación*, no. 428 (August 5, 1829): 2.
17. *Correo de la Federación*, no. 427 (August 4, 1829): 2.
18. Ibid., no. 431 (August 8, 1829): 3; no. 445 (August 22, 1829): 3.
19. Ibid., no. 445 (August 22, 1829): 1.
20. Ibid., no. 448 (August 25, 1829): 1.
21. *El Sol*, no. 76 (August 26, 1829): 227.
22. *Correo de la Federación*, no. 431 (August 8, 1829): 1.
23. Ibid., no. 438 (August 15, 1829): 1.
24. *Voz de la Patria* 2, no. 20 (January 17, 1831): 14; Lorenzo de Zavala, *Venganza de la colonia* (Mexico, 1950), p. 40 (hereafter cited as Zavala, *Venganza*); Dublán and Lozano, *Legislación mexicana*, 2: 162.
25. Zavala, *Venganza*, pp. 39-40.
26. *Correo de la Federación*, no. 428 (August 5, 1829): 3.
27. Ibid., no. 454 (August 31, 1829): 2.

28. *Voz de la Patria* 4 (March 2, 1831): 1.

29. Antonio López de Santa Anna, *Mi historia militar y política, 1810-1874* (Mexico, 1905), p. 22.

30. *Correo de la Federación,* no. 428 (August 5, 1829): 3.

31. Ibid., no. 461 (September 7, 1829): 3.

32. Zavala, *Venganza,* p. 36.

33. Ibid., p. 34.

34. Ibid., p. 46.

35. *Voz de la Patria* 4, no. 12 (November 24, 1830): 3-4.

36. *El Sol,* no. 92 (September 20, 1829): 328.

37. *Correo de la Federación,* no. 476 (September 22, 1829): 3.

38. Zavala, *Venganza,* p. 10.

39. Ibid., p. 62.

EIGHT

Reconciliation

Anastasio Bustamante's coup d'état succeeded because the moderate groups distrusted the popular democracy offered them by the radical *yorkinos*. Most of the republic accepted the Plan of Jalapa in principle, but some states refused to recognize the new govern-ment. The state of Veracruz, for example, authorized Governor Antonio López de Santa to take whatever measures he thought necessary to protect the federal system and preserve public tranquility. In Mexico City the masses also opposed the Bustamante regime, and as a result, the new government had to devote most of its energies to pacifying the country.[1]

Lucas Alamán, minister of internal and foreign affairs and the driving force behind the Bustamante government, sought to protect the regime by discrediting the defeated president. He succeeded, not without some opposition, in having Congress declare Vicente Guerrero "morally incapable" of governing the federal republic.[2] Then Bustamante was officially recognized as the vice-president in charge of the executive power.

Although Alamán had criticized Guerrero's fiscal policies when he was attempting to discredit him, the new government nevertheless proposed a budget of 20,499,680 pesos, of which 15 percent was allocated to service the foreign debt. However, the administration found it impossible to balance the budget and calculated that it would have a deficit of more than 8 million pesos.[3] Unlike the Guerrero government, the Bustamante regime enjoyed the support of Mexico's great capitalists, who were willing to lend money to the government at between 1½ and 2 percent interest.[4] Obviously, a conservative government could expect considerations which a liberal one could not!

In February, 1830, Alamán reported to Congress that Mexico's international relations were primarily concerned with trade, which de-

pended upon internal tranquility. He believed that the defeat of the
Spanish invasion would restore Mexico's international credit, provided the government suffered no further domestic disturbances.
However, he feared that unless civil and military employees were
paid, public order could not be maintained.[5] The commercial
oligarchy heeded his warning and made additional large sums
available to the government.

During its first year in power, the Bustamante administration
attempted to win widespread support by declaring that it favored expelling the Spaniards and that it would never permit their return. The
government's actions, however, failed to live up to its declarations.
Spaniards who were citizens of friendly nations but resided in Mexico
were not deported, although the 1829 law specified that all those born
in Spain were subject to exile. Another example of the regime's
failure to enforce the law was its refusal to banish Europeans who
owed money to the national treasury, claiming that this would be
against the public interest. The administration blamed the previous
government for the difficulties Bustamante encountered in applying
the expulsion law.[6]

In an attempt to distract public opinion and to reduce antigovern-
ment sentiment, Alamán reported that Spain was preparing another
invasion. When questioned by Congress, however, he admitted that it
would be "many months" before the administration could be certain
of Ferdinand's intentions. Still, he said, if the invasion did materialize, he expected the people to rally in defense of their nation.[7]

On March 17, 1830, the opposition paper *El Atleta* claimed that no
such invasion was being prepared.[8] The paper argued that the government did not really expect a Spanish invasion, but feared that the
downtrodden people would attempt to regain their lost rights.[9] And it
warned the government to be more concerned about a possible civil
war if oppression, abuses, and unconstitutional measures continued.[10]

On April 17, 1830, Alamán circulated another report that the
Spaniards were preparing to invade Mexico. He argued that it was
therefore necessary to allow the emigrés to return and to suspend the
expulsion law because Mexico needed men for defense.[11] Although
the minister did not admit it, the implication was that the emigrants
and other Spaniards would defend the republic against their native
land, a questionable proposition at best.

In order to defend its actions, the Bustamante regime founded the newspaper *El Gladiador.* The first issue tried to win public support by endorsing public liberty and federalism. However, it also backed the Plan of Jalapa, which brought Bustamante to power and had restricted civil rights and attacked the federal system.[12] Later it openly criticized the *yorkinos,* whom it described as the "poorest and most prostituted class of citizens."[13] *El Gladiador* also declared that Spain was preparing to invade Mexico. It reported that Bellido, an "expert, experienced, and prudent" general, was in command and that he would be a much greater threat to Mexico than the ill-fated Barradas. The paper urged the insurgents to cease fighting for their "unjust" cause and support the regular army, the only force capable of defending the nation.[14] Carlos María Bustamante also reported news of an invasion in his *Voz de la Patria.* Indeed, he chastised the government for not taking stronger action. Bustamante, who had initially questioned the possibility of an invasion during Guerrero's administration, announced that the first contingent of three thousand Spanish troops had arrived in Havana under the command of General Pablo Maceo.[15] The public, however, remained unconvinced.

Most people were more disturbed by news that individual Spaniards were returning despite laws which were supposed to expel them. When some supporters of the administration also began to criticize, the regime explained that many Spaniards had returned with the permission of the secretaries of the Senate and without the administration's approval.[16] *El Gladiador* attempted to exonerate the Bustamante administration by saying that Europeans were returning because Guerrero had given them permission before he was ousted from office.[17] The paper argued that, in reality, the expulsion law had been passed in order to extort money from the rich. And it accused earlier administrations and their officials, including President Guadalupe Victoria, of having profited from the laws by selling exemptions.[18] On the other hand, *El Gladiador* claimed that the Bustamante administration carried out the letter of the law, citing the example of the Spaniard José Rugido Castejón, deported because he had tried to return illegally.[19]

The Castejón case gave the administration an opportunity to argue on behalf of the Spaniards. *El Gladiador* published an anonymous article warning the authorities that they should exercise great care before accepting "public or secret" denunciations against Spaniards. Often these were made "not because of patriotic motives, but because the victim has a lovely wife or has money that can be taken from him, or [because there is] some injury to be avenged."[20] A writer calling himself "the slave of the law" replied in a special supplement that he did not know Castejón's wife and that the Spaniard could leave the republic taking his wife and his wealth with him. He also suggested that if the anonymous writer had any pertinent information he should reveal it to the government.[21] Days later, "the slave of the law" received a reply stating that the writer had not meant Castejón specifically but the many Spaniards who had suffered persecution because of people who coveted their wives or their properties.[22]

The government also sought to distract popular attention from the Spaniards by publicizing the Banco de Avío, a national development bank. Estaban de Antuñano declared that the establishment of the Banco de Avío, which was intended to promote economic growth, particularly in the textile industry, was the "greatest development" to occur in Mexico since it had become a nation.[23] Many hoped that it would restore the republic to its former prosperity. The bank's capital, however, depended upon custom revenues, most of which were already mortgaged to pay the debts of previous administrations. Therefore, in spite of promises, the government, facing a deficit of 8 million pesos and a public debt of more than 30 million pesos, was unable to give the institution anything more substantial than lip service for support.[24] Nevertheless, the regime managed to survive.

In 1831, after the government seemed more secure, the Bustamante administration warily tested public sentiment toward the peninsulares. It introduced a bill in the Senate modifying the expulsion law of 1829, only to be surprised by the violence of the pamphlets and newspaper articles which took up the hue and cry.[25] Enemies of the government used the opportunity to challenge the administration. Pablo Villavicencio, for example, argued that as long as Spain did not recognize Mexico, Spaniards should be considered enemies because they would surely support "their kin and not strangers," and he asked the government if it had noticed that some exiled Spaniards had returned.[26] Many others, including Friar Sufras, were also disturbed by the emigrés return.

In criticizing the government, the newspaper *El Atleta* warned that other foreigners were replacing the Spaniards and demanded that Congress protect Mexican citizens against foreign competition.

Among the many advantages foreigners enjoyed was the fact that the merchants among them generally preferred employees from their own countries. Like the Spaniards in the past, the new foreigners did not consider themselves Mexicans and thought of the country and its people as something to exploit. In fact, according to *El Atleta,* foreigners believed that Mexicans had no other role than that of "consumers and spectators."[27] The paper charged that the Bustamante administration did not protect the republic's interests and suggested that the regime had entered into disadvantageous commercial relations with other countries for the same reasons that it had relaxed enforcement of the expulsion law, allowing even those who had invaded Mexico with Barradas to enter unmolested.[28] Upon hearing the charges, the Chamber of Deputies passed a bill restricting foreign activities in Mexican commerce. Later, however, it abrogated its own decision.[29]

In presenting his report to Congress that year, Alamán again claimed that the government had strictly enforced the expulsion law. At the same time he justified permitting deserters from the Barradas expedition and from the Spanish warship *Asia* to settle in Mexico, claiming that men who turned against Spain must be allies. He also noted that countries like Chile, the United States, and Peru had granted citizenship to persons born in Spain and that the republic could not expel them from Mexico without insulting those friendly nations.[30] Alamán not only defended his actions, but even asked Congress for funds earmarked for colonization, to pay the return passage of poor exiled families living in abject misery in New Orleans.[31] The measure was apparently approved, because the following year the treasury spent 5,637 pesos to return 130 persons, including women and children, to Mexico.[32]

Although the Bustamante administration seemed to have pacified Mexico enough to begin to defend the Spaniards more openly, this calm was illusory. Many remained hostile to the regime—part of the press, some congressmen, and, most of all, Guerrero. Early in 1831, the government tried to silence the capital's opposition press through fines or imprisonment. It permitted only progovernment newspapers like the *Registro Oficial, Voz de la Patria, La Regeneración, El Sol, El Torito,* and *El Observador* to appear regularly.[33] In the states, the insurgents also suffered setbacks. General Guerrero was betrayed into enemy hands, court-martialed, and executed in February, 1831.[34]

Nevertheless, the regime did not feel completely safe. Throughout March and April, it continued to assert that vice-president Busta-mante was determined to enforce the expulsion law.[35] At the same time, the administration persuaded Congress to strengthen its power by rescinding all Guerrero's appointments and promotions, on the grounds that the extraordinary powers he had received in 1829 were only to be used against the Spanish invaders.[36] The resulting vacancies allowed Bustamante to promote 250 commissioned and noncommissioned officers, a few to field grade and 6 to brigadier gen-eral.[37] He was also able to reward prelates who had rendered dis-tinguished service during the first eleven years of independent national life.[38] In this way he hoped to remove all officials who might have ties with the dead Guerrero and to bind another group to his administration.

Although these actions were meant to neutralize the government's enemies, they produced the opposite result. There had always been a small but important opposition to Bustamante in Congress, and opponents to the government were never eliminated in the states. The administration's repressive actions alienated a powerful group of wealthy moderates who had disliked popular democracy under Guerrero and had been willing to give the Bustamante regime a chance to pacify and unite Mexico. Some of them were members of the oligarchy and others were influential politicians. Late in 1831, they formed a committee in Mexico City to coordinate opposition in Congress with that of the states and, if need be, to finance armed resistance. Newspapers like *El Fénix de la Libertad* and antigovern-ment pamphlets began to appear. By January, 1832, the Mexico City committee convinced various state leaders to direct armed move-ments against the national government. The most important of these was the one to be led by General Santa Anna of Veracruz. Although Santa Anna seemed willing to settle for a cabinet change, the committee refused, insisting from the start that peace could return to the nation only when Gómez Pedraza, the legally elected president, was restored to his office.[39]

During 1832, the antigovernment faction in the states and in Mexico City became more hostile. Zacatecas, Jalisco, and Tamaulipas openly joined the rebellion. In Mexico City, opposition press and pamphlets became more caustic despite government attempts—including murder—to destroy them. The insurgents re-taliated by threatening to take reprisals against the Spaniards if the regime did not end its reign of terror.[40]

Late in 1832, the states fought the national army and prevailed in a series of encounters. Then General Bustamante took to the field, but was unable to defeat the rebel forces. Bustamante decided to negotiate. In December, he and his leading officers met in Puebla with Gómez Pedraza, Santa Anna, Miguel Ramos Arizpe, and Bernardo González Angulo in an attempt to end the conflict. On December 23, 1832, he signed the Treaty of Zavaleta, which provided for mutual protection and the holding of state and national elections, and proclaimed Gómez Pedraza the legitimate president until his term of office expired in mid-1833.[41] Thus the conservative regime fell, in spite of the support it had received from the capitalists, the Church, and the army.[42]

One of Gómez Pedraza's first presidential acts was to reimplement the 1829 expulsion law. Later, in 1833, he banished from the republic those Spaniards who had returned illegally. He announced publicly that only the following peninsulares were permitted to remain: those married to Mexicans; widowers with dependent children; and naturalized citizens of friendly countries who had letters of recommendation from their respective ministers. He also delegated to the state governments the responsibility of implementing the law and authorized the governors to exile any European considered dangerous. No Spaniard was permitted to reside in the coastal states. Finally, he distributed lists of all those exempted because of physical defects, stating that anyone granted a temporary waiver because of illness must have his case reevaluated periodically.[43] Although the new administration seemed determined to enforce the law, its success was minimal. Everyone knew that Gómez Pedraza was to retire within a couple of months, and therefore they prudently waited to see what the new president would do.[44]

Although Santa Anna was elected president, he retired to his estates in Veracruz and allowed his vice-president, Valentín Gómez Farías, to govern. Once in power, the new administration decreed a security law which exiled certain prominent conservatives, among them two Spaniards—a doctor and a priest.[45] Gómez Farías, however, was more concerned with enacting basic liberal reforms than with expelling more Spaniards. When President Santa Anna saw that these reforms displeased an important segment of society, he decided to withdraw the authority he had conferred upon the vice-president and returned to power. But Santa Anna, who had once led an anti-

Spanish movement in Perote, was no longer concerned with persecuting them. As a result, the peninsulares were not officially disturbed during his administration.[46]

Anti-Spanish sentiment was occasionally used by later governments, but no new law against them was passed after 1833. The issue ceased to be important because the Spaniards had lost their power and influence in Mexico. Finally, in December, 1836, Spain recognized Mexico, thus eliminating the rationale for expulsion. In February, 1838, Mexico ratified a treaty of peace and friendship with Spain which was intended to remove the differences that had existed "between the governments and between the citizens of both countries."[47] The following year, the first Spanish minister arrived in Mexico amidst shouts of "Viva España."

With the establishment of normal relations with Spain, the expulsion of the Spaniards, a concern of the masses ever since independence, ceased to be an issue. But during the early decades of Mexican independence the peninsulares had become scapegoats for all the nation's problems. Liberals as well as conservatives exploited popular antipathy toward the Europeans as a way of furthering their political interests. Neither party, however, was willing to expel all Spaniards.

Although the emigration of the Spaniards with their capital did affect the economy, this outcome was not caused by the 1827 and 1829 expulsion laws. Even if one attributes the departure of the peninsulares to the general anti-Spanish feelings engendered by independence, the result should be judged within the context of the times. Although economic considerations were important, they were nevertheless of secondary significance. At that time Mexicans were more concerned with reaffirming their political independence. Moreover, the early period of economic difficulty would more than likely have occurred in Mexico with or without the Spaniards. But some of them, especially those capitalists who were not exiled, did contribute to the financial crisis when they liquidated their investments and kept their funds inactive, or when they loaned them to the government at exorbitant rates of interest.

The elimination of the Spaniards' influence and power in Mexico was the first step toward ending the colonial inheritance and establishing true independence. Efforts to curtail the power of the Church and the army—institutions in which the Spaniards had once been powerful—had to await a new generation and the final triumph of the Reform.

NOTES

1. *El Atleta,* January 2, 1830, p. 53.
2. Jaime E. Rodríguez O., ."Oposición a Bustamante," *Historia Mexicana* 20 (October-December 1970): 199-204; Dublán and Lozano, *Legislación mexicana,* 2: 223.
3. México, Secretaría de Hacienda, *Memoria de Hacienda . . . 1831* (Mexico, 1831), p. 24.
4. México, Secretaría de Hacienda, *Memoria de Hacienda . . . 1832* (Mexico, 1832), p. 19-20.
5. México, Secretaría de Relaciones Interiores y Exteriores, *Memoria . . . 1830* (Mexico, 1830), p. 10; México, Secretaría de Relaciones Interiores y Exteriores, *Memoria . . . 1832* (Mexico, 1832), p. 5.
6. México, Secretaría de Relaciones Interiores y Exteriores, *Memoria . . . 1830,* p. 24.
7. *El Atleta,* March 24, 1830, p. 379.
8. Ibid., March 17, 1830, p. 355.
9. Ibid., March 24, 1830, p. 380.
10. Ibid., March 17, 1830, p. 355.
11. México, Secretaría de Relaciones Interiores y Exteriores, *Oficio de 17 de abril de 1830* (Mexico, 1830). There is a copy signed by Pedro del Valle, government secretary.
12. *El Gladiador* 1, no. 1 (March 27, 1830): 1.
13. Ibid. 1, no. 2 (March 28, 1830): 7.
14. Ibid. 1, no. 85 (June 19, 1830): 337-40.
15. *Voz de la Patria* 2, no. 17 (March 22, 1830): 6; ibid. 2, no. 34 (May 26, 1830): 7; ibid. 2, supplement (June 22, 1830).
16. Alamán, *Historia,* 5: 860.
17. *El Gladiador* 1, no. 23 (April 18, 1830): 88.
18. Ibid. 1, no. 42 (May 11, 1830): 182.
19. Ibid. 1, no. 165 (September 7, 1830): 659.
20. Ibid. 1, no. 166 (September 9, 1830): 664.
21. Ibid. 1, supplement (September 10, 1830).
22. Ibid. 1, no. 177 (September 20, 1830): 706-7.
23. Esteban de Antuñano, *Ampliación, aclaración, y corrección a los principales puntos manifiesto sobre el algodón manufacturado y en greña . . .* (Puebla, 1833), p. 35.
24. Zavala, *Venganza,* p. 169; see also Robert Potash: *El Banco de Avío de México: el Fomento de la industria, 1821-1846* (Mexico, 1959).
25. *Sermón de Fray Sufras, dedicado a los españoles* (Mexico, 1832), pp. 1, 4.
26. Pablo Villavicencio: *O se van los gachupines o nos cortan el pescuezo. Contestación del Payo del Rosario a la Voz de la Patria y a los folletos de Rafael Dávila* (Mexico, 1831), pp. 6-9.
27. *El Atleta,* January 29, 1830, p. 164.
28. Ibid., February 26, 1830, p. 325.
29. Ibid., March 17, 1830, p. 355.

30. México, Secretaría de Relaciones Interiores y Exteriores, *Memoria* . . . *1831* (Mexico, 1831), p. 16.

31. Ibid., p. 17.

32. México, Secretaría de Relaciones Interiores y Exteriores, *Memoria*. . . *1832*, p. 11.

33. Rodríguez, "Oposición," pp. 202-9; *Registro Oficial del Gobierno de los Estados Unidos Mexicanos*, no. 57 (February 26, 1831): 225-26.

34. *Registro Oficial*, no. 53 (February 22, 1831): 209.

35. Dublán y Lozano, *Legislación mexicana*, 2: 317-18, 322-23.

36. *Colección de leyes y decretos expedidos por el Congreso General de los Estados Unidos Mexicanos en los años de 1831-1832* (Mexico, 1833), p. 20; hereafter cited as *Colección de leyes del Congreso General, 1831-1832.*

37. *Registro Oficial*, no. 85 (March 26, 1831): 337-39.

38. *Colección de leyes del Congreso General, 1831-1832*, pp. 1-2.

39. Rodríguez, "Oposición," pp. 212-34.

40. *Si asesinan a Santa Anna no quedará un gachupín* (Mexico, 1833), pp. 1-2; *El Fénix de la Libertad* 1, no. 11 (January 11, 1832): 49.

41. *El Sol*, no. 1,279 (December 29, 1832): 5, 110.

42. *El Indicador de la Federación Mejicana* 1, no. 2 (October 16, 1833): 52.

43. Dublán y Lozano, *Legislación mexicana*, 2: 476-77.

44. *El Telégrafo* 1, no. 33 (February 12, 1833): 1-2; ibid. 1, no. 34 (February 13, 1833): 2; ibid. 1, no. 35 (February 14, 1833): 2-3; ibid. 1, no. 36 (February 15, 1833): 3-4; ibid. 1, no. 37 (February 16, 1833): 1-3; ibid. 1, no. 38 (February 17, 1833): 1-2.

45. *Colección de leyes y decretos del Congreso General de la Nación Megicana en los años de 1833 a 1835* (Mexico, 1840), 7: 35.

46. Alamán, *Historia*, 5: 863.

47. Dublán y Lozano, *Legislación mexicana*, 2: 389.

Bibliography

This work is based on primary sources because, aside from a few references in general accounts, the subject has remained virtually unstudied. The most important archival material for this study came from the sections on Bienes Nacionales, Consolidación, and Expulsión de Españoles of the Archivo General de la Nación in Mexico. Masae Sugawara H. has classified and catalogued some of the material in Bienes Nacionales and Consolidación, and the fruits of his labor, now appearing in the *Boletín* of that archive, will be of great interest to other researchers. Harold Sims of the University of Pittsburgh has organized a tentative catalogue of the seventy-two legajos of Expulsión de Españoles. Other manuscript material important to this study is found in the Latin American Collection of the University of Texas, Austin. Most of these materials are described in C. A. Castañeda and J. A. Dabbs, *Guide to the Latin American Manuscripts in the University of Texas* (Cambridge: Harvard University Press, 1939).

The period discussed in this work was a time of intense political discussion, and therefore, pamphlets and newspapers are indispensable sources. The Hemeroteca Nacional in Mexico is the chief repository for the nation's periodical literature. The most important collections of pamphlets in Mexico are the Lafragua Collection of the Biblioteca Nacional, the Basave Collection of the Biblioteca de México, the pamphlet collection of the Archivo General de la Nación, and the Library of the *Museo Nacional de Antropología e Historia*. Lucina Moreno-Valle Suárez of the *Biblioteca Nacional* has completed a draft of a bibliography on the expulsion of the Spaniards which is available to researchers at that institution.

I. PRIMARY SOURCES

A. Manuscript Materials

Archivo General de la Nación, Mexico City (ramos and volumes)
    Bienes Nacionales: 352, 1,596, 1,604, 1,667, 1,671, 1,777, 1,802, 1,814, 1,832

Consolidación: 1-20, 28
Expulsión de Españoles: 1-20
Historia: 72, 73, 74, 442
Justicia Eclesiástica: 82, 83, 83-1, 83-2, 84
Padrones: 13, 19, 20, 30, 31, 32, 33, 34
Pasaportes: 1, 2, 4, 5
Reales Cédulas: 30, 76, 197, 201
Abad y Queipo, Manuel, Representación a S.M. en 20 de junio de
    1815 por el obispo electo de Michoacán el Ilmo. sr. d. Manuel
    Abad y Queipo, sobre la situación política de nuestras Américas.
    Library of the University of Texas, Austin. Latin American
    Collection, Colección Genaro García, G. 360.
Humboldt, Alexander von. Tablas políticas del reino de la Nueva
    España que manifiestan la superficie, población, agricultura,
    comercio, minas, rentas y fuerza militar, primer bosquejo. AGN
    H, vol. 72.
Representación contra la consolidación del ayuntamiento de la
    ciudad de México. Archivo del ex Ayuntamiento de la ciudad de
    México. Actas del Cabildo, vol. 126.
Voto consultivo del real acuerdo para que se suspenda la junta.
    Biblioteca Nacional Colección Lafragua, vol. 315.

B. Printed Materials

A los españoles americanos. Mexico, 1821
*A los españoles americanos que militan en el ejército imperial de las
    tres garantías.* Tepotzotlán: Imprenta Portátil del Ejército, 1821.
Abad y Queipo, Manuel "Edicto instructivo del obispo electo de
    Michoacán, d. Manuel Abad y Queipo." In *Colección de
    documentos para la guerra de la independencia de México . . . ,*
    Compiled by Juan E. Hernández y Dávalos, vol. 3, doc. 158.
————. "Escrito presentado a d. Manuel Sixto Espinosa del con-
    sejo y director único del príncipe de la paz en asuntos de real
    hacienda, dirigido a fin de que suspendiese en las Américas la real
    cédula de 26 de diciembre de 1804 sobre enajenación de bienes
    raíces y cobro de capitales píos para la consolidación de vales." In
    *Colección de documentos para la guerra de independencia de
    México . . . ,* compiled by Juan E. Hernández y Dávalos, vol. 2,
    doc. 263.
————. "Informe dirigido a Fernando VII." In *Historia de Méjico,*
    Lucas Alamán, vol. 1, doc. 10.

_____. "Representación a nombre de los labradores y comerciantes de Valladolid de Michoacán en que se demuestran con claridad los inconvenientes de que se ejecute en la América la real cédula de 26 de diciembre de 1804, sobre enajenación de bienes raíces y cobro de capitales de capellanías y obras pías para la consolidación de vales." In *Colección de documentos para la guerra de independencia de México . . . ,* compiled by Juan E. Hernández y Dávalos, vol. 2, doc. 262.

_____. "Representación al arzobispo virrey contra le ejecución de la real cédula de 12 de marzo de 1809 sobre préstamo de $20,000,000.00." In *Colección de documentos para la guerra de independencia de México . . . ,*compiled by Juan E. Hernández y Dávalos, vol. 2, doc. 266.

_____. "Representación sobre la inmunidad personal del clero, reducida por las leyes." In *Colección de documentos para la guerra de independencia de México . . . ,* compiled by Juan E. Hernández y Dávalos, vol. 2, doc. 361.

_____. "Representación sobre la necesidad de aumentar la fuerza armada para mantener la tranquilidad pública." In *Colección de documentos para la guerra de independencia de México . . . ,* compiled by Juan E. Hernández y Dávalos, vol. 2, doc. 265.

Ahumada, Juan Antonio de. *Representación político-legal que hace a nuestro señor gobernador d. Felipe V . . . para que se sirva declarar que no tienen los españoles indianos ovices para obtener los empleos políticos y militares de la América; y que deben ser preferidos en todos asi eclesiásticos como seculares . . .* Mexico: Valdes, 1820.

Alamán, Lucas. *Historia de Méjico desde los primeros movimientos que prepararon su independencia en el año de 1808 hasta la época presente. 5 Vols. Mexico: J. M. Lara, 1849-52.*

_____. *Liquidación general de la deuda esterior de la República Mexicana hasta fin de diciembre de 1841.* Mexico: Imprenta Cumplido, 1845.

El Amante de la Unión. *Hastʼque se le vio una al sr. generalísimo.* Mexico: Betancourt, 1822.

El Amante de sus Semejantes. *Ahora si, Ahora si europeos y americanos se hermanaron ya.* Mexico: Benavente, 1820.

Un Americano por todos contra el europeo duelista y contestación al papel titulado desafío del europeo al americano. Mexico: Valdés, 1820.

El Amigo de Todos. *Desafío del europeo al americano.* Mexico: Ontiveros, 1820.

Los Amigos de la Verdadera Independencia. *Triunfo en frente del enemigo, la virtud de Matamoros.* Puebla: El Patriota, 1827.

Andrade, José Antonio de. *Presupuesto general de gastos de 1823.* Mexico, 1823.

Antuñano, Esteban de. *Ampliación, aclaración, y corrección a los principales puntos del manifiesto sobre algodón manufacturado y en greña que escribió y publicó en el mes de abril el c. Esteban de A., que también escribió y publica esta dedicándola asimismo al sr. presidente de la República Mexicana gen. de división A. López de Santa Ana.* Puebla: Oficina del Hospital de San Pedro, 1833.

Arrangoiz, Francisco De Paula de. *Méjico desde 1808 hasta 1867: Relación de los principales acontecimientos políticos que han tenido lugar desde la prisión del virrey Iturrigaray hasta la caída del segundo imperio, con una noticia preliminar del sistema general de gobierno que regía en 1808, y del estado en que se hallaba el país en aquel año.* 4 vols. Madrid: D. A. Pérez Dubrull, 1871-72.

Arrillaga Basilio de. *Informe que dieron los sres. José Ruiz de la Barcena, comisario de guerra honorario a. José Ma. de Echave y Teniente Coronel D. Gregorio Sáenz de Sicilia, prior y consules del Real Tribunal del Consulado de México al exmo. sr. Juan Ruiz de Apodaca, virrey gobernador y capitán general de ésta N. España. Contestando a una representación suscrita por 229 vecinos de Veracruz, que pretendieron se abriera aquel puerto al comercio directo con extranjeros amigos o neutrales contra el dictámen de su consulado, de su junta de gobierno y de otros muchos vecinos de la propia ciudad escrito por . . .* Mexico: Arizpe, 1818.

Aviraneta e Ibargoyen, Eugenio de. *Mis memorias íntimas, 1825-1829.* Mexico: José L. Vallejo, 1906.

Astucia del estranjero para llebarse el dinero o sea, cuento dedicado a los estranjeros Mexico: Canuto Sánchez, 1834.

Aunque corran ríos de sangre no nos damos a la España. Mexico: Moreno Hernanos, 1823.

Azcárate, Miguel María de. *Noticias estadísticas que sobre los efectos de consumo introducidos en esta capital en el quinquenio de 1834 a 1838, presenta el comandante de rentas unidas de México, coronel retirado del ejército, M. M. A.* Mexico: Aguila, 1839.

"Bando sobre embargo de bienes de europeos y que rindan cuentas los empleados de la real hacienda y de las iglesias." In *Colección de documentos para la guerra de independencia de México* . . .,compiled by Juan E. Hernández y Dávalos, vol. 1, doc. 98.

Barandarian, Martín José de. *Ensayo sobre el origen y remedio de nuestros males por . . . alférez de granaderos del regimiento provincial de dragones de Michoacán, y comandante de la compañía de lanzeros de la parcialidad de San Juan de México.* Mexico: Fernández de Jáuregui, 1812.

Barbabosa M. *Memorias para la historia megicana, ó los últimos días del Castillo de San Juan de Ulúa.* Jalapa: Imprenta del Gobierno, 1826.

El Becerro, hijo del buey manso, o el criollo agradecido a la nación española. Mexico: Arizpe, 1820.

Bocanegra, José María. *Esposición documentada que J. M. B. secretario de estado y del despacho de hacienda leyó en la cámara de diputados el día 19 de nov. de 1833 a consecuencia del acuerdo de la misma del día 16 del propio mes, sobre dar cuenta con los contratos celebrados en los 3 últimos meses.* Mexico: Juan Ojeda, 1833.

————. *Memorias para la historia del México independiente, 1822-1846.* 2 vols. Mexico: Imprenta del Gobierno Federal, 1892.

Bosquejo histórico de la revolución de tres días en la capital de los Estados Unidos Mexicanos, o sea las acusaciones del ministro de la Guerra D. Manuel Gómez Pedraza. Mexico: F. Aburto, 1828.

Bravo, Nicolás. *A los Estados y a todos los habitantes de la Federación Mexicana.* Mexico, 1828.

Bringas y Encinas, Diego Miguel. *Impugnación del papel sedicioso y calumniante que baxo el título manifiesto de la Nación Americana a los europeos que habitan en este continente, abortó en el Real de Sultepec el 16 de marzo de 1812. El insurgente relapso doctor José Ma. Cos, escribíala para antídoto de los incautos para desengaño de los ignorantes para confusión de los insurgentes fr. D. M. B. y E.* Mexico: Fernández de Jáuregui, 1812.

Brito, José, comp. *Legislación Mexicana índice alfabético razonado de las leyes, decretos y reglamentos órdenes y circulares que se han expedido desde el año de 1821 hasta el de 1869.* Mexico: Imp. del Gobierno, 1872.

Buscapiés a los españoles y americanos [Tepotzotlán] : Imprenta Portátil del Ejército, 1821.

Bustamante, Carlos María. *Campañas del general d. Félix María Calleja, comandante en jefe del ejército real de operaciones llamado del centro.* Mexico: José Ximeno, 1828.

———. *La Constitución de Apatzingán.* Mexico: Empresas Editoriales, 1960.

———. *Continuación del cuadro histórico de la revolución mexicana.* 4 vols. Mexico: Publicaciones de la Biblioteca Nacional, 1953-1963.

———. *Historia del emperador don Agustín de Iturbide hasta su muerte, y sus consecuencias; y el establecimiento de la república popular federal.* Mexico: I. Cumplido, 1846.

———. *Martirilogio de algunos de los primeros insurgentes por la libertad e independencia de la América Mexicana o sea prontuario e índice alfabético de varios eclesiásticos seculares de quienes se habla en las causas de las conspiraciones de abril y agosto de 1811 . . . sacóse este precioso documento de los originales de la junta de seguridad, presidida por el oidor de la real audiencia de México Miguel Bataller y Vasco . . .* Mexico: J. M. Lara, 1841.

———. *Memorias para la historia de la invasión española sobre la costa de Tampico, Tamaulipas hecha en al año de 1829 y destruida por el valor y la prudencia de los generales d. Antonio López de Santa Anna y d. Manuel de Mier y Terán en el corto espacio de un mes y quince días.* Mexico: Valdés, 1831.

C. D. M. *Resumen histórico de la insurrección de Nueva España, desde su origen hasta el descembarco del sr. d. Francisco Xavier Mina. Escrita por un ciudadano de la América Meridional y traducido del francés.* Mexico: Zuñiga y Ontiveros, 1821.

"El Cabildo Eclesiástico de Guadalajara manifiesta al virrey cual fue su conducta durante el tiempo que mando el sr. Hidalgo, y contestación del virrey." In *Colección de documentos para la guerra de independencia de México . . . ,* compiled by Juan E. Hernández y Dávalos, vol. 2, doc. 189.

Calderón de la Barca, Frances E. *La Vida en México durante la residencia de dos años en ese país.* 2 vols. Mexico: Porrúa, 1959.

El Capitán Cócora. *Observaciones al dictamen de las comisiones de seguridad pública y puntos constitucionales de la cámara de diputados del congreso general de los Estados Unidos Mexicanos, sobre el proyecto de ley acerca de espulsión.* Mexico: T. Uribe y Alcalde, n.d.

Los Capitulados debían morir según la ley. Mexico: Benevente, 1822.

Carta del sr. general mariscal de campo d. José Antonio de Echávarri al sr. Brigadier D. José María Lobato. Puebla: Pedro de la Rosa, 1823.

Castillón, J. A., ed. *República Mexicana informes y manifiestos de los poderes ejecutivo y legislativo de 1821 a 1904.* 3 vols. Mexico: Imprenta del Gobierno Federal, 1905.

Causas que se han conseguido y terminado contra los comprendidos en la conspiración llamada del padre Arenas estractadas y publicadas por disposición del supremo congreso general de los Estados Unidos Mexicanos, tomo primero. Mexico: José María de Alva, 1828.

Cavo, Andrés, *Los tres siglos de México durante el gobierno español hasta la entrada del ejército trigarante . . . publícala con notas y suplementos el lic. Carlos María Bustamante.* 4 vols. Mexico: Luis Abediano y Valdés, 1836.

Cincuenta respuestas de una muger ignorante a otras tantas preguntas del pensador mexicano. Mexico: Mariano Ontiveros, 1821.

Colección de itinerarios y leguarios formada por la sección de estadística militar, que se manda imprimir por orden del supremo gobierno, para que ratificada por las autoridades y personas a quienes corresponde pueda servir a los usos de la administración general de correos de la república. Mexico: I. Cumplido, 1850.

Contestación a las observacientes del señor contador de crédito público, sobre la cuenta y memoria del ramo referente a los 8 primeros meses del año de 1825. Mexico: Aguila, 1828.

Corral, Juan José del. *Dictamen presentado al exmo. señor vicepresidente en ejercicio del supremo poder ejecutivo por el oficial mayor encargado de la secretaría de hacienda, sobre el cumplimiento de la ley de 7 de diciembre de 1833, y uso de la autorización que concede al gobierno la del 21 del mismo para arreglar la amortización de órdenes emitidas sobre las aduanas marítimas.* Mexico: Aguila, 1834.

Cos, José María. "Proclama de Cos a los españoles habitantes de América 21 de octubre de 1814." In *Colección de documentos para la guerra de independencia de México . . . ,* compiled by Juan E. Hernández y Dávalos, vol. 3, doc. 182.

El Cosmopolita. *Oficio del señor Lemaur al señor Echávarri.* Mexico: Juan Cabrera, 1823.

El Coyote Manso. *Manuel Gómez Pedraza, segundo emperador de los mexicanos.* Mexico: Águila, 1829.

Cuaderno que contiene el préstamo hecho a Colombia por d. Vicente Rocafuerte, publicado con autorización del ministerio de hacienda. Mexico: Águila, 1829.

Cuevas, Luis Gonzaga. *Porvenir de México, o juicio sobre su estado político en 1821-1851.* Mexico: Imprenta Cumplido, 1851-57.

Chihuahua (Estado), Gobernador. *Memoria presentada al congreso de Chihuahua por el secretario de gobierno . . .* Chihuahua: Supremo Gobierno del Estado, 1829.

Decreto sobre espulsión de españoles del estado libre y soberano de Querétaro. Querétaro: Rafael Escandón, 1829.

Degradación que causa en los hombres la tiranía. Mexico: Betancourt, 1821.

De La Torre, Ernesto, ed. *Correspondencia diplomática franco-mexicana (1808-1839).* Mexico: El Colegio de México, 1957.

De Ocariz, José. *Declaración legal de la inocencia del ciudadano Antonio de Olarte, acusado calumniosamente de conspiración contra la patria por Andres María, Segismundo Nieto.* Mexico: Martín Rivera, 1826.

Dictamen de los ciudadanos síndicos del escmo. ayuntamiento acerca de si los estrangeros pueden tener carnicerías, panaderías, y otros comercios de esta clase. Mexico: Valdés, 1830.

Documentos justificantes de la conducta del ciudadano Mariano Oyarzabal, sobre el préstamo forzoso que en 19 de septiembre decretó el gob. del estado de Querétaro en uso de las facultades extraordinarias con que se hallaba investido. Mexico: Valdés, 1830.

Don Antonio siempre el mismo se marcha a San Juan de Ulúa. Mexico: Ontiveros, 1821.

Dublán, Manuel, and Lozano, José María. *Legislación mexicana o colección completa de las disposiciones legislativas expedidas desde la independencia de la república.* Official ed. 34 vols. Mexico: Dublán y Lozano, 1876-1904.

Duende Oajaqueño. *Voz de la razón contra los gachupines empleados.* No. 2. Puebla: Moreno, 1824.

E., L. *Una cuarta garantía muy necesaria para el estado.* Mexico: Valdés, 1821.

Eguía, José Joaquín de. *Memoria sobre la utilidad e influjo de la minería en el reino. Necesidad de su fomento y arbitrios para verificarlo.* Mexico: Arizpe, 1819.

Ejecución de justicia en el religioso dieguino fr. Joaquín de Arenas.

Mexico: Ontiveros, 1827.

Espino, Luis [Spes in Livo]. *Barata de empleos consignada a las calaveras y muertos desenterrados.* Mexico: Ontiveros, 1825.

―――. *O muere Bravo en el palo o mueren los del congreso.* Mexico: Ontiveros, 1828.

Espinosa de los Monteros, Juan José. *Documentos relativos al asunto pendiente sobre si se conceden pasaportes para salir del imperio mandados publicar por la soberana junta provisional gubernativa.* Mexico: Valdés, 1822.

Esposición que varias señoras mexicanas presentaron al exmo. señor general d. Vicente Guerrero, electo presidente de los Estados Unidos Mexicanos, sobre la ley general de espulsión de españoles, la noche del 24 de marzo de 1829. Mexico: Galván, 1829.

Estado que manifiesta el ingreso y egreso de caudales que ha tenido esta tesorería general del ejército y hacienda pública en todo el mes de la fecha (julio). Mexico, 1822.

Esteva, Jose Ygnacio [J.Y.E.]. *Rasgo analítico de J. Y. E.* Mexico: Águila, 1827.

Execución de justicia contra los enemigos del estado o garantía tercera vindicada. Mexico: Betancourt, 1821.

F., A. *Ventajas de la independencia.* Mexico: Ontiveros, 1821.

Fernández de Lizardi, José Joaquín. *Cincuenta preguntas del pensador a quien quiera responderlas.* Mexico: Valdés, 1821.

―――. *El conductor eléctrico por el pensador mexicano J. J. F. L.* Mexico: Zuñiga y Ontiveros, 1820.

―――. *El pensador mexicano a los españoles preocupados entre la justicia de nuestra causa y los americanos egoístas y traidores a la Patria.* Puebla: Oficina del Gobierno Imperial, 1821.

―――. *El pensador mexicano Chamorro y Dominguín. Segundo diálogo joco-serio sobre el cuaderno titulado verdadero origen, carácter, causas, resortes fines y progresos de la revolución de Nueva España y defensa de los europeos en general . . .* Mexico: Ontiveros, 1821.

―――. *El pensador mexicano, J. F. de L. sobre diversas materias.* Mexico: Fernández de Jáuregui, 1812.

―――. *Ni están todos los que son, ni son todos los que están o sea justa satisfacción que el pensador mexicano da a los beneméritos europeos, agraviados sin razón por algunos incautos escritores. Especialmente se dirije a favor de los señores oficiales que han servido y actualmente sirven en el ejército imperial.* Mexico:

Celestino de la Torre, 1821.

———. *Primera pregunta al pensador mexicano sobre pasaportes y caballos.* Mexico: Ontiveros, 1820.

Fernández de San Salvador, Agustín Pomposo. *Memoria cristiano política sobre lo mucho que la Nueva España debe temer de su división en partidos y las grandes ventajas que puede esperar de su unión y con fraternidad por el dr. Agustín Pomposo Fernández de San Salvador . . .* Mexico: Zúñiga y Ontiveros, 1810.

"Fragmento de la defensa de Gabriel de Yermo." In *Colección de documentos para la guerra de independencia de México . . .* compiled by Juan E. Hernández y Dávalos, vol. 1, doc. 281.

G., C. A. *Execusión de justicia contra los enemigos del estado o tercera garantía vindicada.* Mexico: Betancourt, 1821.

———. *Sentencia de muerte contra los capitulados o razones que justifican este procedimiento.* Mexico: Betancourt, 1822.

G., V. *Estado actual de las cosas.* Mexico: Benavente, 1821.

Galván Rivera, Mariano. *Nueva colección de leyes y decretos mexicanos, en forma de diccionario, contiene el texto de todas las leyes vigentes de Indias . . . hasta el presente.* Mexico: Tomás F. Gardida, 1853.

García, Santiago. *Bando publicado en esta capital el día de su fecha sobre espulsión de españoles, Santiago García Coronel del Activo de Tres Villas.* Puebla: El Patriota, 1827.

García Cosme, Diego, et al. *Exposición de los europeos dirigida al General Dávila, pidiéndole la entrega del Castillo de San Juan de Ulúa.* Mexico: Ontiveros, 1822.

Giménez, Manuel María. *Memorias del coronel Manuel María Giménez, ayudante de campo del general Antonio López de Santa Anna, 1798-1878.* Mexico: Librería de la Vda. de Ch. Bouret, 1911.

Gómez Pedraza, Manuel. *Manifiesto que M. G. P., ciudadano de la República de México dedica a sus compatriotas; o sea una reseña de su vida pública.* New Orleans: Benjamin Levy, 1831.

Gondra, Isidro Rafael. *Voto particular del que suscribe al dictamen de la comisión inspectora de la cámara de diputados, sobre varios contratos celebrados por el gobierno en 1829.* Mexico: Correo, 1830.

Guanajuato State, Gobernador. *Memoria que presenta el gobernador de Guanajuato de su administración pública correspondiente al año de 1829.* Guanajuato: Imprenta del Gobierno, 1830.

Guerra, José Basilio. *Representación que el comercio nacional y estrangero de esta capital dirige al supremo gobierno de la unión para que se sirva pedir al congreso general la derogación de la ley de 11 de junio de 1822, que establecío el dos por ciento sobre moneda que sale de las aduanas de la republica formada por el lic. d. José Basilio Guerra.* Mexico: Rivera, 1831.

Hardy, Robert W. H. *Travels in the Interior of Mexico in 1825, 1826, 1827, and 1828.* London: Henry Colbourn and Richard Bently, 1829.

Hernández y Dávalos, Juan E. *Colección de documentos para la historia de la guerra de independencia de Mexico de 1808 a 1821.* 6 vols. Mexico: J. M. Sandoval, 1877-82.

Herrera, José Joaquín de. *Lista de los españoles exceptuados publicada por ordenes de José Joaquín de Herrera, general de brigada y gobernador del Distrito Federal, 23 de enero de 1833.* Mexico, 1833.

Hidalgo, Miguel. "Bando del sr. Hidalgo aboliendo la esclavitud, deroga las leyes relativas a tributos, impone alcabalas a los efectos nacionales y extranjeros, prohibe el uso del papel sellado y extingue el estanco del tabaco, pólvora, colores y otros." In *Colección de documentos para la guerra de independencia de México . . . ,* compiled by Juan E. Hernández y Dávalos, vol. 2, doc. 145.

El Hijo de la Constitución. *Primera pregunta al pensador mexicano sobre pasaportes y caballos.* Mexico: Ontiveros, 1820.

Humboldt, Alexander von. *Ensayo político sobre el reino de la Nueva España, edición crítica con una introducción bibliográfica, notas y arreglo de la versión española por Vito Alessio Robles.* 6th ed. 5 vols. Mexico: Pedro Robredo, 1941.

———. *Población de N. E. Censo general hecho en 1793, progresos de la población en los 10 años siguientes, proporción entre nacidos y muertos.* Mexico: Zuñiga y Ontiveros, 1820.

———. *Tablas geográfico-políticas del reino de N. E. que manifiestan su superficie, población, agricultura, fábricas, comercio, minas, rentas y fuerza militar. Por el Barón de Humboldt, presentada al Ecmo. señor virrey Don José de Iturrigaray.* Mexico: Ontiveros, 1822.

Ibar, Francisco. *Muerte política de la República Mexicana, o cuadro histórico crítico de los sucesos políticos acaecidos en la república desde el 4 de diciembre de 1823 hasta el 25 de agosto de 1829.* 3

vols. Mexico: T. Uribe y Alcalde, 1829-30.

Impugnación al papel titulado consejo prudente sobre una de las garantías. Mexico: Zúñiga y Ontiveros, 1821.

El Indio con la coscolina riñendo por el papel moneda. Mexico: José Eugenio Fernández de la Peña, 1823.

Iniciativa de un mejicano a todos los españoles en defensa de la que se publicó en la península reclamando el número de diputados de ultramar para las presentes cortes hecha en Valladolid en 30 de marzo de esta año: E Impugnación de los errores y proposiciones sediciosas del artículo inserto en el suplemento al Noticioso General de 27 de septiembre. Mexico: Valdés, 1820.

Unos Insurgentes. *Nuestro mote es religión, independencia y unión.* No. 4. Mexico: Martín Rivera, 1826.

Unos Insurgentes. *Nuestro mote es religión, independencia y unión.* No. 5. Mexico: Martín Rivera, 1826.

Unos Insurgentes. *Se quedarán los gachupines sin costarles el pescuezo.* Mexico: Martín Rivera, 1826.

Intereses de Puebla de los Angeles bien entendidos. Puebla: Valdés, 1821.

Iturbide, Agustín de. *Breve diseño crítico de la emancipación y libertad de la nación mexicana, y de las causas que influyeron en sus más ruidosos sucesos, acaecidos desde el grito de Iguala hasta la espantosa muerte del libertador en la villa de Padilla.* Mexico: Ontiveros, 1827.

_____. *Carrera militar y política de D. Agustín de Iturbide o sea memoria que escribió en Liorna antes de haber hecho la malhadada espedición a su patrio suelo donde terminó sus glorias perdiendo su vida en un cadalso a manos de los violentos. Tamaulipas en la Villa de Padilla el mes de julio de 1824.* Mexico: Ximeno, 1827.

_____. *El generalísimo almirante a los habitantes del imperio.* Mexico: Valdés, 1822.

_____. *Papel de s. m. imperial dirigido al consejo de regencia en 15 del corriente del mes de mayo.* Mexico: Pedro de la Rosa, 1822.

_____. *Proclama: el primer gefe del ejército imperial de las tres garantías a los españoles europeos habitantes en esta América.* Mexico: Valdés, 1821.

Juárez, Benito. *Documentos, discursos y correspondencia.* Edited by Jorge L. Tamayo. 11 vols. Mexico: Secretaría del Patrimonio Nacional, 1964.

Lagranda, Francisco. *Consejo prudente sobre una de las garantías.* Mexico: •Betancourt, 1821.

La Junta del perro contra la del gato. Mexico: Valdés, 1821.

Lemaur, Francisco. *Proclama de San Juan de Ulúa.* Mexico: Valdés, 1822.

López Cancelada, Juan. *Conducta del excelentísimo señor d. José de Iturrigaray durante su gobierno en Nueva España. Se contesta a la vindicación de don Facundo Lizarza cuaderno tercero y segundo en la materia por el Lic.* Cadiz: Imprenta del Estado Mayor, 1812.

————. *Ruina de la Nueva España si se declara el comercio libre con los extranjeros. Exprésanse los motivos. Quaderno segundo y primero en la materia por D . . . redactor de la Gazeta de México.* Cadiz: Manuel Santiago de Quintana, 1811.

López de Santa Anna, Antonio. *Mi historia militar y política, 1810-1874.* Mexico: Librería de la Vda. de Ch. Bouret, 1905.

Llegada de D. Francisco de Paula a Veracruz. Puebla: El Patriota, 1827.

Maniau, Yldefonso. *Balanza general del comercio marítimo por los puertos de la república en el año de 1827, formada por orden del gobierno . . .* Mexico: Jimeno, 1829.

Manifiesto de la nación americana a los europeos que habitan este continente. Mexico; 1814.

Manifiesto del supremo poder ejecutivo a la nación. Mexico; Imprenta del Supremo Gobierno, 1823.

M. de A., J. *Somos Libres pero aún nos falta el rabo por desollar.* Mexico: Herculana del Villar y Socios, 1822.

Medina, Antonio de. *Apéndice a la exposición al soberano Congreso sobre el estado de la hacienda pública, y conducta del ciudadano Antonio de Medina en el tiempo que fue a su cargo el ministerio.* Mexico: Aguila, 1824.

————. *Documentos que tuvo presentes la comisión de hacienda de la Junta Instituyente para formar el plan de contribución del año de 1823.* Mexico: Imprenta Imperial de Alejandro Valdés, 1823.

Mendibil, Pablo de. *Resumen histórico de la revolución de los Estados Unidos Mexicanos; sacado del "cuadro histórico" que en forma de cartas escribió el Lic. D. Carlos María Bustamante, i ordenado en cuatro libros . . .* London: R. Ackermann, 1828.

México, Congreso, Cámara de Diputados, Comisiones de Policía y Segunda de Hacienda. *Dictamen de la mayoría de las comisiones de policía y segunda de hacienda de la cámara de diputados sobre derogación de la ley de 26 de nov. del año anterior que aumentó el derecho de consumo y voto particular de los señores que disintieron del mismo dictamen.* Mexico: J. M. Lara, 1840.

México, Congreso, Cámara de Diputados, Comisiones de Seguridad Pública y Puntos Constitucionales. *Dictamen de las comisiones de seguridad pública y puntos constitucionales de la cámara de diputados del congreso de la unión, sobre el proyecto de la ley de expulsión de algunos españoles presentado a la cámara, hoy 5 de diciembre y cuya discución se ha señaldo para mañana.* Puebla: El Patriota, 1827.

México, Congreso, Cámara de Representantes, Comisión Inspectora. *Dictamen de la comisión inspectora de la cámara de representantes del congreso general sobre la cuenta presentada por el ministro de hacienda correspondiente a los primeros meses del año 1825, en la parte de aquella respectiva al crédito público.* Mexico: Ximeno, 1827.

México, Congreso, Cámara de Representantes, Sección del Jurado. *Expediente instructivo formado por la sección del jurado de la cámara de representantes sobre la acusación que los sres. Aburto y Tamés hicieron contra el vicepresidente de la república. d. Nicolás Bravo.* Mexico: Ximeno, 1828.

México, Congreso, Cámara de Senadores, Comisión de Hacienda. *Análisis de la memoria presentada por el secretario del despacho de hacienda al primer congreso constitucional de los Estados Unidos Mexicanos.* Mexico: Martín Rivera, 1825.

——————— *Contestación que da la comisión de hacienda de la cámara de senadores al impreso titulado crisol de la memoria de hacienda, en el examen de los análisis de ella.* Mexico: Martín Rivera, 1825.

——————. *Dictamen de la comisión de hacienda de la cámara de senadores de los Estados Unidos Mexicanos sobre la memoria presentada por el secretario del despacho de hacienda al congreso general en el año corriente de 1826.* Mexico: Ontiveros, 1822.

México, Congreso, Comisiones de Hacienda y Comercio. *Dictamen de las comisiones de hacienda y comercio reunidas sobre préstamos forzoso y arbitrios para subrogarlos.* Mexico: Ontiveros, 1822.

México, Congreso, Comisión Especial para Regularizar los Derechos . . . *Dictamen de la comisión especial para regularizar los derechos y deberes de los españoles europeos residentes en el territorio de la federación, leida en la sesión pública del día 14 de febrero de 1824, y mandado imprimir por orden del soberano congreso constituyente.* Mexico: Imprenta del Supremo Goberno, 1824.

México, Congreso, Comisión Ordinaria de Hacienda. *Dictamen de la comisión ordinaria de hacienda sobre la instancia que hacen los individuos de las secretarías de estado para que se les exhonere del descuento que sufren conforme al soberano decreto de 11 de marzo último.* Mexico: Ramos Palomera, 1822.

México, Congreso, Comisión Sobre Vinculaciones. *Dictamen de la comisión de legislacion sobre vinculaciones leida en la sesión del 26 de julio.* Mexico: Ramos Palomera, 1822.

México (Estado), Gobernador. *Memoria del gobierno del estado de México, año económico corrido desde el 16 de octubre hasta el 5 del mismo mes de 1829, presentada el 20 de marzo de 1829.* Mexico: [Aguila, 1829].

México, Leyes y Estatutos. *Colección de decretos y órdenes que ha expedido la soberana junta provisional gubernativa del Imperio Mexicano, desde su instalación en 28 de septiembre de 1821 hasta 24 de febrero de 1822.* Mexico: Valdés, 1822.

———. *Colección de leyes fundamentales que han regido en la República Mexicana, y de los planes que han tenido el mismo carácter desde el año de 1721 hasta 1857.* Mexico: Imprenta Cumplido, 1857.

———. *Colección de leyes y decretos del congreso general de la nación megicana en los años de 1833 a 1835.* Mexico: Imprenta Galván, 1840.

———. *Colección de leyes y decretos espedidos por el congreso general de los Estados Unidos Mexicanos en los años de 1831 y 1832.* México: Juan Ojeda, 1833.

———. *Colección de los decretos y órdenes del soberano congreso mexicano, desde su instalación en 24 de febrero de 1822, hasta 30 de octubre de 1823, en que cesó.* Mexico: Imprenta del Supremo Gobierno, 1825.

———. *Colección de órdenes y decretos de la soberana junta provisional gubernativa y soberanos congresos generales de la Nación Mexicana.* 2d. ed. Corregida y aumentada por una comisión de la Cámara de Diputados. Mexico: Galván, 1829.

México, Secretaría de Guerra y Marina. *Memorias de los ministros, 1824-1836.*

México, Secretaría de Hacienda y Crédito Público. *Memorias de los ministros, 1821-1838.*

México, Secretaría de Justicia y Negocios Eclesiásticos. *Memorias de los ministros, 1824-1836.*

México, Secretaría de Relaciones Interiores y Exteriores. *Memorias de los ministros, 1821-1838.*

México como nación independiente: Descripción de su presente estado moral, político, intelectual, etc. y esperanzas de su condición futura. Artículo traducido del periódico literario intitulado Revista Trimestral de Filadelfia correspondiente al mes de diciembre de 1827. Mexico: José A. Marqués, 1828.

Mier, Servando Teresa de. *Historia de la revolución de Nueva España, antiguamente Anáhuac, ó verdadero origen y causas de ella con relación de sus progresos hasta el presente año de 1813.* London: Guillermo Glindon, 1813.

Mora, José María Luis. *El Clero el estado y la economía national.* Mexico. Empresas Editoriales, 1950.

———. *El Clero, la milicia y las revoluciones.* México. Empresas Editoriales, 1951.

———. *Méjico y sus revoluciones.* 3 vols. Paris: Librería de Rosa, 1836.

———. *Obras sueltas.* 2d ed. Mexico: Porrúa, 1963.

Navarro y Noriega, Fernando. *Catálogo de los curatos y misiones de la Nueva España, seguido de la Memoria sobre la población del reino de Nueva España (primer tercio del siglo XIX).* Mexico: Publicaciones del Instituto Mexicano de Investigaciones Histórico-Jurídcas, 1943.

———. *Memoria sobre la población del Reino de Nueva España, escrita por don F. N. y N. Contador general de los ramos de arbitrios de estos reinos.* Mexico: Arizpe, 1820.

N. C., J. *Observaciones a los europeos por un americano: Segunda parte.* Mexico: Betancourt, 1821.

Negrete, Pedro Celestino. *D. José Antonio de Andrade y Baldomar . . . El exmo. sr. capitán general d. Pedro Celestino Negrete, se ha servido dirigirme . . . [La] representación que los generales y gefes del ejército reunidos la noche del 11 del corriente en la junta presidida por el capitán general de la provincia, dirigieron al serenísimo señor almirante, para que S. A. tomase las providencias oportunas, a fin de proceder legalmente contra el autor del papel intitulado: "Consejo prudente sobre una de las garantías," y evitar los males que pudiese producir la circulación de tan escandaloso folleto* . . . Guadalajara: Imprenta Imperial del Gobierno, 1821.

Nieto, Andrés María. *Traición de unos gachupines, sabida por uno de ellos.* Mexico: Ontiveros, 1825.

Noriega, Juan de. *El Sr. d. Juan de Noriega sobre la difamación que le arroja el papel titulado: Vindicación del exmo. sr. Iturrigaray. Oficio de d. José Ignacio Negreiros.* [Mexico; 1820].

Noticia estraordinaria de la completa derrota de la nueva espedición española. Mexico: Valdés, 1833.

Ocursos de los acreedores al ramo de peages del camino de Veracruz dirigidos al congreso general y suprema corte de justicia; y pedimento del señor fiscal sobre la contrata del mismo camino hecha por la secretaría de relaciones con d. Manuel Escandón, Anselmo Zurutuza, y d. Antonio Garay. Mexico: Galván, 1835.

Oficios del consulado de Veracruz al escmo. Ayuntamiento referentes al estado de la plaza y disposiciones del gobierno; con otras contestaciones ocurridas posteriormente. Veracruz: Imprenta del Gobierno Imperial Mexicano, 1821.

Ornoz, Luis Gonzaga. *Religioso franciscano a la nación española.* Mexico: Ontiveros, 1820.

Ortiz de Ayala, Tadeo. *México considerado como nación independiente y libre, o sean algunas indicaciones sobre los deberes mas esenciales de los mexicanos.* Burdeos: Carlos Lawalle Sobrino, 1832.

————. *Resumen de la estadística del Imperio Mexicano, dedicado a la memoria ilustre del sr. d. Agustín I, emperador de México por d.* . . . Mexico: Herculana del Villar y Socios, 1822.

El Pastor de las Gallinas. Mexico: Ontiveros, 1825.

Parecer de los tres fiscales sobre el voto consultivo pedido por el exmo. sr. virrey, sobre la real orden relativa a la sucesión del mando de México. Mexico; 1807.

Paz, José Ignacio. *Estupendo grito en la Acordada, y verdadero Detal* [sic] *de sus inmarcecibles sucesos desde el domingo 30 de noviembre del año próximo pasado hasta el día 4 de diciembre del mismo* . . . Mexico: Correo, 1829.

Pérez y Comoto, Florencio. *Discurso patriótico contra la rebelión que acaudilla el cura Hidalgo, y ventajas que ofrece la unión de todos los buenos ciudadanos por El dr. d. Florencio Pérez Comoto, de la real sec. patriótica de la Habana.* Mexico; Imprenta de Arizpe, 1820.

———— *Impugnación de algunos errores políticos que fomentan la insurrección de Nueva España por el dr. d. Florencio Pérez de la Habana y consultor de la económica de Guatemala.* Mexico: Arizpe, 1812.

Perros y Gatos. *Análisis económico iniciativo al amigo de la patria.* Mexico: Manuel Antonio Valdés, 1812.

El Piadoso con los Gachupines. *Que mueran los gachupines y la patria será libre.* Puebla: Moreno, 1827.

Plan formado en Tlaxcala para nuestra total independencia y pacífico establecimiento de los E. U. M. Puebla: Moreno, 1827.

Pradt, Dominique G. F. *Ideas políticas Escritas por Mr. de Pradt. Tomo II de las colonias, cap. 10, fol. 126. De la separación preparada o no preparada entre colonias y metrópolis. Peligro y ventajos entre ambos casos.* Mexico: Ontiveros, 1821.

Prieto, Guillermo [Fidel]. *Memorias de mis tiempos.* Mexico: Editorial Patria, 1958.

La Prisión de los generales Echávarri y Negrete. Puebla: Moreno, 1827.

Pronunciamiento de Perote, por el general Antonio López de Santa Anna, y sucesos de su campaña hasta la derogación de la ley que lo proscribió (escrito por un ciudadano que no tomó la más mínima parte en aquellos acontecimientos). Mexico: Águila, 1829.

Pronunciamiento en San Andrés Chalchicomula. Puebla: El Patriota, 1827.

Provisión de Empleos. Mexico: Benavente, 1821.

Proyecto sobre un establecimiento de papel moneda. Mexico: José Ma. Ramos Palomera, 1822.

Quejas del pueblo contra el papel moneda. Mexico: Fernández de Lara, 1823.

La Quema de los papeles contra la independencia, publicados por el anterior gobierno y por particulares es necesaria para mantener nuestra unión. Mexico: [Betancourt], 1823.

Quintana Roo, Andrés. *Informe del apoderado de los acreedores a los fondos del establecimiento de minería en un recurso dirigido al supremo gobierno por los responsables a las cuentas de aquel ramo, y algunos otros sobre el nombramiento de una comisión interventora.* Mexico: Arévalo, 1834.

Quirós, José María. *Ideas políticas económicas de gobierno. Memoria de instituto, formada por d . . . secretario de la junta gubernativa cuya lectura han de abrirse sus sesiones en el año venidero de 1822.* Veracruz: Imprenta del Gobierno Imperial Mexicano, 1821.

Quirós, José María. *Memoria de estatuto. Idea de la riqueza que daban a la masa circulante de Nueva España sus naturales producciones en los años de tranquilidad y su abatimiento en las presentes conmociones por J. M. Q. secretario del real consulado de Veracruz y leída en la primera junta de gobierno celebrada en 24 de enero de 1817.* Veracruz, 1817.

Ramírez Sesma, Joaquín, comp. *Colección de decretos, órdenes y circulares espedidas por los gobiernos nacionales de la federación mexicana desde el año de 1821, hasta el de 1826 para el arreglo del ejército de los Estados Unidos Mexicanos, y ordenados por el teniente coronel de caballería J. R. S.* Mexico: Martín Rivera, 1827.

Ramos, Manuel. *Grito de un americano amante de sus compatriotas.* Mexico: Benavente, 1821.

Ramos Arizpe, Miguel. *Memoria, que el doctor d. Miguel Ramos de Arízpe, cura de borbón, y diputado en las presentes Cortes Generales y Extraordinarias de España por la provincia de Coahuila, una de las cuatro Internas del Oriente en el Reyno de México, presenta a el augusto Congreso, sobre el estado natural, político, y civil de su dicha provincia y las del Nuevo Reyno de León, Nuevo Santander y los Texas, con exposición de los defectos del sistema general, y en particular de sus gobiernos, y de las reformas, y nuevos establecimientos que necesitan para su prosperidad.* Cadiz: José María Guerrero, 1812.

Razón de los préstamos que ha negociado el supremo gobierno de la federación; en virtud de la autorización concedida por los decretos del congreso general de 21 de noviembre del año de 1827, 3 de octubre y 20 de noviembre de 1828 que se publica con autorización del escmo. sr. ministro de hacienda ciudadano Lorenzo de Zavala. Mexico: Correo, 1829.

Reflexiones al bando de 16 del corriente sobre la repartición que gratis se ha de hacer de los impresos a las corporaciones y sugetos que en el se espresan. Mexico: Valdés, 1821.

Reflexiones del patriota americano lic. Fernando Fernández de S. Salvador, asesor ordinario por S. M. de esta intendencia. Mexico: Zuñiga y Ontiveros, 1810.

Reflexiones sobre las leyes de españoles. Mexico: Agustín Guiol, 1833.

Representación al honorable congreso del estado, sobre espulsión de los gachupines. Puebla: El Patriota, 1827.

"Representación americana a las cortes de España, en [primero] de agosto de 1811, con notas del editor inglés." In *Colección de documentos para la guerra de independencia de México* . . . , compiled by Juan E. Hernández y Davalos, vol. 3, doc. 149.

Representación del comercio solicitando una indemnización de las pérdidas que sufrió en los primeros días de diciembre de 1828, por conducto y con el correspondiente apoyo del escmo. ayuntamiento del gobierno al congreso general de los Estados Unidos Mexicanos. Mexico: Correo, 1829.

Representación del escmo. ayuntamiento de Mégico al comandante accidental de armas de la misma ciudad mariscal de campo d. Fco. Novella. Mexico: 1821.

Representación hecha a la soberana junta provisional gubernativa. Mexico: Valdés, 1821.

Robinson, William Davis. *Memorias de la revolución de México y de la expedición del general d. Francisco Javier Mina, á que se han agregado algunas observaciones sobre la comunicación proyectada entre los dos oceános, Pacífico y Atlántico. Escrita en inglés por . . . y traducida por José Joaquín de Mora.* Paris: St. Ferrez, 1888.

Segunda Parte de tanto le pican al buey hasta que embiste. Mexico: Ontiveros, 1820.

Semblanzas de los miembros que han compuesto la cámara de diputados de congreso del la unión de la República Mexicana, en el bienio, 1827-1828. Mexico: Valdés, 1829.

Sermón de Fray Sufras, dedicado a los españoles. Mexico: Rafael Núñez, 1832.

Si Asesinan a Santa-Anna no quedará un gachupín. Mexico: A. Guiol, 1833.

Sivrob, Juan José. *Prevenciones a los europeos descontentos.* Mexico: Betancourt, 1821.

————. *Representación al exmo. sr. virrey sobre la independencia de América.* Mexico: Betancourt, 1821.

Suárez y Navarro, Juan. *Historia de México y del general Antonio López de Santa-Anna: Comprende los acontecimientos políticos que han tenido lugar en la nación, desde el año de 1821 hasta 1848.* Mexico: I. Complido, 1850.

La Suprema Junta Gubernativa del Reyno. *A la nación española.*

Mexico: Mariano Zuñiga, 1809.

Tanto le pican al buey hasta que embiste. Mexico: Ontiveros, 1820.

Tornel y Mendivil, José María. *Breve reseña histórica de los acontecimientos más notables de la Nación Mexicana desde el año de 1821 hasta nuestros días.* Mexico: I. Cumplido, 1852.

Torrente, Mariano. *Historia de la independencia de México.* Madrid: Editorial América, 1918.

Triunfo en frente del enemigo, la virtud de Matamoros. Puebla: El Patriota, 1827.

Unzueta, Juan Antonio de. *Informe presentado al Exmo. señor presidente de los Estados Unidos Mexicanos por el Contador mayor gefe de la oficina de rezagos . . . en cumplimiento de la Comisión que le confirió S. E., para que le manifestase el manejo y estado que guardó la Hacienda pública en los años 1830, 1831, y 1832.* Mexico: Águila, 1833.

[Uribe y Alcalde, T.] *Ya el soberano Congreso declaró la guerra a España.* Mexico: Herculana del Villar y Socios, 1827.

Various españoles al señor Tornel, última respuesta. Mexico: J. M. Lara, 1841.

[Venegas, Francisco Javier]. "Bando del virrey [Francisco Javier Venegas] publicando el de la regencia de la Isla de León, libertando de tributo a los indios." In *Colección de documentos para la guerra de independencia de México . . . ,* compiled by Juan E. Hernández y Dávalos, vol. 3, doc. 70.

Via crucis de los coyotes, que su autor dedica, consagra y ofrece a los editores del Sol. Mexico: Ontiveros, 1827.

Victoria, Guadalupe. *Mensaje del presidente de los Estados Unidos Mexicanos a sus conciudadanos.* 2d ed. Monterrey, 1828.

Villaurrutia, Jacobo. *Voto que di en la junta general tenida en Méjico en treinta y uno de agosto de 1808, sobre si se había de reconocer por soberana a la junta suprema de Sevilla y papeles que escribí por las contestaciones ocurridas en la ley del nueve del siguiente septiembre sobre la necesidad de una junta de diputados del reyno y autoridad para convocarla.* Havana: Arzoza y Soler, 1814.

Villavicencio, Pablo [El Payo del Rosario]. *Carta del Payo del Rosario al general Bravo vicepresidente de los Estados Unidos Mexicanos.* Puebla: I. J. de Arroyo, 1828.

————. *Comedias para la unión de criollos y gachupines.* Mexico: Ontiveros, 1827.

————. *Los coyotes de España vendrán pero los de casa nos la pagarán.* Mexico: Ontiveros, 1826.

———. *O se destierra al coyote o mata nuestras gallinas.* Puebla: Moreno, 1824.

———. *O se van los gachupines o nos cortan el pescuezo. Contestacion del Payo del Rosario a la voz de la Patria y los folletos de Rafael Dávila.* Mexico: Agustín Guiol, 1831.

———. *Si vienen los godos nos cuelgan a todos.* Mexico: Ontiveros, 1826.

Ward, Henry G. *Mexico in 1827.* 2 vols. London: Henry Colburn, 1828.

Zavala, Lorenzo de. *Albores de la república.* Mexico: Empresas Editoriales, 1949.

———. *Ensayo histórico de las revoluciones de México desde 1808 hasta 1830.* 2 vols. Paris: P. Dupont et G. Laguione, 1831-32.

———. *Juicio imparcial sobre los acontecimientos de México en 1828-1829.* New York: C. S. Van Winkle, 1830.

———. *Manifiesto de los principios políticos del ecsmo. sr. d. J. R. Poinsett por su amigo el c. Lorenzo de Zavala.* Mexico: Correo, 1828.

———. *Umbral de la independencia.* Mexico: Empresas Editoriales, 1949.

———. *Venganza de la Colonia.* Mexico: Empresas Editoriales, 1950.

C. Periodicals

El Águila Mexicana (Mexico), 1823-28.
El Amigo del Pueblo (Mexico), 1827-28.
El Atleta (Mexico), 1829-30.
Correo de la Federación Mexicana (Mexico), 1826-28.
Correo Semanario Político y Mercantil de México (Mexico), 1809-10.
Diario de México (Mexico), 1805-08.
El Fénix de la libertad (Mexico), 1831-34.
Gaceta del Gobierno Imperial de México (Mexico), 1823.
Gaceta del Supremo Gobierno de México (Mexico), 1823-25.
Gaceta Imperial de México (Mexico), 1821-22.
Gazeta de México (Mexico), 1800-10.
El Gladiador (Mexico), 1830.
El Indicador de la Federación Mejicana (Mexico), 1833-34.
Jornal Económico Mercantil de Veracruz (Veracruz), 1806.
El Noticioso General de Méjico (Mexico), 1815-23.

El Observador de la República Mexicana (Mexico), 1827-28; 1830.
Registro oficial del gobierno de los Estados Unidos Mexicanos (Mexico), 1830-33.
Repertorio Mexicano (Mexico), 1827-28.
Semanario Económico de Noticias Curiosas y Eruditas Sobre Agricultura y Demás Artes y Oficios (Mexico), 1808-10.
Semanario Político y Literario de Méjico (Mexico), 1820-22.
El Sol (Mexico), 1821-29; 1830-32.
El Telégrafo, periódico Oficial de los Estados Unidos Mexicanos (Mexico), 1833-35.
Voz de la Patria (Mexico), 1828-31.

II. SECONDARY SOURCES

Anes, Gonzalo. *Las crisis agrarias en la españa moderna.* Madrid: Editorial Taurus, 1970.
Artola, Miguel. *Los Afrancesados.* Madrid: Sociedad de Estudios Políticos, 1953.
Bancroft, Hubert H. *History of Mexico.* 6 vols. San Francisco: A. I. Bancroft and Co., 1883-85.
Bazant, Jan. *Historia de la deuda exterior de México, 1823-1946.* Mexico: El Colegio de México, 1968.
Benson, Nettie Lee. "The Contested Election of 1812." *Hispanic American Historical Review* 26, no. 3 (August 1946): 336-50.
————. *La diputación provincial y el federalismo mexicano.* Mexico: El Colegio de México, 1955.
————. "The Plan of Casa Mata." *Hispanic American Historical Review* 25, no. 1 (February 1945): 44-56.
————. *The Provincial Deputation in Mexico, Precursor of the Mexican Federal State.* Ph.D. dissertation, University of Texas, Austin, 1949.
Benson, Nettie Lee, ed. *Mexico and the Spanish Cortes, 1810-1822.* Austin: University of Texas Press, 1966.
Berry, Charles. "The Election of the Mexican Deputies to the Spanish Cortes, 1810-1822." In *Mexico and the Spanish Cortes, 1810-1822,* edited by Nettie L. Benson, pp. 10-42. Austin: University of Texas Press, 1966.
Bosch García, Carlos. *Problemas diplomáticos del México independiente.* Mexico: El Colegio de México, 1947.
Bulnes, Francisco. *La Guerra de independencia: Hidalgo—Iturbide.*

Mexico: El Diario, 1910.

Carreño, Alberto María. *Los Españoles en el México independiente: Un Siglo de beneficiencia.* Mexico: Manuel León Sánchez, S. C. L., 1942.

Costeloe, Michael P. *Church Wealth in Mexico: A Study of the "Juzgado de Capellanías" in the Archbishopric of Mexico, 1800-1856.* Cambridge: Cambridge University Press, 1967.

Cué Cánovas, Agustín. *Historia social y económica de México (1521-1854).* Mexico: Editorial F. Trillas, 1960.

Cuevas, Mariano. *Historia de la Iglesia en México.* 3d ed. El Paso, Texas: Editorial Revista Católica, 1928.

Cunniff, Roger. "Mexican Electoral Reform, 1810-1822." In *Mexico and the Spanish Cortes, 1810-1822,* edited by Nettie L. Benson, pp. 59-86. Austin: University of Texas Press, 1966.

Chávez Orozco, Luis, ed. *El comercio exterior y la expulsión de los españoles.* Mexico: Banco Nacional de Comercio Exterior, 1966.

————. *Historia de México (1808-1836).* Mexico. Editorial Patria, 1947.

————. *Historia social y económica de México.* Mexico: Botas, 1938.

De la Torre Villar, Ernesto. *La Constitución de Apatzingán y los creadores del estado mexicano.* Mexico: UNAM, 1964.

Delgado, Jaime. *España y México en el siglo XIX, 1820-1830.* Madrid: Instituto Gonzalo Fernández de Oviedo, 1950.

Domínguez Ortiz, Antonio. *La sociedad española en el siglo XVIII.* 3 vols. Madrid: Instituto Balmes de Sociología, 1955.

Farriss, Nancy M. *Crown and Clergy in Colonial Mexico, 1759-1821.* London: Athlone Press, 1968.

Fernández de Recas, Guillermo S. *Mayorazgos de la Nueva España.* Mexico: UNAM, 1965.

Florescano, Enrique. *Precios del maíz y crisis agrícolas en México, 1708-1810.* Mexico: El Colegio de México, 1969.

García Cantú, Gastón. *El Pensamiento de la reacción mexicana: Historia documental, 1810-1965.* Mexico: Empresas Editoriales, 1965.

Gonzáles Obregón, Luis. *La Vida de México en 1810.* Mexico: Vda. de C. Bouret, 1911.

González y González, Luis, comp. *El Congreso de Anáhuac, 1813.* Mexico: Cámara de Senadores, 1963.

————. *Los Presidentes de México ante la nación: Informes*

manifiestos y documentos de 1821-1966. Mexico: Cámara de Diputados, 1966.

Haddick, Jack A. "The Administration of Viceroy Iturrigaray." Ph.D. dissertation, University of Texas, Austin, 1954.

Hamill, Hugh M. *The Hidalgo Revolt: Prelude to Mexican Independence.* Gainesville: Florida University Press, 1966.

Hamilton, Earl J. *War and Prices in Spain, 1651-1800.* Cambridge: Harvard University Press, 1947.

Hann, John H. "The Role of the Mexican Deputies in the Proposal and Enactment of Measures of Economic Reform Applicable to Mexico." In *Mexico and the Spanish Cortes, 1810-1822,* edited by Nettie L. Benson, pp. 153-84. Austin: University of Texas Press, 1966.

Herr, Richard. *España y la revolución del siglo XVIII.* Madrid: Aguilar, 1964.

Lafuente Ferrari, Enrique. *El Virrey Iturrigaray y los orígenes de la independencia de Méjico.* Madrid: Instituto Gonzalo Fernández de Oviedo, 1941.

León Portilla, Miguel, et al. *Historia documental de México.* 2 vols. Mexico: UNAM, 1964.

Lerdo de Tejada, Miguel. *El Comercio esterior de México desde la conquista hasta hoy.* Mexico: Rafael Rafael, 1853.

Lerner, Victoria. "La Población de la Nueva España." *Historia Mexicana* 28, no. 3 (January-March 1968): 327-46.

López Cámara, Francisco. *La Génesis de la conciencia liberal en México.* Mexico: El Colegio de México, 1954.

Macauley, Neill. "The Army in New Spain and the Mexican Delegation to the Spanish Cortes." In *Mexico and the spanish Cortes, 1810-1822,* edited by Nettie L. Benson, pp. 134-52. Austin: University of Texas Press, 1966.

Mateos, Juan A. *Historia parlamentaria de los congresos mexicanos de 1821 a 1857.* 25 vols. Mexico: Vicente S. Reyes, 1877-86.

Miquel I. Verges, José María. *La diplomacia española en México (1822-1823).* Mexico: El Colegio de México, 1956.

————. *La Independencia mexicana y la prensa insurgente.* Mexico: El Colegio de México, 1941.

Moreno-Valle Suárez, Lucina. *La Expulsión de españoles en México (1821-1833).* Master's thesis, Universidad Nacional Autónoma de México, 1967.

Otero, Mariano. *Ensayo sobre el verdadero estado de la cuestión social y política que se agita en la República Mexicana.* Mexico: I. Cumplido, 1842.

Palavicini, Félix F. *México, historia de su evolución constructiva.* 4 vols. Mexico. Distribuidora Editorial "Libro, S. de R. L.," 1945.

Potash, Robert. *El Banco de Avío de México: El Fomento de la industria (1821-1846).* Mexico: Fondo de Cultura Económica, 1959.

Rabasa, Emilio. *La Evolución histórica de México.* Mexico: Porrúa, 1956.

Reyes Heroles, Jesús. *El Liberalismo mexicano.* 2 vols. Mexico: UNAM, 1957-61.

Reyes Heroles, Jesús, ed. *Mariano Otero obras.* 2 vols. Mexico: Porrúa, 1967.

Riva Palacio, Vicente, ed. *México a través de los siglos.* 5 vols. Mexico: Gustavo S. López, 1940.

Rodríguez O., Jaime E. "Oposición a Bustamante," *Historia Mexicana* 20 (October-December 1970): 199-234.

_____. "Rocafuerte y el empréstito a Colombia," *Historia Mexicana* 18, no. 4 (April-June 1969): 485-515.

Romero Flores, Jesús. *Comentarios a la historia de México, (1821-1861).* Mexico, Libro México, 1958.

Sierra, Catalina. *El Nacimiento de México.* Mexico: UNAM, 1960.

Sierra, Justo. *Evolución política del pueblo mexicano.* Mexico: FCE, 1950.

Smith, Robert S. "Shipping in the Port of Veracruz, 1790-1821." *Hispanic American Historical Review* 23, no. 1 (February 1943): 5-20.

Torrente, Mariano. *Historia de la independencia de México.* Madrid: Editorial América, 1918.

Tribunal del Consulado. "Noticias de Nueva España publicadas por el tribunal del consulado." *Boletín de la Sociedad Mexicana de Geografía y Estadística* 2 (1950): 3-52.

Vasconcelos, José. *Breve historia de México.* Mexico: Cía. Editora Continental 1960.

Vicens Vives, Jaime. *Historia social y económica de España y América.* 5 vols. Barcelona: Ed. Teide, 1959.

Vilar, Pierre. *Crecimiento y desarrollo. Economía e historia: Reflexiones sobre el caso español.* Barcelona: Ediciones Ariel, 1964.

Villoro, Luis. *El proceso ideológico de la revolución de independencia.* México: UNAM, 1967.

Whitaker, Arthur P. *The United States and the Independence of Latin America, 1800-1830.* New York: Norton, 1964.

Zamacois, D. Niceto de. *Historia de Méjico desde sus tiempos más remotos hasta nuestros días* . . . 22 vols. Barcelona: J. F. Parrés y Cía., 1879-1903.

Zerecero, Anastasio. *Memorias para la historia de las revoluciones en México.* Mexico: Imprenta del Gobierno en Palacio, 1869.

Zúñiga y Ontiveros, Mariano. *Calendario manual y guía de forasteros en México para los años de (1810-1828).* Mexico: M. Zúñiga, [1810-1929].

————. *Lista de los señores que voluntariamente han contribuído con las cantidades que se expresan para el vestuario de las tropas del Gral. Guerrero.* Mexico: Zúñiga y Ontiveros, 1821.

Index